Anatomy of Me

Books by Fannie Hurst

NON-FICTION

Anatomy of Me

NOVELS

The Man with One Head
Anywoman
The Hands of Veronica
Hallelujah
Lonely Parade
Great Laughter
Anitra's Dance
Imitation of Life
Back Street
Five and Ten
A President Is Born
Appassionata
Lummox
Stardust

SHORT STORIES

We Are Ten
Procession
Song of Life
The Vertical City
Humoresque
Gaslight Sonatas
Every Soul Hath Its Song
Just Around the Corner

MISCELLANY

No Food with My Meals
Back Pay
Land of the Free
It Is to Laugh

Anatomy of Me

A WONDERER

IN SEARCH OF HERSELF

Fannie Hurst

The Temple Library
UNIVERSITY CIRCLE AT SILVER PARK
CLEVELAND, OHIO 44106

DOUBLEDAY & COMPANY, INC.   GARDEN CITY, NEW YORK 1958

89-129

Library of Congress Catalog Card Number 58–10025
Copyright © 1958 by Fannie Hurst
All Rights Reserved
Printed in the United States of America
First Edition

To My Friend
The Anonymous Public

Foreword

THE chasms in the path of the autobiographer lead to pitfalls of egotism and egoism.

The autobiography of I saw, I did, I came, I went lifts from the pages of memory as easily as a cake from its greased pan.

Then there is that hardy perennial, the personal history, lively with name dropping and resurrecting an era.

But if these are fraught with hazards, the way of the explorer into the Himalayas, into the tropical and arctic zones of the inner life, is a venture into tracklessness.

When the mind's eye turns inward, it blazes upon the dearly beloved image of oneself.

Nevertheless, another wanderer, with the perpendicular pronoun "I" as her alpenstock, sets out in search of herself.

Either the mental and spiritual processes of all human beings rate scrutiny, or no one's processes are worth the telling. Rich man, poor-man-beggarman-thief, Albert Einstein, and the Jukes family share some of the same inner experiences.

The chemistry of each inner life, as it fuses in the test tube of body and soul, becomes a study in similarities and differences.

This recital of this microcosm, me, attempts nothing more.

The historical background of the era which frames this telling is deliberately subordinated to the clinical analysis of a traveler, who happens to be me, detained, along with billions of fellow travelers, in this strange interlude between birth and death known as span-of-life. My life.

This is the way it was and is with me.

Imagine a sliver off the top of my head. Look down into the "fearful and wonderful" crater of the human mind and spirit. My mind and spirit. It is in unceasing processes of change: smoke, flame, eruption.

But Mama's interpretation of the sound and fury of a child adolescing was more potent and succinct:

Growing pains.

Book One   1
Book Two   81
Book Three   145
Book Four   311

Book One

F ROM the hour I gave Mama my first stare from her bed of my birth, I must have braced my new spine against being overpowered by the rush of her personality.

When Mama walked into a room filled with ladies, she doused them like so many candles blown out on a birthday cake.

Yet, on the other hand, no sooner had I left the warm cove of her body than we committed the anachronism of becoming one again.

Despite the fact that we had neither temperamental nor intellectual compatibility, I loved her in a deep uncomplicated way that was never to waver throughout storm and stress.

And storm and stress it was. Mama's temper, fiery as lightning, terrible as thunder, was a matter of periodic blitz in our home, my own kitten of a temper, like Papa's, managing to keep its claws in.

In a way, however, Papa and I were a pair of terrible meeks, huddling and waiting for the storm to pass like a pair of wayfarers, our mute surrender to her fury serving only to increase the gale which could rage out of a trifling or fancied hurt, and a clear sky.

Mama, who emerged from these outbursts contrite, darling, and her usual warm self, was a "natural," uninhibited, sparkling with a wit both unique and exhilarating, an "extrovert" in a community that had never heard the word.

Bashful, and what Papa termed "reserved," I grew up in the lavishness of her maternalism, recipient of the heavy spill of her easy emotions.

Mama doted on me with an animal kind of fierceness. A rebuke from a schoolteacher was sufficient to cause her to lift a paw like a big cat, lay back her lips and hiss.

Mama lived in a world of bric-a-brac and realities.

My laundress steals soap. Fannie is hard on pantywaists. Fifteen cents a dozen for "cooking-eggs," but Mr. Hurst doesn't believe in them. Says they go into our stomachs even if they are in a cake, the same as better grade eating-eggs. I always say it doesn't pay to economize. It's the extravagant women who are most respected by their husbands. You can't tell me she keeps a clean kitchen. She has ants.

Mama's world was composed of tiny mosaics, seven days a week of things you could eat and touch and smell and do.

On the other hand, to her voiced mystification, I moved in a world you could not see.

Mama said: The sooner you come down to earth the better. You are not a rich man's daughter, although you could be, if your father didn't put every cent back into leather bellies.

The phrase "leather bellies" ran like a bitter threnody through my childhood. Papa, it seemed, as president of a fair-sized shoe factory, withdrew as little as possible in salary from the business. No amount of his placating or explaining could mollify Mama: It is just a matter of your wife and child coming last was her invariable counter.

By "come down to earth" Mama meant be more tidy, read less, play more, take better care of your clothes, although her mania was for keeping me oversupplied with new ones.

Papa was as soft as silk and as gentle to the touch, although I came within physical touch of him but few times during the several decades his life extended into mine.

Our rare kisses were light pecks of greeting or farewell, his mustache clean as snow and, in his later years, as white.

His reserve, against which he was constantly warning me as if it were something he could not bear for me to inherit, was exaggerated to a degree. Papa slid from his double-breasted business coat into the black "seersucker" he wore at home as if shirtsleeves were vulgar exposure. He never permitted me to see him in so little as his undershirt, although I do seem to remember that he wore nightshirts trimmed in rickrack, three-quarter length with little slits on the sides and, like everything else in our house, immaculately clean.

Born in Vicksburg, Mississippi, reared in Memphis, Tennessee, he married Rose Koppel of Hamilton, Ohio, whom he met while she was visiting relatives in St. Louis, Missouri, and he was a traveling salesman. If ever a couple validated the adage that opposites attract, they did.

My father's nobility was built into his handsomeness. Six feet, heavy but not obese, his kind brown eyes were clean through and through. I do not remember the time when his heavy black hair, which stood upward on his head like the bristles of a brush, was not salted with gray.

His southern speech had worn off to only an occasional "I reckon" or "you all." With no more than half a Memphis high school education, Papa nevertheless gave the impression of culture. His mind and spirit reached for it. Like a broken record, his dusty cliché: Remember, Fannie, knowledge is power, reverberated through my growing years, motivated by that immemorial compulsion of the parent to extend his offspring beyond himself.

An inveterate addict of newspapers, Papa read little else. Nothing could have been less characteristic of each of my parents than book-in-hand.

Mama, so given to overstatement, would exclaim as she came across books that were in my current reading, face down and scattered about the house: I wish I could throw out every book in this house, and probably in the next breath would inquire:

I'm going downtown today. Do you want me to bring you any books from the library?

While it is true that Papa's reading was chiefly confined to the St. Louis *Post-Dispatch* and the Republican morning paper, the *Globe-Democrat,* he must have lived a rewarding life of introspective satisfactions far removed from Mama and, for all I know, from me. I had immense respect and admiration for him and I think I loved him. Yet we remained such strangers! I lived in his home, yet I was locked out of it by his great reserves. I realize too late that had I so much as knocked at Papa's door or dared slip my hand into his I could have found my way to him.

If only I had put my hand out to him! But a dirge old as the human race is vested in those broken words—if only . . .

Papa is gone now these many years, but the quiet and the goodness and the remoteness of him come to life even more vividly than when I saw him in life.

The two quiet men in my life are gone now. Papa and my husband.

I am impatient for this tell-all recital of the infinitesimal universe known as me to reach the stage where my husband enters it. Because what had passed before I met him as sunlight was to become by comparison gray as a slow dawn.

However, at this point, fifteen or twenty years lie between a rather spoiled, overweight brat of a child, living snug as a bug in the middle-class middle-western so-called security of a pre-first-world-war era, and the romantic figure of a poetic looking young man who was then studying music in Paris.

Papa and Jack shared no qualities except their quietness and inherent goodness, although now, to be sure, they share death. Otherwise, they might have dwelt on different planets.

Papa's was my first close-up encounter with death. Already the imponderables were at me. I had browsed in the valley of youthful attraction to the theme of death. . . .

"Approach the grave like one that wraps the drapery of his couch about him, and lie down to pleasant dreams."

ANATOMY OF ME

Years before Papa's going, I had pondered, perhaps because I so loved life: Death, where is thy sting?

My youth cried out: Thy sting is in loving life even when you are as old as Papa—Death, where is thy sting? Everywhere! I find Alexander Pope's lines copied by me in vertical handwriting on the flyleaf of a Fisk's *American History:* "Years following years steal something every day. At last they steal us from ourselves away. This subtle thief of Life, this paltry Time, what will it leave me . . . Death?"

Papa, when you died and I flew to your side from the midst of a lecture tour, I thought I knew what grief was, or did I? Not in view of the grief for a death that was to come to me long, long after. . . .

Looking back, I believe I was only saddened by Papa's going. There is a timetable for death, and you, Papa, in your seventies, were inevitably close to its schedule. I grieve for you now chiefly because of what you missed in the son-in-law you deserved, but whom you rejected.

In the beginning I suffered so because you would not open your mind and heart to him. A foreigner! you said bitterly. But now I have only pain for you. Never in your long and not too eventful life, Papa, did you know his like, and except for one of those hairline turnings of a corner, for which I have you to thank, neither would I.

But this is far ahead of my story.

Until I was four years old, I had a sister, Edna. I think Mama must have wanted her, because otherwise, after the unpremeditated coming of me, Mama being Mama would not have let it happen. There were exactly eleven months between us. From an enlarged photograph I can no longer lay hands on, I remember Edna feature by feature. She had large black eyes set rather closely together under straight black bangs. She was small-boned and the photograph showed her face to be heart-shaped and dimpled. Her lightness of build must have been in sharp contrast to my squareness. The enlarged photograph of the heads of the two of us together, cheek to cheek, framed in carved silvered wood, used to hang in our parlor. It is gone into that limbo of things you wish you had kept.

This child, who, like a butterfly, had alighted in our house for a brief four years, had a strange effect upon me, not admirable.

Even after her death, in the days when diphtheria ranked high as a killer, I still strove to be more than what she might have become had she lived.

Was she as pretty as she appeared to be in the cheek-to-cheek portrait? That meant she would have been prettier than I as she grew older. Her oval face against my round one indicated as much. Would she also have been smarter? Were Mama and Papa sorry that I had not been the one to get diphtheria? Tormenting questions relating to Edna buzzed through those early years.

The time Edna fell ill of her fatal disease I was disturbed by these buzzes. The household revolved around her, the doctor came and went. I was not allowed in the room and went generally unheeded.

Then came the day when Edna's illness was pronounced contagious and Mama announced that I must go and stay with the Mannheimers until she recovered, because the door of the house was being placarded and no one could come or go after that.

The Mannheimers were German-born friends of Grandma Hurst. They lived in a large oldfashioned apartment over their prosperous retail grocery store in South St. Louis. Mr. and Mrs. Mannheimer were in their seventies and had given the store over to their sons. Old Mr. Mannheimer sat in the back of the store, munching what St. Louisans called "rat cheese and crackers," and watched the till. The upstairs apartment smelled of cold boiled potatoes. The old folks must have felt helpless about me, because Sydney, the stubby kindly son, kept me most of the time down among the cracker barrels and striped candies in jars. And there was a cat.

Every two or three days Mama and Papa came, and Sydney held me at the upstairs window as they called to me from the sidewalk because they did not want to bring possible infection into the house.

Mama always cried and said Edna was a very sick child and that I was her life and it was terrible to be away from me. Sweetheart, Papa called up to me, using one of his rare endearing terms, be good and say your prayers for Edna; and then he too cried and held Mama's hand, and I stood at the window, silent but with a tight feeling and remorse for all the times I had taken things away from Edna and secretly drunk her condensed milk.

I realized something dreadful known as death was at hand. Prayer was so seldom used at our house. One was ashamed to speak of such matters. To be sure, Papa frequently asked: Do you say your Now-I-lay-me? Never go to sleep without it. Sometimes he stood at the foot of my bed and listened and I felt more ashamed than ever.

What had happened to my smooth world? What was happening to Edna? What was dying? The question took supremacy in my mind and was to grow. . . .

They came for me about a week later, Mama all in black. She cried unceasingly as she talked to Mr. and Mrs. Mannheimer; and Papa stood by, again holding her hand and looking big and helpless.

All the way back home Mama continued to cry and I said nothing. No one had told me directly that Edna had done the thing called die. I had just listened and knew. A kind of horror swooped at me when we entered our house. It was darkened and smelled of roses. Upstairs in the room where Edna and I had slept everything was in order, there was nothing about that suggested my little sister, except her rocking chair with two of her dolls seated upright.

I never mentioned Edna. I never asked a question. I went to bed on my side of the one I had shared with her and Mama and Papa tucked me in and I said Now-I-lay-me, with all the God blesses, including Edna as usual, and Mama and Papa cried some more and said if I felt lonesome I could come into bed with them.

I snuggled my face down into my pillow and shook my head no.

Papa said: After all, why should she be afraid? Her little sister is in heaven.

I recall so clearly that I awoke at dawn and for no reason in particular crept downstairs. Mama was in the front hall scraping away at the outside of the front door where the health department quarantine sign had been posted. Keep Out. Diphtheria.

The waters of time closed swiftly over little Edna Hurst. She had been with us so briefly. But for the first few years following her going Mama's eyes would fill at the mention of her. Time dried them, but with Papa it was not so.

Mr. Hurst will never get over Edna's death, Mama used to say, and at that some of the old jealousy pangs still assailed me. Once or twice a year we drove ten miles to the fine cemetery to visit her grave.

Had they liked this gone child better than they liked me? Was I glad to be left the only one? Or sorry? The bad thoughts frightened me, but they buzzed. What if Edna had lived . . .

Mama would place the potted plants we had bought on the way to the cemetery on the small grave and then would take me by the hand to wander away, leaving Papa alone. With Edna.

Later he would join us, red-eyed, and Mama would suggest that on the way home we stop at Schneider's German Garden for rye bread and *schmierkäse*.

Would Papa, so reserved so strong so silent, have cried over my grave?

What did this child have . . . to make Papa cry. . . .

I am back in St. Louis, living the first dozen years of my life, tucked into the somnolent world of phony security which antedated the world wars.

Barring a few sporadic ups and downs in Papa's business life, my childhood was spent in middle-class well-being, nice home, and after I had begun my teens and Papa's factory prospered we moved from better house to better house to better house, from Morgan Street to West Belle Place to Cates Avenue.

Papa was not one to initiate change or expenditure. Mama's repetitive voice of grievance beats through my memory like rain on a roof: When I see how other men indulge their wives I could cry my eyes out.

Papa, drawing about ten thousand dollars a year out of the business, was what might be termed, his era considered, well fixed. We paid forty-five dollars a month rent, about four dollars a week for a "girl," bread was five cents a loaf, a newspaper cost one cent. Mama, who voluntarily "stinted" and felt martyred about it, could, in her own idiom, make a dollar stretch three ways; one way was in the direction of overdressing me. Papa, who detested what he called ostentation, used to remonstrate.

You've taken all the gaiety out of me, Sam, Mama would counter, but I don't propose for you to do it to your child. Mama bubbled with gaiety but chiefly, it is true, when Papa was not about.

We are not allowed to laugh at our house, Mama used to remark semihumorously to the neighbors in Papa's presence.

Now, Rose, what a thing to say.

To me, if I transgressed: You wouldn't act this way if your father were home. You're a changed child when he enters the house. With him it is "Yes sir" and "No sir." But no respect for me, the one who does the scrimping and sacrificing.

As a matter of fact, Papa's arrival home evenings did douse things. I never knew him to raise his voice, he was kindness and courtesy personified, his rare rebukes to me were more in pain than in anger, yet his very entrance into a room sobered all present.

Papa did not like the immense pompadours that were the fashion of the period, nor the large ribbon bows that surmounted them. Just before his arrival I would remove the "rat" and slick my hair, thus deflating myself and my spirits. The neighbors used to say: Mr. Hurst is a prince among men. Such a gentleman. Henpecked, but a prince.

To this last Mama would retort:

Yes, I get my way in the little things and Mr. Hurst gets his in the big.

Mama had a half-humorous way with her, but the bones of truth protruded.

With no notes to guide me, not a scrap of diary to refresh me, my chronology wide open to challenge, the memories spill as if from a cornucopia of time.

Mama, big as life before me, simultaneously tormented by obsessive love and antagonism to my father.

What do I get out of it all? What do any of us get? I stint and save and here we huck, while that old leather business down there sucks everything deeper and deeper into it.

Rose, we have our health.

We wouldn't if it cost anything.

You're the one, Rose, who objects to having Fannie's teeth straightened.

It isn't the five hundred dollars and you know it. I don't want the child to suffer through it. Dentistry isn't my idea of recreation.

Fannie, your mother got up on the wrong side of the bed this morning.

It's all sweet talk before your daughter. When I see what other women expect and get from their husbands . . .

Papa's soft eyes would trouble up at these only half-meant invectives, and my heart would rush out to him but, alas, I made no move.

You don't mean all you say, old lady.

Don't I! Better say I don't say half I mean.

She didn't mean everything she said, except for those moments when her quick temper boiled up. I think she enjoyed our way of life. I even suspect a melody of contentment ran through it.

If ferment was at work in Papa, he revealed so little of it that only the antenna of the child in his house moved a little.

He occasionally said wishful hungry things to me without ever taking me into intimacy.

Mama insisted she knew him like a book. She knew him like a closed book. For that matter, so did I. Papa lived so separately within himself that I retreated to Mama, who wore herself on the outside. Everything about her hung in view like peasant adobe houses with green peppers and little shrines, drying diapers and cooking utensils, on the façade.

But she was darling and as easy to read as the great colored letters in a child's book, and she was correct when she insisted that I was a changed child in the presence of my father.

A child of different temperament might have found her way to him. If only . . .

To be sure, Papa occasionally said defeated things: Learn to think carefully before you leap. Remember, many of our most important decisions are made in youth and often our greatest mistakes.

His voice was full of his greatest mistake. I wondered what it was, and was afraid I knew.

For a decade after the century had turned, St. Louis was still vying with Chicago for the majestic place of "Gateway to the West." Destined ultimately to lose the race, she nevertheless maintained her identity as a highly respected and well-to-do member of the summit cities of the nation. Her interesting compound of German and French beginnings is probably the answer to the stability and conservatism which characterize her.

Papa fitted into that stability and conservatism like a round peg into a round hole. His compatibility with environment must have been part of his capacity for monotony. Intellectual curiosity was languid at our house.

Looking back, I realize that the insulation of our lives could scarcely be equaled today, even on a desert island. Local and national issues, the temper and temperature of the world found slow if any entry into our home or consciousness. Radio and television were not yet common methods of communication, or we might have had glimpses of considerable goings on beyond our little acre. The world might have caught our eye.

Some of it doubtless caught Papa's eye from the pages of the St. Louis *Post-Dispatch* and *Globe-Democrat* and from his discussions with men. But these were male concerns to which Mama and I scarcely listened.

However, at the mention of business conditions between Papa and his porch confreres, a listening look would come into Mama's face and she would stop rocking.

Every evening she met Papa with the same anxious question: How is business, Sam?

I never knew him to answer other than cheerfully. All right.

It is not. I can tell by your voice.

All right, if you prefer it that way, then it isn't.

I heard you talking to the men across the porch the other evening. From what you said to them, things aren't so good.

Mama's dread of poverty was little short of obsessive. Money matters plagued her out of all proportion.

The paradox of a woman generous to the extreme in so many ways, yet parsimonious to that same extreme, was to harass Papa and me all through the years.

The circumstance of dwelling in the same city with various relatives on her father's side, who lived in those fine private places enclosed in stone gates, was humiliating to her.

They only invite me out of charity. I'm a poor relation. I can't entertain the way they do, and I don't intend to be beholden.

But Rose, these people go out of their way to be nice to you. For Fannie's sake, we should cultivate more Jewish people.

My child is not going to be humiliated by having her cousins visit her here. If you can't earn the kind of living Henry Sayres does for his family, we stay right here where we belong.

Mama, I feel sure, had no conception of her biting cruelty, and fortunately Papa and I seemed to sense that.

Because of Mama's repetitive indoctrination, I too felt insecure among our eager-to-be-friendly "rich relatives." Their fine homes impressed but did not depress me as they did Mama.

I liked our little seven-room house with its white rock front and on our modest tree-bordered street, especially following the years during Papa's business depression which we had spent in Mrs. Cleveland's boardinghouse on West Belle Place.

Mama always kept the house darkened, conditioning me for life to like gray days and escape sunshine wherever possible. The double shades, white outer and green inner, were drawn low and with precise evenness, the furniture placed so that each caster fitted into the dent it had made in the carpet.

My room was the second-story front with alcove, which contained a double brass bed. Evenings, we used the main section as sitting room. There Papa used to read his newspaper, Mama telephoned her friends or mended, and I sat in the alcove and pored over homework, books, or wrote stories which I showed to Papa, who without reading them somehow managed to show great interest: That's right, Fannie, study and improve yourself. Knowledge is power.

Mama was given to interjections: I wish she would straighten her dresser drawers or get her desk in order, instead of scribbling day and night.

Had Papa, who never uttered them, said things like that to me they would have meant humiliation, deep and painful. From Mama, somehow they glanced off me harmlessly.

Mama may not have been her inimitable self among her wealthy relatives, but in the Iberian village of her own neighborhood she was supreme.

I could listen to Mrs. Hurst talk all day!

Laugh! I thought I'd die! The way she says things. Such wit.

And so generous. Last time at her house I came away with five yards of that lovely eyelet embroidery she uses on Fannie's petticoats, and two pounds of that fresh butter she gets from the farmers as they pass her house at five in the morning on their way to Union Market.

Imagine! If I had her money, I'd sleep until ten.

It embarrassed Papa to have Mama shout to the early morning farmers, or for her to come home laden with marketing packages. He cared a great deal what people said. Mama's talk made Papa seem small. We both wished she would not dwell so much on money and its scarcity. Her friends would react in a way she apparently enjoyed. It's too bad about you, Mrs. Hurst, I wish I had half your bank account.

But when children were carrying pennies and nickels to school, I had dollar bills, and on through upper grades and college was more liberally endowed than young people of far higher income brackets.

It was Mama's way with me. In spite of her taunts, I could not bring myself to ask anything of Papa. Why don't you go to your father for that new bicycle? Why don't you go to your father for book money? He's the one who is always telling you knowledge is power. You act like strangers together.

I knew Papa would not have refused me, but for the life of me I couldn't.

I notice you don't hesitate to come to me.

I didn't. She was so warm in her volatile, unpredictable way. I loved her. I believe that most of the time Papa did too.

A cloud no larger than my pudgy hand began to form on the horizon.

A chain of us girls were walking arm in arm in the bricked schoolyard at recess.

Suddenly, one of them—I recall her name, Hazel Thompson—sang out: What religion is everybody? I'm Lutheran! Instantly the line took it up like a singing regiment. Left foot, right foot, each girl snapping out in turn: Lutheran. Catholic. Baptist. Lutheran. Presbyterian. The exception was the girl at the far end. Me. I opened my mouth to speak in turn, but no sound came. I opened my mouth again, in the silence that had fallen, unloosed my encircling arm from the the girl next to me and stood apart. Suddenly I had become different.

That night at the dinner table I asked a difficult question.

Is being Jewish one's religion?

Certainly, said Mama with prompt sureness. Why do you ask such a question?

Can you be the Jewish race and be Lutheran or a Catholic the way you can be American and also be a Lutheran or a Catholic?

Of course not.
Why not?
Because you can't.
But why?
Ask your father.

Papa began to moralize. That's a mighty difficult question, Fannie, and I'm glad you are thinking about such matters. I hope you say your prayers nightly. Always be proud of your religion.

I wasn't. It was difficult to be what no one else was, even though it was never talked about.

Your mother and I aren't as observing as we might be. I think the time has come, Rose, when we should join the temple and Fannie attend Sunday school.

I don't intend to join the temple and be stuck in the back pew so I can see my rich relatives up front. Besides, aren't you the one who always says you can say your prayers as well at home as in temple?

A child should have religious training.

But I don't want to join the temple, Papa, I hastened to intervene. I can learn Bible history at school if I want to. I was just asking . . .

Since you are a great reader, Fannie, I am sure your teacher or the librarian can give you books on the subject. I don't feel competent to answer your question, except to impress upon you that the Jews are both a race and a religion, and you are both.

I'm an American.

Always be proud of being that, too.

I notice, Sam, interposed Mama, you always say of yourself that when men you meet in business speak of "that damn Jew" you keep silent. That does not sound as if you are proud.

This kind of repudiation, especially in my presence, must have been bitter to Papa. He gave no sign.

When there is nothing to be accomplished, Rose, except embarrass the other fellow into admitting that he has his "pet Jews," I keep quiet.

But when Papa was not present, Mama would speak admiringly

to her Jewish friends: Mr. Hurst never makes it an issue when someone in business who doesn't know his religion refers to the damn Jews. He says the embarrassment caused only increases prejudice.

I realized that I was not proud but furtive, or I would have answered Hazel Thompson's question in the schoolyard.

In our middle-western world of assimilated German Jews, and comparatively few of them, this race consciousness had been slow to awaken and then only languidly. The small incident of the schoolyard was quickly laid back into the silence, although I was to come to know from talk at home that prejudice could lift its head.

Our neighbor, a Mrs. McCaffry, had once made a disparaging remark to which Mama had been the one to reply proudly: You may as well know, Mrs. McCaffry, that we are Jews.

Oh, Mrs. Hurst, I was only speaking generally. I knew a lovely girl in Keokuk before I was married. Babette Levy. You couldn't meet a lovelier person.

I always suspected, said Mama relating the incident to Papa, that she had *richus*.

Such people are to pitied for their ignorance.

I could tell a few things about the Irish Catholics, too. And I wish you could see the condition of her kitchen. Unwashed dishes piled to the ceiling.

That's no way to talk, Rose. It puts you in a class with her.

That's right, make me small.

You make yourself that way by using her methods.

We can't all be as noble as you are.

All right, Rose, you win. Get into an argument with such people and belittle us all, if that's what you prefer.

No, I want to be made small by my husband. Everybody in the world is in the right but me. If it wasn't for my child, I would wish myself out of it altogether. . . .

This was typical of the kind of circumstance that would send Mama off into one of her volcanic eruptions that could last for an hour or a day, as the case might be. The quarrels in our house began that way.

People tell me what a fine husband I have. They should know. Fine words outside his home, but abuse on the inside. The mistake of my life was not to have gone home to Hamilton with my child, while my parents were alive. Thank God they never knew. . . . My child—what comfort is she! I sacrifice my life for her and she takes sides with her father.

The psychology of Mama's quick temper fascinated me. The explosion would seem to come out of the blue from an innocent remark or unintended implication. Housemaids scurried before the gale of Mama like chickens before a storm, and we too hurried before the hurricane, closing windows and doors.

There must have been times when the spectacle of Papa and me, fearful for rather than of her, presented a sorry sight. Like Papa, I seemed to lack the capacity for flying off the handle; neither am I the slow-to-anger-but-oh-my-when-I-get-going type. I contain my anger neatly, with scarcely a spill. Again, like Papa, I think my anger takes the form of pity, combined with an embarrassment before the exposure of emotions of those in uncontrollable temper.

Time and time again the reserves which Papa had passed on to me boomeranged: Fannie, I would try not to appear so reserved before people. They misjudge. You appear unfriendly. This, from Papa of all people!

Be that as it may, except for Mama's eruptions I grew up in a quiet house of evenly drawn window shades, impeccable cleanliness, geometrically placed conventional furniture, middle-class respectability.

I adored Mama. I liked Papa. I hated the quiet house.

In that quiet house I spent years that put me together in a quiet way. In it, unhampered, a child could cogitate and ruminate and wonder in ways so separate from Mama and Papa and yet so within their boundary.

Without being aware of it, and through indulgence rather than motivation, both Mama and Papa, a generation or two ahead of themselves, practiced on me the techniques of so-called progressive education.

"Permissive," which had not yet reached even pedagogical vocabulary, was the word. What Fannie liked, Fannie did, breaking down parental opposition where it existed.

Allowed unrestricted choice of mental diet, I read at will and willy-nilly, strewing the house with library books not on the list of selected reading for children, a proportion of them likewise not worth adult consumption.

The titles or authors of these strewn books meant little if anything to either Mama or Papa. As a matter of fact, except for those included in school curriculums, I picked them at random, attracted and often misled by titles. I recall Spenser's *Faerie Queene* turned out to be meaningless verse in unintelligible dialect. *Anna Karenina* was a find! Also, poems by François Villon, and another that lived up to its title, *The Scarlet Letter*.

The librarian at the St. Louis Public Library once asked me if I selected these books for my mother. Yes, I lied, and it was through some of her subsequent suggestions that at twelve and thirteen my reading habits were an adult hodgepodge, ranging from Hall Caine, Marion Crawford, Mrs. Humphry Ward to Robert Louis Stevenson, Tolstoy, Maeterlinck, William Dean Howells, Dumas, Pushkin, and Hardy.

The quiet house offered opportunities to one of whom no household duties were demanded. After-school hours were for reading and scribbling down fanciful stories.

There were, however, exceptions to the unimpeded way of life. The piano and dancing school.

Mama, like many a mother, yearned for a musically accomplished daughter. I can see her now in the reception hall which contained the upright piano that she played in the identical sequence every evening while we waited for Papa's footsteps down the quiet street. "Angel's Serenade." "Alice, Where Art Thou." "The Maiden's Prayer." Chaminade's "Scarf Dance." Nevin's "Narcissus."

Mama liked music. Miss Lee, an extremely unfastidious teacher who sniffed, came biweekly to give me piano instruction.

Mama would remain in the house to hear my practice hour, which she frequently interrupted with calls from upstairs. Fannie, that's pretty. Play it over a little slower. And remember, Miss Lee says you should play more scales.

I would peg away, an alarm clock at one end of the keyboard and a bag of little salt pretzels at the other, munching through the slow minutes as I made my bored way up and down the keys, sometimes propping a book against the rack and reading the while.

I have always suspected that Papa was not only indifferent to music, but would find a pretext to take himself to another part of the house when Mama or I were at the piano.

On one occasion, when Ignace Paderewski played at the St. Louis Odeon, Mama insisted that the three of us attend. During the intermission, Papa went out and did not return to the auditorium. This resulted in a scene as we rode home in the streetcar.

Now, Rose, don't take it like that. I went out for a smoke and when I realized the second half had begun I didn't like to disturb the people in their seats.

Don't tell me. You hate music. Your mother hated music.

We will leave my mother out of this. Paderewski is a fine piano player. I enjoyed it.

You enjoyed it! I'll bet if he had played the Leather Bellies Symphony you would not have stayed out.

Rose, the entire streetcar doesn't have to hear you.

Papa never even had the compensation of seeing the ludicrous in scenes such as this. His sense of humor just would not reach. There were times in the midst of these storms when uncontrollable laughter would bubble in me—a kind of hysteria—the comic in Mama combined with the indescribable loneliness and sobriety of Papa. . . .

I had the feeling as we rumbled homeward that night that the Paderewski performance had rolled off or rather past me too. If only his great and grand musical phrases had been words—that I had written!

By the time we reached home, Mama's threatened tantrum had passed.

There is something about it, she observed, that I just can't explain. But a man piano player, even if he is a Paderewski, goes against my grain.

Now, if I had said that, Rose, you would jump on me. I must say, it seems to me to be a strange profession for a man.

If they could have known that off in the dim reaches of years to come was a young man whose hands were already making the keyboard sing! Unbeknownst to himself, he was to lead me across the borderline of the dim world, in which I was to live until I met him, into the world he was to irradiate for me for all the lovely years he was my husband.

I would not choose to live over again these early years because they did not contain him. However, now I joyfully relive them in retrospect because I know, as I could not then, that they were leading me to him.

Papa's rigid credos encased us: Liberals and Socialists were anarchists.

The theater was Bacchante in pink tights. Artists, long-haired depraved Bohemians.

Russian Jews were "kikes."

Negroes, all right in their place.

Keep our national nose out of international affairs.

See America first and, possibly, only.

Foreigners beat their wives and wear small collar sizes.

Modesty is a girl's finest raiment.

To this last, Mama said: It costs money to keep a girl dressed, modestly or immodestly.

Fannie understands what I mean, don't you?

Yes, Papa.

Yes-Papa-yes-Papa!

Papa and I smarted under this recurring observation. It embarrassed us. But bafflingly, Mama entertained a kind of sporadic fury toward the two she best loved!

Mama and Papa, to be sure, had their private existence together, shutting me out into an arctic loneliness when they retired to their bedroom at night, closing the door behind them.

Meanwhile, my public school life was beginning to open up an outside world. To a child who had experienced few playmates, the competitive world was disquieting.

In it, my importance receded.

Even at that time, the St. Louis public schools were overcrowded, the classes overlarge. Teachers for the most part were impersonal although obviously more interested in their outstanding pupils. I was not one.

Looking back, I regard with some puzzlement the anatomy of a little girl who happened to be me. Inhibited, I was simultaneously enough of an exhibitionist, and still am, to attempt to step out of the herd in order to attract attention. Failing, I resorted to out-of-order procedures, instigating class unruliness. Teachers became aware of me chiefly for infractions, my scholarship being only average, except in English where I excelled.

Psychiatry has new names for the same old adolescent symptoms of cosmic itch, frustration, yearning, intimations of sex, depressions, elations, despairs, egocentricity, love, infatuations, crushes, passions unrequited. Naturally, I knew them all, shame, secrecy, self-pity, forbidden thoughts, family antagonism, fear, envy, preoccupation with death, the slow demise of innocence, budding maturities—the flowering . . .

I doubt if either Mama or Papa had ever put more than a toe across the border of the imagination. However, Mama must gropingly have sensed something of my whereabouts when she reiterated: You are woolgathering. You act as if you don't live here. Other daughters chat with their mothers or sit and sew with them. What does mine do? I wish you thought as much of your family as you do of that public library.

Rose, what kind of talk is that? You should be glad Fannie wants to improve herself.

What about me? We have no interests in common. She doesn't

even want to come into the dining room when I have a card party. I am ashamed for the people. Is that what books do for her?

Fannie, you should have more regard for your mother. She certainly doesn't deserve anything but the best from you.

I know that, Papa. It's just that I haven't anything to say to Mrs. Stettheimer and Mrs. Calvert.

Not good enough for her ladyship. They don't have their noses in books all day. But I notice when I go to their houses their children don't have to be coaxed to come in and say how-do-you-do to their mother's friends. I don't know what kind of a child you are. If it isn't books, it's scribble-scribble, and when all is said and done, what does it amount to? A lot of writing that doesn't make sense.

That meant Mama had been into my desk and among my papers and she could not have mortified me more.

I rushed from the room, shamed, humiliated, and loaded with young unhappiness.

Papa's sighs echo. He had a habit of emitting long tired ones on occasions such as this. They come to me down through the years and fill me with ineffable pity for all the things I should have been and was not.

He understood me with a part of his nature he had never developed but had passed on to me.

But we had our good times. In her rollicking moods, Mama's sense of humor was so enlivening that friends declared her better entertainment than many of the professionals who appeared at our local Keith's Vaudeville Theatre.

Once, one of Mama's first cousins, Hattie Heller, a clubwoman and at that time president of "The Pioneers," a literary society composed of Jewish ladies of the higher social and intellectual echelon of our community, came to visit us, but with a purpose. An aggressive capable woman of high intent, she came to the point over Mama's excellent home-baked *schnecken*, apple *kuchen*, and coffee.

Rose, we want you in "The Pioneers." You've a good mind

which you don't use. I've never seen you with a book in your hand. I'm surprised Sam permits you to mix so much with the *goyim*. It's quite an honor to be asked to join "The Pioneers" and I have come with the club's authority to invite you.

I had just come in from school and was stealing up the back stairs when Mama called me in to share the coffee and cake. For some reason, probably because the two strong minds frequently met head on, Mama was fond of Hattie Heller.

Join "The Pioneers!" exclaimed Mama, withdrawing as if an ugly epithet had been hurled. You must think I'm crazy. I am surprised, knowing me as you do, that you would even suggest it. Where do I come in with a literary society. That's all I need, a literary society.

Literary society! The phrase had magic!

You should join for Fannie's sake, so that when she grows up she can join too and share the cultural background, like my Irma.

Don't worry about our daughter, Hattie. She is not going to be deprived.

But you've a good mind yourself, Rose, that you have allowed to go to seed, pursued Hattie Heller with characteristic brusqueness. You should improve it by reading and discussion.

I don't attempt to run your life, Hattie, and I'll thank you not to run mine.

Well, if that's the way you take it.

It is. I know you mean well, but we just aren't literary and make no bones about it.

I was mute and miserable during the *Kaffeeklatsch* that day, without knowing just exactly why.

I met your father on the streetcar the other day, Fannie, continued Hattie Heller, and he tells me that you get very good marks for your essays.

That's all we need, a writer in the family, said Mama.

How did a writer know she was one? I asked myself. I had never seen, much less met, a live writer or known anyone who had. Charlotte Brontë, I had read somewhere, was a "born writer." Did you get born that way?

I would no more have asked Mama or Papa than I would have asked them how babies get born. They had never set me straight on the stork.

Like most children of my era, I dwelt in rigid and ashamed silence concerning the facts of life. Pregnancy was something not to be discussed in the presence of a child, unless smeared over with evasion.

But of course I knew vivid truths from my miscellaneous reading, although, strangely enough, never from the little girls in the neighborhood or schoolyard. I was deeply ashamed that people were made the way they are and shied from the whisperings of awakening youngsters that took place in schoolyards or at recess, or the horridness of small boys.

Ugh, echoed through my growing awarenesses.

Regarding Mama and Papa and their intense preoccupation with the things you could see and smell and taste, it seemed incredible that they had had that strange other life together—in the next room from me—divided only by a closed door. . . .

And yet I was the answer to the fact that they had.

But what processes begot writer-babies? Could you be born one if you were like us? Grandma and Grandpa in Hamilton, Ohio? Uncle Gus or Aunt Jennie? Uncle Ben or Mich on Papa's side?

I loved these people with the predatory cling of a little monkey to its mother's back. I was not alien to my unremarkable family. They were my people. They were my security. They were my world and already they were my vast unhappiness.

I doubt if it occurred to either of my parents to give more than passing perplexity to aspects of me which they considered varied from the norm.

I don't know what ails the child! She never complains of an ache. Just the same, I imagine it must be growing pains. She mopes.

Papa approached the situation something like this: You certainly worry your mother, Fannie, and show very little consideration. She would go through fire for you and yet you seem to be a dissatisfied child.

ANATOMY OF ME

How could I cry out to Papa, who awed me: I love it here, but I don't like it here. It's warm and nice being with you and Mama, but I have no one to talk to. I cannot say to you or anybody the kind of things I think inside. Where are the beautiful people like Romeo and Lancelot and Elaine and Isolde and the Lady of the Lake, Helen and Cleopatra? Why don't we talk nicer? Why don't we talk about the lovely things, instead of leather and money and what Mrs. Moss says and what shall we have for supper? Why are we the way we are, when somewhere there are the lovely people who think beautiful thoughts or write them?

Flocks of such highfalutin vagaries fluttered within and pestered me, as they doubtless torment the average imaginative child. A passionate phrase from a second-rate novel. The heartbreak of: *I wish I were where Helen lies*. The loveliness of such a line as: *Oh weep for Adonais for he is dead*. Or, *Trailing clouds of glory do we come* . . . earliest memory gems that I collected. Not necessarily for their content. Reading beyond my years, I often did not even understand. But words were sensuous, like music. They were my colored sands, my bright beads, my little hummingbirds.

In our geographies and in the song books stamped "Property of the School Board of St. Louis, Missouri," there were wonderful words, Zanzibar, Bali, Malta, Excelsior, Ave Maria . . .

I was a word lapidary, interested not so much in their values as in their colors. Ruby was a word that glowed. Serene was like a pearl.

I used to evoke words as I lay in bed. Think about them over and above Mama's kitchen chatter to our Willie, maid-of-all-work: Willie, go down in the cellar and bring up some potatoes. Willie, do you call this pan scoured?

Probably these measles of the spirit were indicating that a little later I was to begin my long stubborn apprenticeship to words. Today, they torment and delight as they did then, fly through the mind in bright flocks. Only now, as then, by the time I capture them on paper they too often prove to be little sparrows.

The grand canyon which yawns between the writer's concept

of what he wants to capture in words and what comes through is a cruel abyss.

That explains why it is so often the case that the writer's most rewarding creative period is gestation, when the ideas are abornin' and the book but a concept. . . .

Thus the scratching uneases were already at work in an overweight, pampered adolescent tucked away in the dangerous security of the pre-world-war middle-class Middle West.

This matter of overweight.

Had it ever occurred to Mama and Papa to analyze beyond: I don't know what ails the child; she mopes; they might have hit upon one or two contributory causes.

First, the special climate that surrounds the only child. Usually, they move in an adult world of overemphasis upon them. Their oneness invites introspection, and for want of the sharing family life of brothers and sisters, the give and take, rather special conflicts set in.

Second, and by no means less in my case, was the psychology of the fat child.

Intimations of my rotundity came to me slowly. Occasionally a small boy would call out as I passed: Hello, Fatty. Mr. Lazarus Scharff, a rotund friend of Papa's, used to pinch my cheek and say: Hello, little Fatso. In the beginning, this made no more impression upon me than the yanking of one of my heavy brown braids by one of the small boy pests, which I met with a glare or a stuck-out tongue.

Three healthy uninhibited appetites had their way at our house and enough was left over of Mama's rich cookery to send out to the neighbors as much again as we consumed. Little wonder that girth consciousness came to me slowly.

The first conscious prick I recall was on the occasion of Mama's decision to send me to Mr. Jacob Mahler's select dancing school.

I protested.

But I thought you wanted it.

I did last year, but not now.

Why?

I'm too—fat.

I think it must have been about the first time the humiliating phrase crossed my lips.

What do you want to be, a skinflint like Marian Flitcraft!

That evening Mama said to Papa in my presence: Your daughter doesn't want to go to Mahler's now that she has pestered me into it.

Papa, reading his newspapers, looked up over his eyeglasses.

Well, I don't know that I blame her. Fannie is serious-minded.

Oh, so you want her to be a wallflower. Your daughter's reason is that she thinks she is too fat.

Why, Fannie, said Papa gently, handsome is as handsome does. Besides, you should be grateful that you are healthy. You have flesh on your bones and that is nice. Surely you don't want to look sickly.

In the end I attended Mr. Mahler's dancing school, but immediately I began to scrutinize the other girls. They were slender, with small waists and no dimples in their hands; and their legs, above black patent-leather dancing pumps, were slim.

When we knew our steps sufficiently to have partners for the waltz and schottische, I began to notice with sinking heart that when Mr. Mahler clicked his cricket and snapped, Take partners! the boys broke row on the opposite side of the room and began to slide across the polished dance floor, each racing for the girl of his choice. I was not among the first they made for. Sometimes the last, or almost.

That was terrible. I not only wanted to be among the first, but the first. That or nothing, and any old little boy would have sufficed.

Dancing school began to be a dread. When I demurred, Mama said: I have paid Mr. Mahler one hundred dollars in advance and I don't intend to throw it away. Money doesn't grow on trees.

Once, when I had been left over, Mr. Mahler drew me out on the floor to dance with him.

Fannie is very light on her feet, he said, addressing the class. If she can handle herself gracefully, there is no excuse for the rest of you. Watch us.

I knew what he meant! If a fat girl could do it, the thin ones surely could.

Nevertheless, I continued to be chosen last, or among the last, and that major frustration of childhood, feeling out of the herd, began to take shape.

I saw everyone in relation to my pudginess. In the cloakroom I stealthily tried on the girls' jackets. Almost invariably they spanned me tightly, and the armholes cut in.

It never occurred to me that you could do anything about it. You were fat as uncompromisingly as your eyes were brown.

It helped make me a tight little island. I was fat and all the other girls in the world were thin. To isolate me further, everybody else had sisters or brothers or both.

Not that I coveted them, but nevertheless it was another difference. There was still another. We were Jews. Almost everybody was not Jewish.

Hamilton, Ohio. My Grandpa Koppel's home in this industrial town of about twenty-five thousand people, twenty-five miles west of Cincinnati—Mama's birthplace and mine—was my summer palace.

Here, where Mama had taken me from St. Louis for the purpose of being born where she first saw the light of day, dwelt the lusty family of my lusty mother.

Grandma Koppel, a spare mirthless woman who died when I was about five. Grandpa, roaring, vulgar, packed with native wit, unlettered, high-minded, foul-spoken, generous.

He had married Grandma in their native Bavarian town, migrated that same year to America, where she subsequently bore him four sons and three daughters in healthy succession. Lusterless as her husband was gusty, she mended, baked, scrubbed, laundered, reddened the brick sidewalk, did menial work in the chicken house, and nurtured an angry kind of self-pity because of overwork which Grandpa, like Papa, neither encouraged nor desired.

On those mornings when Grandpa on horseback drove a herd of his cattle to the Cincinnati stockyards, she would rise at three o'clock to prepare his breakfast.

During my summer visits I could hear him from my bed, in the room where Mama and I had been born, roaring his rage against his stalwart sons, also still in their beds.

Lazy louses! he would shout in his broken English as he made his way to the barns. Lazy good for nothing louses, and Grandma would shush him in German.

Mama once said to me upon our arrival one summer, as I held back from Grandma's outstretched arms and unsmiling face: Go to Grandma, she loves you but doesn't show it.

She reared her own children the unsmiling scolding way, her labor of love bittersweet. She died, I feel sure, without regret, even for the noisy boisterous husband, a man as beloved in his community as she was icily respected.

The summer following her death we went as usual to Hamilton for our annual visit. Grandma Koppel seemed scarcely missed. Time had flowed quickly over what small dent she had left, Aunt Bettie, Mama's unmarried sister, taking up where she left off. Taking up, as they would say it in Missouri idiom, with a vengeance.

Grandpa shivered before and roared against Aunt Bettie's restraining hand even more than he had at Grandma's. A dark, gypsy-looking woman of big heart and high hand, Aunt Bettie controlled her father and four stalwart brothers with greater skill and far more warmth than her mother before her.

Aunt Jennie, the homeliest of the family and, I might add, of almost any family, was that strange paradox, so plain that she fascinated. Married to a handsome and successful business man who spread himself as a red carpet before her long feet, Aunt Jennie insisted upon living at home, thus necessitating a twenty-five-mile commuting trek for Uncle Joe.

Those were the summers! Usually Mama and I arrived in Hamilton when the school vacation began. Two enormous trunks, a wardrobe and a flat, packed for the most part with my finery, were tossed off the train at the depot where Aunts and Uncles were assembled to meet us, Grandpa waiting at the curb in a shabby old basket-phaeton with which he defied and excoriated traffic.

The Aunts and Uncles crowded around the only child the flock of them had produced.

Rose, I can't get over how she has grown!

Fannie, come here to your Uncle Kaufman, and let me measure how much longer your tongue is.

Kaufman, don't begin teasing her!

Rose, why don't you pin up the child's hair in summer? Those heavy braids must be hot.

Come here, Pudgy, and I'll show you what I have for you.

Charley, don't go loading her up with jewelry. Sam hates it.

Uncle Charley, who was bald and the least comely of my handsome Uncles, traveled for a Pittsburgh jewelry firm and covered me with baubles. But it was Uncle Gus to whom I turned most eagerly.

He would wink at me mysteriously, pat his pocket or jerk his head and say: It meows. It barks. It eats tin cans. Guess.

Gus, Mama would remonstrate, no cats or dogs or animals. She makes my life miserable enough on account of them. I won't have my house cluttered with them and she knows it. You remember last summer how she carried on to take the billy goat home with her.

I, who could break down almost any opposition in Mama, had little success when it came to pets. There seemed no way to convey to her the intensity of my craving.

Uncle Gus was a handsome hunk of a man who had rejected schooling from twelve on and according to his sisters was a "hayseed" at heart. Unmarried like all of the Uncles, he was quite a beau, chiefly among farmer maids. You could trace his course by the following odor of bay rum with which he doused himself. But even then it did not quite cover up the strong effusions of Grandpa's cattle.

Hamilton was an industrial town, predominantly German, set in a farming area. Grandpa did his trading in high German, which was little more cultivated than his pungent English. Grandma employed only German girls and spoke German to her children. Sometimes, when Grandpa saw red over his sporty citified sons, with the exception of Uncle Gus, who wanted no part of the cattle business and who had to be watched where the hired girls were concerned, the house rang with German and English.

Old Katrina, lame and wrinkled, who came to help out and remained thirty years, was the solution to the problem of my naughty uncle and the young and pretty farm girls who hired out to Grandma. Katrina used to call me Rosie Koppel's Fanchon, and when she hugged me she felt and smelled like the bag through which Aunt Bettie squeezed her sourish cottage cheese. If one of my uncles even came within teasing reach of her, she began to flay with her arms—*Schweinnerie*, she would shriek—whatever that meant—although obviously built into her synthetic epithet was the word "swine."

Many years later, while still in college, I wrote a short story, "The House of Wrath," one of the few pieces of fiction I have ever consciously created out of actual circumstances. Like most authors, I am repeatedly asked if I glean my characters from real life. Almost invariably no, but "House of Wrath" stemmed directly from Grandpa, in chronic and violent conflict with his four sons, the daughters, as usual, being more conformable.

He certainly contributed most of the virility, the personality, the sparkling if crude wit to his marriage, qualities which made him a state-wide "character." People said: old Dave Koppel, with his inimitable malaprop vocabulary, was worth his four sons put together. That was not entirely the case. My Uncle Charley, urban and urbane, sporty Uncle Kaufman, Uncle Abe, stormy looking as a young Beethoven, of no earning capacity, and with an immense fascination for women, Uncle Gus, even more peasant than his ancestry, to say nothing of the three girls, were all of a basic middle-class respectability.

We were bourgeois through and through and the bourgeois in me must have responded. I liked the coarse texture of life at my grandfather's. Even while I was already rebelling against the fate of having been thrust into a world so alien to my yearnings, I felt at home there. . . .

You did not worry about being fat in Hamilton. In Hamilton you had pets. Dog, goat, rabbit, pony. The Aunts dressed me up in the overloaded finery in the trunks, and I was taken around to the *Kaffeeklatsches* given by Mama's one-time school friends to honor her return.

Grandpa drove me in the rickety phaeton to the homes of the farmers, who admired my heft and fed me.

She's a good one? Grandpa would inquire of them.

They pinched my chubby legs above the sock line and guffawed.

Against admonitions from his daughters, Grandpa usually stopped at one or two of the town's taverns, stood me on the bar and let the beer-smelling, tobacco-stained denizens admire me.

Rosie's child. She's a good one, not?

She is another Rosie, Dave, and Rosie Koppel was the prettiest girl in this town.

How much you think she weighs? She's a good one, not?

I was a good one, in Hamilton.

Just as Mama used to say: You are a different child when your father comes into the house, so Hamilton seemed a different place when Papa came to call for Mama and me after our summer sojourn.

It was as if someone had removed a boiling kettle from the stove. The house quieted. Aunt Jennie did not yell at Uncle Abe over what was destined to be his tragic liaison with her best girl friend. Grandpa did not insist upon sitting in the side yard in his socks, with his suspenders dangling. Aunt Jennie and Aunt Bettie wore dresses instead of "wrappers" in the house. They spoke in measured tones.

Mama beamed, although her fun, too, was curtailed. I reflected her pride. Papa had elegance, or perhaps dignity is the word. He was gracious and tried to ease the tensions he seemed to sense he introduced into the household. He even tried to joke.

But persiflage sat on Papa like a ton of coal.

Those summers in Hamilton were practically my first taste of nature in the close-up. While Mama and her sisters napped and the wheat-growing Ohio sun beat into the white dust of Hamilton streets and against the closed green shutters of Grandpa's white frame house, I was free to roam through meadows, pastures, and along streams to smells that were new to me. The acrid ones of heat into vegetation, weeds and cow droppings. The sounds of bell-sheep, of frogs plopping into the creek, cattle lowing in a motionless scene, and that throat-catching whistle of a distant train.

Long afternoons of wandering alone in middle-western heat stored themselves away in my mind like Aunt Bettie's winter apples in the cellar. In the deep places of my memory, her winter apples have kept firm and round through the years. I can taste them and smell them. I can taste and smell Hamilton.

Recently, at the invitation of civic groups, I revisited Hamilton for a return-of-the-native celebration. Three, four, or five Fannie Hursts, age seven, eight, nine, ten, were at my heels. All of my early selves following me into my yesterdays and fitting into one another like a Russian toy.

The town, meanwhile, has grown from twenty to fifty-eight thousand inhabitants. Aerials stalk the roofs of the humblest houses, multicolored automobiles line its streets, motion picture theaters with fine marquees are on High Street, the Five and Dime store is red-fronted, the White Tower Lunch Room is plate-glass-fronted, Strauss' Clothing Emporium is gone, and a five-story department store is on the site.

But the old courthouse on High Street stands, and three times a week the market wagons, piled with the same fresh Ohio produce, line its curbs, just as in the days when Aunt Bettie used to take me to market for live fowls, fresh country butter wrapped in cheesecloth, watermelons that you plugged before purchasing.

The farm wagons are trucks now, and the twenty-five-cent watermelons are a dollar, unplugged.

As part of the gala two-day celebration marking the return

of this prodigal, "they" drove me past the site of the old Koppel homestead, which is now a lumberyard.

Grandpa bequeathed the homestead to his only unmarried daughter, Aunt Bettie, who sold it the last year of her life. Why I did not find some way to preserve the lovely old house, I will never understand. I feel sure I could have stayed Aunt Bettie's hand. I was beginning to write then, quite lucratively, and might have contrived to purchase it. As a matter of fact, in all probability Aunt Bettie would have given me the place. I don't believe I even knew of its sale until after the event.

Besides, by that time Jack was already in my life and my cup of interests was full to overflowing.

Hamilton memories are stamped into me as firmly as Grandpa used to mash down tobacco into his smelly old pipe.

Grandpa is gone, his four sons and three daughters are gone. The white frame house is gone. Koppel bones, in the pretty little cemetery beyond the creek, must by now be dust to dust.

Only I remain. With me goes the last member of an emigrating family which, a century ago, came to put its roots down into a brave new world.

The turbulent song of the Koppels is finished, but I hope and believe that through all their dissonances a thread of melody lingers on. They were simple, they were crude, they were fundamentally good.

They helped build their era, lived by faith and law. The good in them outweighed their shortcomings. America is better, not worse, for them.

I am glad that, despite the vulgarities and petty violence of my background, a modicum of the magnesium of Ohio soil is built into me.

Papa prospered. Our house was refurnished in the Mission style then in vogue. Brass beds, stained-glass dome over the round dining-room table, and a three-piece velour, upholstered "set" for the living room.

Mama gained weight, and my adolescence quickened.

Outside the small universe into which our lives were cemented, a great sprawling city on the banks of the Mississippi was gathering strength.

Theodore Roosevelt into Taft into Wilson!

As far as awareness or discussion went, our home never turned a hair. Papa read politics assiduously and discussed it with us not at all. I do recall the man on horseback riding figuratively and literally through the era, sparks flying, but the memory is by way of a large Teddy bear, which I kept in a child-size rocking chair, and the Teddy Roosevelt roughrider hats which boys and girls alike wore jauntily.

To Mama and to me politics and national affairs were practically nonexistent. We knew election time chiefly because the St. Louis *Globe-Democrat* arrived with a row of roosters across the first page. Mama once admonished me: If any of the children should ask you what your father is, say Republican.

By now, French, English, and American history were part of my school curriculum, but I could not have told you the current Vice-President of the United States, the Secretary of State, or even the name of the Mayor of my city.

William Jennings Bryan, yes. Everyone talked about "free silver" and "The Cross of Gold." His daughter, Ruth Bryan, who was later to become my intimate, and who monopolized the front pages of the *Nation* by eloping at sixteen from her school in Monticello, Missouri, had the small girls of my world goggle-eyed.

Papa exchanged "man talk" with our neighbors summer evenings, as we sat on our veranda wielding palm-leaf fans against heat and mosquitoes, while the Cates Avenue dusk thickened and the trees blackened. Mark Hanna, roughriders, Chauncey Depew, Henry Cabot Lodge, and those "anarchists," the "socialists," are some of the references that bounced from porch to porch in the successive years of my little girlhood. But inside our house there was little talk to which a child could listen to her cultural advantage. No one ever read a book or attended a lecture or a concert, although come evenings, while waiting for Papa, Mama in her crisp "dressing sacque" would seat herself at the upright piano in our reception hall and render—yes, "render" is the word for it—her repertoire, tried and true.

I would sit on the stairs and let the tunes infiltrate while Mama pounded at the keyboard, the bisque girl and boy on top of the piano rattled, and the odors of pot roast and German fried potatoes drifted into the sounds; and fantasy had its way with me: I visualized myself as beautiful, slender, and desired. Older men were in love with me. My essays were read at teachers' meetings as the finest that had ever been done. I was voted the most popular girl in school . . . teachers singled me out . . . my dance program was the first one filled . . .

Whatever the aridity of our lives, it did not seem so in the living. But looking backward, I realize how little fun, aside from Mama's flashes of wit, we had at our house.

Whatever inner life of the spirit existed was secretive. In our lives a spade was a spade was a spade.

The neighborhood motion picture was an occasional outlet, but we seldom ventured into downtown where the Olympic Theater often presented St. Louis with New York's two- or three-year-old Broadway successes. Distances were great, we had no automobile, and the late walk from the streetcar to our house could be cold and dark or, as the case might be, humid and dark.

Neither Mama nor Papa had hobbies, such as photography, golf, fishing, travel. We celebrated no anniversaries or holidays. I used to come to the breakfast table on Mama's or Papa's birthday stiff with apprehension at having to express anything so bordering on sentiment as "Happy Birthday," with accompanying kiss. Picnics I do not recall at all, although sometimes on Thursdays or Sundays, the "girl's" day off, we dined out. Papa much preferred meals at home. So did Mama, who said it was "a shame for the money" as she could serve a better and less expensive meal in her own kitchen. Usually, it was for my sake that we went to a restaurant.

When Papa did things at all, he did them nicely, but with one persistent and embarrassing flaw. He would order with a lavish hand, Mama nudging him under the table: Sam, one portion of asparagus is enough for two. Why order fresh fruit? We have plenty at home.

But he abhorred the system of tipping, declared it demeaned a big strapping man to be given loose change, which it literally was in a day when twenty-five cents was a munificent gratuity.

Mama said: I should be so demeaned. But we exchanged apprehensive glances when Papa took out his wallet to pay the check: Sam, if you don't leave that waiter a tip I'll do it myself. I don't intend to be humiliated.

Papa would sigh, dig into his pocket for coins, and reluctantly slap them down.

Mama, on the other hand, contributed her own irritants. I recall one evening as we rode the streetcar home after a restaurant repast, she suddenly exploded: That halibut tonight wasn't fit to eat. Three dollars and sixty cents for our meal and what did we have? I can give you better food at home for less than half. . . .

Rose, you don't need to tell the entire streetcar.

Well, provide me with an automoblile and your wife won't embarrass you in public. Next time I'll stay at home and then you won't have a problem.

Now, old lady, don't get on your high horse.

A depression would steal over me. Why weren't we like other people! Why didn't we have more fun? Papa was never so heavy as when he tried to lighten our lives. You somehow knew it was forced. He never really wanted to go out to dinner or take a vacation or buy a gewgaw or play around, the way some fathers did. He made a brave show of desiring divertissement because he knew Mama's tendency to pull back in the name of economy would come to his rescue. But once Mama had capitulated, Papa's lukewarmness began to assert itself.

Papa must have been sedate at twenty. People who knew him that far back queried: How in the world did Sam Hurst and Rose Koppel ever get together? The last girl in the world I should think he would have married.

No, by way of objective analysis, there is not too much in my childhood, secure and pampered though it was, to invite nostalgia.

Holiday celebrations, family birthday parties, Christmas invoke no dear memories in me because we never practiced them. We had fireplaces in our house but no open fires. No family circle to gather. We were undemonstrative, minimizing any show of our feelings toward one another. I lived alone, walked alone, read alone, despaired alone.

Again, to be appraisingly factual, I was not even a wanted child and knew it by way of overhearing Mama talking with a friend whose daughter was about to be married: I hope Rosalie doesn't have a baby the first year, the way I did. I cried my eyes out. We weren't ready for it, couldn't afford it. I had Fannie before Mr. Hurst and I had time to get to know one another. . . .

I may not have been wanted; but, once arrived, love, security, and more were my portion.

According to today's theories, I was reared consistently wrong by parents who had never read or studied child psychology, heard a lecture, or reckoned with psychiatry or Parent-Teacher Associations.

When Mama reiterated: I don't know what ails the child, she has it too good if the truth were known; the elaborate and complicated vocabulary of psychiatry was already on its way toward us, but the name Freud had scarcely infiltrated.

Despite their bewilderment, they gave me love, and more love.

I am blessed to have had them, and they, in turn, lie buried where I know they would want to be, deep in the heart of their only child, who gave them so little in return for all the things they were.

To be sure, pleasure and some pride in my doings were in store for them. But they were never to be on relaxed terms with the inexplicable things that were to happen to me.

A writer in the family!

My junior year in college, when my first published opus appeared in the famous St. Louis weekly, *Reedy's Mirror*, Papa reacted as if his daughter's name were Balzac.

I always told you, Fannie, knowledge is power. You'll show them! Mama's reactions were mixed. Pride was out all over her, but so was her dubiousness. It doesn't pay to be too smart. It frightens people off.

Papa saw through the thinly veiled implication.

Fannie has too much sense to be boy crazy. She lets the other girls push themselves forward.

I dared not be boy crazy because I felt fat. The incidents of Mr. Mahler's dancing school were seared into me. I avoided boys even when they showed some disposition to take note of me. Besides, so many of them had sour-smelling hands and pimples. I hated that.

After this first publication in *Reedy's Mirror* and our friends were buzzing about me, Mama remarked to a neighbor:

It's just wonderful. Her father and I are naturally proud. But, as I say to Mr. Hurst, men are afraid of smart girls.

When the time came for me to enter high school we became a household divided.

Mama wanted me to attend one of the town's select private schools, Mary Institute or Harperly Hall. Papa was for Central High School.

Inwardly I leaned in his direction, but somehow when he put it into words it set up in me that mysterious amalgam, family antagonism.

I am willing to scrape and stint myself, blazed Mama, but I don't intend to do it on my child.

The public schools of the United States are good enough for me, contended Papa.

And what about the riffraff your daughter may encounter? I want her to have the best.

I have nothing more to add, said Papa, and retired behind his newspaper.

Despite his unusually decisive manner, Mama held out. I was entered at Harperly Hall. It seemed more like a handsome private residence, which it had once been. Potted palms everywhere, framed Anderson prints of the Colosseum by Moonlight, Michelangelo's David, and Murillo's Madonna and Child, following the wall space of the great winding staircase.

The headmistress, a large woman with a wide shelf of bosom, and salt-and-pepper hair which she wore in a high stern pile, received us.

She had my application and school grades before her.

Mr. Hurst's occupation? Age. Grandparents, maternal and paternal, names and places of birth. And here it came! Religion?

Jewish, replied Mama, as if she were biting off a thread.

The headmistress's pen paused an almost imperceptible second and so did my breathing, then both proceeded.

What else could Mama have said! But, punily, I would have given anything not to have had her say that word to this lady whose professional graciousness seemed to curdle for the instant and then turn back into cream.

She questioned me. Yes, I liked school. English and history were my favorite studies. No, I don't ride horseback. Yes, I hoped to learn French.

Sports? I didn't know anything about them, except tennis. Travel in the United States or Europe? Only in America. Where? Hamilton, Ohio. Have you ever been to Vicksburg, your father's birthplace? No.

It occurred to me how little I knew of Papa's youth. Mama's family was near and dear. Papa's somehow remote.

The headmistress then talked tuition and all the extras with Mama. Harmony, horseback riding, voice, fencing, concerts, textbooks; and then said that we would hear from her, as the school was quite crowded and the waiting list long.

On the way home, Mama was explosive. The nerve of her! You would think we had come asking something for nothing. Where, how, and why were we born? What has that got to do with education? I guess your father was right, only don't let him know I said so.

I felt one major burning apprehension but could not bring myself to speak about it. Girls from the boulevards and the big houses in the outlying towns came there for culture. I suddenly wanted

Harperly, except for that burning and challenging apprehension.

As we neared home, Mama, still fuming, spoke it out for me.

And on top of it all, I think she was *richus*.

When Mama used that word, it grated against me like sandpaper.

To have *richus*, I knew from Mama's and my Aunts' lips, was to have "race prejudice", a phrase which never failed to strike dread and humiliation into me.

I did not say as much to Mama, but I wondered if I would be accepted. If only that terrible question had not been asked. What did it matter? Neither by appearance nor manner were we typed. The horrid little thoughts crawled all through me, and on they crawled.

A week later we were notified of my acceptance, and I entered Harperly Hall the following autumn. It proved a heartbreaking experience of short duration. From the beginning, my separateness from the Harperly girls, even though it had nothing to do with creed, asserted itself.

I doubt if it was due to anything more than my own self-conscious aloofness, quickened by the fact, soon apparent, that I had little in common with these girls. They were Schwachts, van Blarkoms, Baumgartens, Kunkles, brewery, banking, real estate, railroad names in our city. The Kunkle twins had been registered for Vassar the day they were born. The van Blarkom girl lived in one of the finest Victorian mansions in Vandeventer Place. Most of the pupils arrived at Harperly Hall in family limousines. They knew one another out of Harperly, attended the same dancing classes, conducted privately in the ballroom of the Kunkle home in Westmoreland Place, and went with their families to the same summer resorts, Bar Harbor or Kennebunkport, Maine, or Europe.

It is not improbable that nothing more or less than my contrast to these plainly dressed girls was responsible for some of my isolation. Mama sent me out in clothes geared, so she thought, to Harperly. I arrived my first day in plaid, the skirt ruffled to the waist, and an enormous hair bow of corresponding plaid accenting my high pompadour. Shoes, patent leather with plaid tops.

It had been a lovely outfit when I left home, but at Harperly I was hot in it, bothered in it, and suddenly furious with Mama.

To be sure, there was something at Harperly I lacked at home. Certain amenities, I suppose, but they did little if anything for the wide lonesome places within my growing self.

Mama said: No wonder you're lonesome, you don't mix.

The dark word "lonely" had not yet moved into my consciousness. It was not that I was lonesome at Harperly for the girls who did not make up to me. I was lonely for what Harperly could not give me. For what my kind of life could not give me . . . It was rather the beginnings in me of that endemic ailment of the lonely spirit and youth . . . that indefinable hunger . . .

I endured silent and miserable weeks at Harperly, Mama's eagle eye probing.

Either you don't feel well or something is bothering you.

Please, Mama, I tell you I'm all right.

It's that school. You don't like it.

Did I say anything!

What don't you like?

But I do.

Fannie, is there *richus?*

That dreadful word again!

No.

I guess your father was right. I made a mistake in sending you there.

At the end of the third month I broke down.

Don't make me go back there. What I want isn't there!

What do you want?

I don't know, only I know it isn't there.

Five hundred dollars for tuition and now she discovers that what she wants isn't there. . . .

I entered high school a semester late, with private lessons to help make up for the delayed start.

At the time, St. Louis, a city of six hundred thousand, boasted one high school, a huge red brick structure, midtown. Fourteen hundred pupils streamed through its wide corridors.

Here were the masses! I swam into their midst like a delighted duck into new waters.

Subconsciously, I suppose, I was already seeking the people, and Harperly Hall had been a matter of persons.

At Central High you said "tomato" and "can't" without the broad *a*. I wore my plaid dress with the ruffles and it drew admiring eyes. In contrast to Harperly Hall, the teaching staff seemed alive and stimulating. No one heeded whether you crossed your legs, or saw to it that the young ladies were hatted and gloved before leaving the building.

Almost immediately, one of the male teachers, a Mr. Heide, history department, became my secret passion and inner excitement. I don't believe even when I tried to capture his interest by laborious attempts at originality when called upon in class that he ever gave me a sustained look.

Mama said: You would think you were going to the Veiled Prophets' Ball the way you waste time in front of the looking glass dressing for school.

The sweet pain of Mr. Heide moved through my first weeks of Central High. I thought of life for us both. I thought of death for us both. Death, where is thy sting, with Mr. Heide. . . .

Mama said and said: That Harperly Hall with its *richus*. I'm going to ask them to refund the tuition money I paid in advance.

Papa put his foot down. Rose, you cannot do that. Business is not conducted that way.

It's not the money, it's the principle, insisted Mama stubbornly.

But there was something in Papa's voice and frown that Mama did not further controvert.

For years afterward, whenever we passed Harperly Hall, Mama would let go: Robbers!

Central High School, a red brick Victorian pile, then outstanding for its modern innovations, was situated on Grand Avenue, a midtown crosstown artery.

A horde of white segregated children surged upon it from the four corners of the city, swarming in before 9 A.M. and avalanching out at three-thirty.

When people said, as they were wont, and still are for that matter: St. Louis is a slow town, give me Chicago or New York; it seemed to me they must know nothing about Grand Avenue.

Besides Central High, Grand Avenue boasted the Odeon Concert Hall, next door, Christian Brothers' College, and the massive stone entrance to the then exclusive Vandeventer Place. There was even a bookstore near Central High where, to be sure, only Christian Science literature was dispensed.

In years to come, Americans were to be shocked by the mass illiteracy of its draft-age young men, an alarming percentage of them unlettered and worse.

Zest for learning, teaching standards, and teaching salaries were low. Teachers faced up to classes of sixty or seventy. Anonymous faces on the day's crowded murals, we were chiefly identifiable by stacks of cards from which the teacher read your name when calling upon you. When you had completed your recitation, she marked your grade on the card. This sum total made up your monthly report. It was not unusual for a teacher, in whose presence you sat for five hours a week, to pass you on the street without recognizing you.

This mass manifestation, ungood educationally and functionally, proved to be providential for me. I felt at home here.

A turn of mind that was to influence many of my later attitudes began to take shape. People en masse, even these public school youngsters coming as they did from varied social, economic, and cultural backgrounds, struggling, squirming, pushing, filled me with a kind of pity or a warm glow. On the other hand, small groups stiffened me to a degree that caused Papa to reiterate: Don't be so reserved. People will think you are proud or indifferent.

I was neither.

Suddenly finding myself part of a human family composed of the swarms I encountered in my overcrowded school of mass education, mass evaluation, and mass graduation, each one of us so mysteriously separate, was as if a dormant part of me had come to life. As a matter of fact, people had come to life. Fourteen hundred of them.

From the beginning I strove for leadership in this new world, and the race became more important to me than the education itself. But, taking my assigned place in alphabetical order, Miss Alper, Mr. Askenasay, Miss Blut, Miss Gronfelt, Mr. Heymeier, Miss Hurst, Miss Imseipen, I was as anonymous as a prisoner behind his number.

It irked. An only child, her swollen ego produced largely by home conditions, was stunned by her gargantuan unimportance in, or to, rank and file.

Seldom at peace with my world, I itched through these early teens as if they were woolens.

Intolerable from the beginning was the fact that the teachers paid me little or no heed, although several pupils were promptly singled out for superior scholarship. No matter how I strove, chiefly without study but by what I considered personality, I seemed unable to arouse interest, except in the form of an occasional rebuke for violation of a rule or careless preparation of an assigned lesson.

Mama said: I can see you aren't any happier at high school than you were at Harperly Hall.

Papa said: Fannie, I am afraid you do not know what you want.

She's got it too good, said Mama.

Be that as it may, I was rigid with a sense of rejection.

Every day that I remained content to be just one more pair of marching feet, I was more certain to remain sunk in anonymity.

I yearned for these underpaid, overworked teachers to pay me special attention. When it did not happen I resorted to the most obvious exhibitionism.

Where hitherto I had discouraged Mama's attempts to overload me, I now accompanied her on frequent trips to the downtown department stores, where it was a simple matter to excite her into a shopping spree.

You want those red shoes? Don't you think they will scuff up for school wear? No? All right, then, let's get some red material and I'll have Miss Stutz make you a red dress to match.

Presently I began to be noticed, but for the largest this, the reddest that. On one occasion a titter ran through history of art class when our instructor paused to remark: Miss Hurst, would you mind flattening down your huge hair bow, those in back of you cannot see the blackboard.

Testing Mama's indulgence, I now managed to appear as many as ten successive days in different apparel.

One day I realized I had indeed broken through the ice of anonymity, when one teacher remarked to another as I passed in a throng: There she goes! That is Fannie Hurst, the heavy-set girl in the checked dress.

At last! "Heavy-set" or not, once they knew of my existence and the way I was, we could share thoughts. It did not matter to me so much that the boys passed me by. I wanted the attention of these teachers who, I believed, lived in the world of the mind.

I wanted them to regard me as the most interesting girl in the school. I felt and thought so much that I could never discuss with the girls on my block or in my classes, or at home with Mama and Papa. No one except me really knew the kind of person I was. I wanted to share me, to exhibit me, the way I was . . . inside. . . .

I became outstanding quickly enough, but not in the manner I craved. Overdressed, overglib in class, my recitations laboriously "different," I too often excited the laughter of class or teacher or both. But it was laughter at me rather than with me. I realized it, and the fires of my tortured teens burned high.

Perversely I went my way, hating the reasons for my becoming a conspicuous pupil among the fourteen hundred. Nevertheless, even if ignominiously, outstanding I was.

Periodically, Mr. Bryan, principal of Central High School, sent word to Mama he would like to see her. In a strange way I exulted in these conferences, which took place in my presence, and I don't think Mama or Papa minded too much.

Fannie has a good mind except for the fact . . .

When a strong personality like Fannie sets a bad example to her classmates . . .

Fannie is quite exceptional in some respects but . . .

I felt secretly flattered.

Mama and Papa did too. I could tell by the indulgent way in which they voiced disapproval of me.

Boys. Toward the close of my freshman year at Central High, they began to bother me. Not by overtures, but by their very existence.

I found myself wishing there were none in our school. The girls were more likable when there were no boys around them. Their mere presence seemed to excite them into curvaceous behavior. A wide variety of artifices appeared: a trick of throwing the eyes never practiced between girls, a pout that in some mysterious way seemed to have boy appeal, laughter in a much higher key.

No sooner would I meet up with a girl who seemed promising, someone to walk home from school with or eat lunch beside, than, presto, the relationship would be impeded by this boy and girl thing. The new friend would acquire a boy "date" to carry her books and accompany her home. From then on, something alienating to the friendship had happened. You shared only half interests.

Despite the fact that one wanted nothing more than an invitation to a baseball or basketball game, it was humiliating not to be boy-asked. For a time I employed the old device of inventing a boy friend who "worked downtown," but how long could one sustain the lie without producing him?

My vanity yearned, but no one was going to know it. If one of the boys, even the football heroes who walked in glory, so much as threw me a glance, I turned away with a haughty dropping of eyelids. Actually, I did not like them. By the mere fact of their maleness they were accorded a superiority which irked me. Most of them were knobby and picked their fingernails. Those in the short pants of the era were beneath my dignity, those in long were gangling, and the big-shouldered athletic darlings of the girls looked and were, for the most part, dumb.

We were still many a year in arrears of the unwashed, ungroomed adolescents of both sexes who, following the world wars,

were to set the fashion for dirty denim, slovenly outside shirts, and revealing sweaters.

Nevertheless, I searched within the reaches of myself to explain the obvious preference of the boys for girls I considered of no particular distinction.

People usually said I had a pretty face, which to me meant the completed saying: Too bad she is so fat, she has such a pretty face.

Obviously the boys preferred thin girls.

Despite the fact that I yearned not at all for their company, the boy and girl aspect of Central High was ruinous to peace of mind.

Why? I kept asking myself.

I began forcing. Not athletically inclined, I joined up with tennis and basketball teams, ultimately excelling in both. Swallowing distaste for it, I seldom failed to answer a call for volunteers to deliver the platform greeting to the weekly assembly of all fourteen hundred pupils.

I wrote jingles about various teachers, passing them during study hours among the snickering students. I jockeyed for a conspicuous place even in the areas of misbehavior. But a calm star with a twinkle was shining over my flamboyance, in the form of William Schuyler, a man with his head wreathed in clouds, who had committed the immense incongruity of finding himself assistant principal of a middle-western high school.

The day I was sent to his office on a charge of inciting study hall misbehavior was remarkable because of two circumstances. First, the moment I clapped eyes on Will Schuyler something exceptional began happening to me. In addition, an intoxicating incident had previously occurred which was partly responsible for the spurt of exhibitionism which landed me in William Schuyler's presence.

My English teacher, a maiden lady who must then have been close to retirement age, announced to the class: I have a composition this week from one of you which is so good it should be read aloud.

My heart missed a beat. . . . Could it be!

It was.

ANATOMY OF ME

That is how exultation got the better of me in the study hall, inciting me to write the faculty-spoofing jingles.

Schuyler was a slightly built man, humorous and very grave. I had never encountered his like. For two hours he talked to me as if I were the only person in that huge hive of swarming youth. Bells rang. Corridors thundered. School let out.

He did not refer to my misdemeanor. Barely glanced over my record in the files. Asked me about myself. My parents. What interested me? What troubled me? What pleased me? Showed me small animals he had fashioned out of clay. There were framed poems and quotations on the walls of his office. I remember two: "They are never alone that are accompanied with noble thoughts. Sir Philip Sydney." The second was a quotation on parchment-like paper, illuminated with painted flowers: "The man that hath no music in himself, nor is not moved by concord of sweet sounds is fit for treason, stratagems, and spoils: . . . Let no such man be trusted." Nonsense! Papa was to be trusted. But the words, I knew not whose, were strung together with beauty. . . . Was Mr. Schuyler strung together with beauty? Papa certainly was not fit for treason, stratagems, and spoils, nor were we at our house strung together with beauty. . . .

People who seemed to live on another plane from us were strangely depressing. Here was someone with framed poetry on his walls and Mama's laundress stole soap. . . .

I talked those long hours in Mr. Schuyler's office as I had never talked before, told him of my confusions and of my undisciplined reading which had led me either into shallow literary waters or those beyond my depth. Two or three aspects of the complex business of being fourteen years old I could not bring myself to tell him. The secret humiliation regarding boys. And the business of being fat. Or about things such as the terrible aloneness experienced at night when Mama and Papa went into their room together and closed their door.

He asked to see the composition that had skyrocketed my day, read it without comment, and my recently laid miseries sprang back into position.

Now about this matter of deportment. Of course you want to apologize to Miss Wayne. He read the ditty aloud: Miss Waney things I'm zany. I think Miss Waney isn't too brainy. Your punishment is inherent in your couplet, Miss Hurst. It could not be duller or less funny.

My punishment stung.

You may also explain to Miss Wayne that you are being further penalized by sitting in my office for the next two weeks, instead of attending her English class, and writing me a daily theme each time.

Mr. Heide flew out of the window of my affections. Now I was in love with a man in his sixties, father of three grown sons.

Looking back upon the fomenting period of adolescence, I seem to have been just another squirmer with an itch I could not scratch. If I have carried over from these conflicts of early life such elaborate impedimenta as hostility, depression, guilt, conflict, ambivalence, euphrasia; if I be manic, defensive, compulsive, or merely obsessed, then I say to these termites of my subconscious, sleep on. . . .

I had known for some time that Papa's brother Mich's wife, Aunt Minnie, was going to have a baby. Her silhouette told me. I had read in an anthology of verse off the public library shelves, "That listening look on the face of her with child, as if by the voices of heavenly angels beguiled." The combination of the birds-and-the-bees mishmash that Mama in my early teens was actually still feeding me and my garbled knowledge of the processes had boiled up into a sense of revulsion against the whole business.

In vain I studied Aunt Minnie's brownish face, which was beginning to look bloated, for the listening angel's look. God, I told myself, was at work on Aunt Minnie and His ways are inscrutable. Nevertheless, I could scarcely bear to so much as glance at her during these months. Once she asked Mama in German, which I understood, if I "knew," to which Mama replied in the negative.

Mama saw to it, poor dear, that I learned the hard way.

It was about this time, at Mama's anxious behest, that a neighboring girl several years older than I asked me over to her house one day after school, because she had something to tell me.

Flattered, and no little curious, I went. Seated on the stairs of her back porch, she dumped her information clumsily, stunning me further into a sense of revulsion. Mama and the way of thought of her era did something to me this time that it was to take me years to overcome. Mama's harbinger of the facts of life went at me with the vocabulary of the abattoir, conditioning me with a kind of revulsion against most physical manifestations, including those of persons indisposed or ill.

I doubt, contemporary way of thought to the contrary notwithstanding, that I was the worse because of the false and foolish shames that existed between parents and children of that era. Had my precocity not denied it to me, I think I might have enjoyed believing the fantasy of the stork flying the babe on its three-cornered magic carpet over the sooty city roofs of St. Louis, in order to deposit Cecile Hurst in Aunt Minnie's black walnut bed on Finney Avenue.

Sooner or later the cobwebby legends of childhood must strain and break apart. The stork, the bees and the flowers, Santa Claus, and the fairies at the bottom of the garden are doomed to early death. Paradoxically, I mourn the passing of the birds-and-bees era even as I hail the clear-eyed youngsters of today to whom the facts of life are the understood and natural results of the facts of life.

I doubt if Mama or Papa had ever heard of a Parent-Teacher Association. Most of us were reared "by ear," Froebel and Montessori becoming important only in more knowing circles, although private Montessori kindergartens were already beginning to spot the town.

I used to feel a pang of envy for girls or boys who could discuss varied subjects with their parents. Myra Frankel's mother, who lived across the street from us on Cates Avenue and had once been a schoolteacher in Worcester, Massachusetts, used to do Myra's homework with her because, she said, it refreshed her mind. Mr. and Mrs. Frankel belonged to a Culture Club. Mama said she wished Mrs. Frankel would use some of her culture toward keeping her lace curtains from looking like dirty strings. At that, Mama's friends would go into gales of laughter. For that matter so would I. Mama's humor was certainly not in what she said, but in her manner of saying it. However, it was at times such as this that Papa would glance over the top of his newspaper and his glasses at Mama's laughing audience and then at Mama, with that puzzled look of trying to fathom her appeal to risibilities.

There were days when I returned home from school glowing with a good experience in history or English, or from a poem or a bit of prose read aloud to me by William Schuyler. But somehow the curtain dropped on this phase of me when I entered our house.

When I changed from my too elaborate school clothes to the simpler ones Mama had waiting for me, I also slipped back from mental stimuli to the way it was at our house, where the cleavage was clean between home life and growing intellectual interests outside.

But, make no mistake, I liked both my worlds.

When I went downstairs into the kitchen where Mama or Willie fed me out of our larder stocked with heavy foods, I reverted.

The strain fell away of needing to impress Mr. Schuyler, the teachers, the girls and boys, some of whom were now showing head and shoulders above the herd. A girl named Ned Steiber was already in my way, some of the boys also showing disquieting and unsuspected aptitudes.

When Mama used "ain't," I continued to feel irked but I was glad I did not say Mammah and Pappah the Harperly Hall way, with accent on the final syllable. I liked Mama's garlic potatoes, despite the fact that I was already beginning to squirm over our mahogany and green velours "parlor set" that I had selected with so much gusto a year or two before. Coming home from school to it was like walking into open arms.

And, in reverse, when I stepped out mornings into that outside world in which I was determined to excel somehow, some way, I felt release. A small cluster of girls in the neighborhood usually met at a corner for the long walk to Central High. After three or four blocks I frequently deserted them to run ahead. They used to say, there goes Hurry-Up-Fannie.

The sense of hurry was and is strong. Perhaps that accounts for a lifetime of early rising. Hurry, hurry to meet the new day . . .

We lived through two business crises.

In the light of looking back I realize now that without Mama's staying hand Papa would have been somewhat of a promoter. His Oklahoma oil holdings were the source of her perpetual pessimism. Every so often he and a group of St. Louis and Kansas City businessmen would travel in a special car to inspect the Gladys Bell Oil Well.

What I get out of Gladys Bell, Mama would declaim bitterly, will be nothing but worry and regret. This unfortunately proved to be the case: The twenty-five hundred dollars I inherited from my father is gone. Next, I suppose, everything else will go.

In a measure this, too, proved dismally true.

There came the time when Papa was forced to admit that between drought and ruined tomato crops his venture in the canning industry was facing bankruptcy. How they watched the cloudless summer skies during this crisic period. Night after night, often into dawn, Papa talked in low troubled tones as they lay in bed, Mama quieter than I ever remembered her.

Ears strained, I eavesdropped long into those nights, sometimes sensing more than hearing, as their voices rose and fell, something wrong with affairs that had to do with money.

This much became clear to me. Papa was in danger of "failing" because the tomato crop had been ruined by the hot dry summer. To "fail," I eked out, meant not to be able to pay your bills. Well, Sam, Mama said, if the worst comes to the worst, you'll have to do the way other men do and go into bankruptcy. Never! said Papa. I'll find a way to meet my creditors one hundred cents on the dollar.

He did, but part of saving the situation was our move to Mrs. Cleveland's boardinghouse.

Mama cried the entire time we were packing.

I have the feeling that this Mrs. Topel is a *schlomp*, bemoaned Mama. I could tell by the way she sat on the bed, when there was a chair next to it. Mama was referring to the wife of the wholesale coffee salesman who had rented our house furnished. This move we are making to save money will cost us more in the end.

It was your idea, Rose.

Another man who had to choose between his wife and going bankrupt would go bankrupt.

Rose!

Both Papa and I realized that Mama's barbs came at you with speed but, like theatrical rapiers, were made of rubber.

Personally, I contemplated the move to Mrs. Cleveland's boardinghouse with excitement. The address, "West Belle Place," was high-sounding. Actually, the street was one that had seen better days, its one-time fine residences coverted into piano showrooms or boardinghouses.

Nevertheless, to me the move was adventure. We had been so few places, seen so little, deviated so little.

Mrs. Cleveland's boardinghouse proved to be two shabby brick residences joined by a bridge. The second floor front and alcove, which we were to occupy, seemed shabby the day Mama took Papa and me to see the place she had previously inspected. But we passed a little girl in the hall with a small black dog in her arms.

Perhaps now that we were to be no longer surrounded by our own furniture Mama would permit me to have a dog. I wanted one almost to obsession, but in this instance Mama's holdout was adamant and unique.

Even the food smells that permeated Mrs. Cleveland's boardinghouse were new! So was the design of my bed, a folding one that looked like a chiffonier during the day.

Mrs. Cleveland herself was short, stout, mussy, and kind. A puny little boy, her grandchild Harry, trailed her every step.

The day Mama brought Papa and me to inspect, she sealed the bargain with Mrs. Cleveland, while Papa and I stood by: Mr. Hurst likes grits in the morning and three fried eggs, turned over, and please see that we have our own bottles of ketchup and Worcestershire on the table. My daughter is accustomed to bread and butter with applesauce and a glass of milk after school. Mr. Hurst is a great one for plenty of towels. After all, we are paying forty dollars a month.

We moved into Mrs. Cleveland's on a rainy November day, Mama crying.

There we remained two years, instead of the six months planned.

Dear Mrs. Cleveland. An intaglio of her is sunk fondly into my memory. Racked with rheumatism, she swayed from side to side; her shoes had scissored cutouts on the side to relieve pressure against her tortured feet, and her legs were taped.

Day in and day out, she traipsed upstairs, downstairs, through her twenty-two-room pair of houses joined by the bridge, baggage lugging, towel laden, ice water laden, hot water laden, breathing short, her heaving bosom above the V neck of her spotty black basque pushed upward and as wrinkled as crepe.

Upstairs, downstairs, and then into the basement where Mr. Cleveland, tall as Abraham Lincoln and as spare, sat in what he called his office, a partitioned affair of a three-walled room beside the coal bin. A tin bucket of beer was part and parcel of his meaninglessly cluttered desk, his idleness piled as high about him as his stacks of unread books and newspapers.

All day long Mrs. Cleveland served him and their tubercular little grandson Harry.

I loved her, so to speak, with my pity, which, however, was tinctured with some of Mama's outspoken intolerance of her servility toward what Mama termed her "nix-nux" of a husband, who sat all day on his "tokas" while his wife "slaved her fingers to the bone."

"Tokas" was a coarse word out of Hamiltonian idiom which caused Papa to writhe and me with him.

Rose, if you have no respect for me, at least have some for your child.

But Mama continued to pour her disrespect upon Mrs. Cleveland's tired head.

Don't come to me to advance you money, Mrs. Cleveland. It doesn't grow on trees for us, the way you seem to think it does. My husband works hard for a living, the way yours should. If the water is going to be shut off, that is your husband's worry, or should be. Don't come to me.

But Mrs. Cleveland did come, knowing, as I knew, that Mama, over and above any of the other boarders, was going to succumb to the rheumy eyes and the pathos of those calloused hands.

Mrs. Hurst, I hate to have to ask you, but the Barnesconis are owing me for two months back, until he gets on his feet after her operation, and the egg and butter man says tomorrow is his last delivery until he gets paid at least half of the eighty-five dollars I owe. Mr. Aschen promised to pay up his back board on Saturday, but didn't come in from off the road.

This is the last time, Mrs. Cleveland. I am not the National Bank. My husband works while your husband sits with his beer and his books.

You wouldn't say that, Mrs. Hurst, if you could hear the way Mr. Cleveland speaks of Fannie. . . .

Poor dear soul, I suspect she knew the shortcut to Mama's capitulation.

. . . he says she is so bright and unusual. He prefers conversation with her to most grownups. You must remember that in our good days back in Boston Mr. Cleveland was a college professor.

It was about here that Mama's advance was as good as in Mrs. Cleveland's pocket.

It is true that despite the beery fumes of the dark hole Mr. Cleveland called his study, and the pallid spectacle of poor little Harry at play near the coal bin, I spent more time in the company of Mr. Cleveland than Mama, had she known, would have tolerated.

Surrounded by dusty stacks of books on philosophy, theology, ancient and modern history, classical lore, the Latin poets in Latin, long unopened, Mr. Cleveland, groggy most of the time, whiled away the hours playing solitaire, brooding over the figure of his grandson, and dozing.

Attracted by the books, I would creep down to him frequently, instead of playing jacks or hopscotch with neighborhood girls. Finally he came to keep a backless kitchen chair cleared for me; and, as long as I dared for fear of Mama leaning out of her window to find me not among those present at sidewalk games, I would listen to his reminiscences of student life at Harvard, of his teaching days in a boys' school outside Boston, and later at a small midwestern college.

An agnostic whose views and addictions had cost him both positions, Mr. Cleveland had evidently stopped dead in his intellectual tracks, his books mere symbols of his past, his mind stewing in the bitter waters of memory.

But when he found me fingering the books which included antichrist, anti this, anti that diatribes, and asking him what must have been bewildered questions, he broke his long days of silence for occasional spots of after-school conversation with me. It was in Mr. Cleveland's dark cave that I first encountered the name Plutarch, whose chief virtue according to Mr. Cleveland was that he had never heard of Christianity. From those same shelves Lecky's *History of European Morals* and Gibbon's *Decline and Fall of the Roman Empire* soared above my head like skyscrapers, with me absorbed and scarcely able to get my feet off the ground floor. Novels were there too, which Mr. Cleveland allowed me to carry up to our room. *David Copperfield, Père Goriot, The Scarlet Letter.* Norse mythology in the form of a huge book, *Twilight Tales*, which had been removed from the kitchen chair to make room for me. I thought the title *Anatomy of Melancholy* the most wonderful brace of words I had ever heard. Mr. Cleveland read me parts of it, translated the many Latin phrases, and explained Robert Burton's analyses of love and art, tearing to shreds his ideas on religion. Benjamin Franklin's *Autobiography* was there, unexpurgated, which I drank in while Mama still spoke such words as pregnant and prostitute in German in my presence.

But Mr. Cleveland's co-New Englanders, Longfellow, Whittier, Emerson, also sat in that dingy basement; and Mr. Cleveland, who had a voice like a basso talking in an echo chamber, and that echo chamber his own skull, would read from his thumbed copies.

Mama admonished: I don't want you to go down in that dirty basement and waste time talking to Mr. Cleveland. He doesn't even dust his books, much less read them. You can't eat books. Never saw a highbrow in my life who could earn his salt, and let me tell you, young lady, it is as easy to fall in love with a rich man as a poor one. Wish I could have remembered it for myself.

Papa, bless his patient heart, would glance up from his omnipresent newspaper and say: Now, old lady, you know you don't mean that.

Don't I, Mama would retort, her voice belied by her smile. I'd show you if I had it to do over again.

These were nice soft moments when the realness crept out over Mama, and the three of us, tucked into Mrs. Cleveland's boardinghouse, felt gratefully aware of something not analyzable.

In no time at all Mama was queen of Mrs. Cleveland's. A Mrs. Townsend, down the hall from us, complained that she saw special dishes come to our table and that our ketchup was a better brand. A hall closet that had been dedicated to the use of the boarders for raincoats and umbrellas was suddenly cleared and given over to Mama, for her private stock of fruit, relishes, and special foods for us in our room. Also, it leaked out among the boarders that Mrs. Cleveland supplied us with a better grade of coffee, separately brewed.

Four or five girls and boys about my own age boarded at Mrs. Cleveland's. Evenings, while Mama and Papa played whist with the other parents, we sat on the front steps or in the dining room after the tables had been cleared.

Two of the boys were pimply and callous-handed, but the third, a sickly but rather beautiful boy, was exciting to me. He said little, but he had a delicate look that placed him apart from us. I knew I was "stuck on" Floyd Chivvis. Abashed by the very idea, I averted my head and dropped my eyes if he so much as glanced at me, which was seldom enough. Conscious of him every instant, I pretended to ignore his presence.

I dressed for this lad, who was chiefly remarkable, his later life was to reveal, for his great degree of unremarkableness. I posed for Floyd, haunted the hallways when I judged he might be passing, and, when his mother came to visit Mama, hung about eager for every word concerning Floyd, which had chiefly to do with the chronic state of his bronchitis, which kept him out of school our first winter at Mrs. Cleveland's. Even this was exciting. It gave him a specialness. I could scarcely keep my eyes off his long frail hands. When he was not looking in my direction, I studied his pallor, his thin and not happy looking profile, and longed to write a story that would properly express his poetic frailty.

A captive indoors, Floyd sat at his front window most of the time, looking out. After school, instead of curling up in the alcove with a book or huddling with Mr. Cleveland, I would dance about on the sidewalk at hopscotch, jump rope, or play with a rheumy-eyed little terrier owned by one of the boardinghouse children, ogling all the while for Floyd's attention. Conscious of him every moment, I lingered about with elaborate unconsciousness, until Mama would put her head out the window and call: Come up and take off your good clothes. Since when do you wear them for play?

My "good clothes" were part of strategy Floyd.

Then one day in the gloomy hall of Mrs. Cleveland's boardinghouse he said to me as I passed: Hello, Fatty-Showoff.

I stood frozen, my conception of myself dropping like a garment about my ankles, leaving me facing the stark reality—fatty-showoff . . .

The adolescent's capacity for pain is usually mature. Racked with humiliation, I crept through the aftermath of that hallway encounter without Mama once querying: Is something wrong?

Yes, something was wrong, but so secretly, privately, and humiliatingly wrong that to confide it would have been like exposing an open wound.

I was once more a fat girl.

It was shortly after this episode that Mr. Schuyler, who read all my weekly themes, remarked in that quizzical way of his: Why are all of your heroines as long and lean and droopy as Aubrey Beardsley's ladies? Why not some round and rosy ones for a change?

What Mr. Schuyler meant, of course, and nothing could have convinced me otherwise, was: What about someone round rosy and—fat, like yourself?

People in the boardinghouse began to say to Mama: Fannie is very aloof and studious, isn't she?

Mama began to say: For goodness' sake, Fannie, I wish you wouldn't huck in the room all the time. Go out and mingle, the way you did when we first moved here. It's not natural to be tied to your mother's apron string.

Papa said: Let her be. Knowledge is power.

Were we a more innocent, less mature teen-age generation than today's? Or did my aloofness seal me away from the boy-meets-girl aspects of my time.

You "got stuck" on a boy, or vice versa. A girl was quickly branded as "fresh" or "fly" if she permitted boys to kiss or maul her. But throughout four years in one of the largest high schools in the country at that period, not more than one actual irregularity came to my ears, although in all probability they were more or less recurrent in a large institution of mixed and mixed-up adolescents.

As a matter of fact, I felt, rather than knew, the nature of a situation I accidentally walked into one day as I entered Mr. Schuyler's office. One of the older girls, a lanky sophomore whom I knew by sight but not name, was crying hysterically, an equally lanky Central High boy standing dejectedly beside her. Papa says he'll have to marry me or he'll kill me. . . .

Mr. Schuyler hurried me out of the office by the shoulders, but I knew what was happening, knew it with wonder and terror.

It was one thing to encounter the conflicts between men and women in books like *Lady Audrey's Secret, Othello, Wuthering Heights,* or *Dee Dee of the Lowlands.* It was another to encounter this girl in the flesh, whom I passed daily, in trouble with a boy.

Following the incident, I kept wondering what it would be like to be involved in something so mysterious, so forbidden. The girl's sobs were not the kind I had ever heard from anyone. The sound of them kept following me long after I was back in the normalcy of our room at Mrs. Cleveland's. Somehow, and guiltily, I felt lonesomely on the outside of something as tremendous as the act of life itself, which was taking shape in this girl's body and experience.

She was more real and in a sordid kind of way more exciting to me than Paris and Helen, David and Bathsheba, Lord Nelson and Emma. I thought of the lanky stringy-haired girl in the terms of a fragment of poetry from Christina Rossetti I had picked up at the public library: "This is the birthday of my life. My love has come to me."

Ah me . . .

Adele Chipley, who lived in the boardinghouse with her widower father, was seventeen when I was fourteen. In love with love, she used to regale me with stories of her conquests in the hospital where she was apprenticing for trained nursing.

Mama said: I want you to stop sitting on the steps evenings with that Chipley girl. I think she has it behind her ears. Most nurses do.

I wanted to have it behind my ears, from wherever I could glean it. Not necessarily from boys—they had dirty hands and cracked their knuckles—but from books, if need be, from the sobbing anguish of a girl, from Adele Chipley's shabby recitals and the sotto voce conversation of the women in the boardinghouse.

My thoughts followed my teachers and classmates into their homes and the boarders into their rooms. They followed Mr. Schuyler and even Mr. Cleveland, who thought thoughts so different from Mama and Papa.

The tormenting sense of being trapped into mediocrity, while some sort of a caparisoned parade was passing me by, drove me inward upon myself and outward from myself.

Extracurricular activities began to push me into the frontal ranks of the student body. Literary society, dramatic society, tennis, basketball, yearbook editor.

During study hours I wrote surreptitiously; in streetcars, in bed, prematurely born ideas pouring down the sides of a young volcano that was erupting adolescence.

Papa said: Don't read so far away from the light. You'll ruin your eyes.

Mama said: It's a shame for the wasted paper.

Papa said: Rose, if Fannie wants to be studious you should encourage it. Knowledge is power.

If you say that once more, Sam, I'll scream.

And then, likely as not, I would come home from school the next day to find my little writing desk laid out with new pads of paper, by this beguiling unpredictable mother of mine.

What a woman. Spreading her warmth through us, and her chill.

If I had it to live over again, I would not change it. Mama was naughty, difficult, darling.

I yearn for the power to write her in full dimension, but my pen clogs.

The tenants in our Cates Avenue home agreed to renew their lease, enabling us to economize further by remaining at the Cleveland's another year.

There are wheels within wheels within wheels at Mrs. Cleveland's. Mama and a Mrs. Greiner have a major falling out over who monopolizes the greater portion of time in the bathroom, Papa or Mr. Greiner. Mama and the Katzenbergs feud because it came to Mama's ears that Mrs. Katzenberg made the remark that she had it on good authority my marks at school were not as high as her niece's.

Mama was all for confronting Mrs. Katzenberg with her calumny.

The talebearer wept and pleaded with Mama not to and Papa said sternly: Don't make a spectacle of yourself, Rose. Mrs. Katzenberg is entitled to her own opinions.

I meant well, sobbed the recalcitrant talebearer.

I'm sure you did, said Papa dryly.

Mama was held in control, but her moment came sooner than she dared hope.

Shortly thereafter, Mr. Katzenberg knocked at our door. The long, lean wholesale grocery salesman, suspenders hanging down, looked perturbed.

Mrs. Hurst, I've lost my mug. Left it in the bathroom when I was shaving. I thought you might have seen it.

Mr. Katzenberg, said Mama in an ice-coated voice and regarding his face intently, if I were to find your mug I could not return it quickly enough.

Strangely, Papa was interested in the minute local happenings that crammed our lives, although he dismissed most of Mama's tremendous trifles in the key of there-there or now-now.

She would greet him when he came home evenings, receive his kiss, while I stood by stung to the core as usual by his unconscious omission of me.

What do you think! That skinny Miss Lilly in the third floor back said to me—you know, the one who teaches burnt wood—she wishes she knew how I charm Mrs. Cleveland.

Well, she was paying you a compliment.

Oh she was, was she! She's the one who made the remark that we demand so many face towels daily that the rest of the boarders have to do with an every-other-day supply.

I'm afraid we do use a good many, Rose.

You mean, you do. For the number of favors I do Mrs. Cleveland, she can afford to give us a few extra towels.

I wouldn't talk about that side of it, Rose.

You wouldn't, but I will.

Well, Fannie, what have you to say for yourself?

Tell your father what Mr. Schuyler said at school today.

He says he thinks I am talented, and that he would like to meet my parents.

Papa's handsome face broke into a smile of deep-seated pleasure.

Well now, that's mighty fine. That is certainly mighty fine.

We'll have to ask him to come to supper, said Mama. He's a widower, isn't he?

Oh no, Mama—not supper—here . . .

You hear that, Sam? I always tell you she's ashamed of her surroundings.

I am not!

Well now, Rose, if Fannie doesn't want it, we can take him out for supper.

I did not want that either, although I did not dare say as much. Papa was elegant, I figured in my snide little snobbery, and his English for the most part all right. Never an "ain't" out of him and his occasional "I reckon" and "you all" were acceptably, even pleasantly, southern.

Mama, however, had all the unpredictability of a "natural."

Mama's callow little brat, not worth her Mama's little finger, did not want to risk a boner or a possible "ain't."

Alas, even as I juggled about on the horns of my dilemma, Mr. Schuyler, my mentor and friend, whose blue eyes I now realize must have crinkled with mirth at my malignant case of adolescence, died suddenly of a heart attack while waiting for a streetcar.

Our school flew its flag at half mast and held memorial services in the assembly hall. I said little and displayed no emotion.

Mama said: What are you made of, Fannie? One would think you didn't even know, much less fairly dote on, this Mr. Schuyler.

Papa said: Let the child alone, Rose. She knows how she feels.

I knew how I felt deep down into the inhibited reaches of me. . . .

I once burst forth to Mama: I wish I were married to Uncle Gus!

Mama made a gesture toward me as if to clap her hand over my mouth.

Don't you ever let me hear you say a thing like that again. Where did you hear such talk?

From myself. Then I could have all the animals I want in the house.

Don't you know that's bad talk? Married to Uncle Gus. The idea!

Why is it bad?

Never mind why.

I did not press. Adele Chipley would tell me. Besides, it came over me that I knew the reason. It was a sin to marry your father or your uncle.

Notwithstanding her capacity for overindulgence, Mama held out against pets. In vain I compromised. A kitten? Cats scratch at the upholstery. A bird? They scatter seed. White mice? I buy traps to get rid of mice.

Once when we were back in our own home I brought home a kitten in sheer defiance. When Mama saw the little gray creature, she made such a violent gesture to prevent it from jumping on a sofa that it made a dash for the back stairs and down into the basement.

For days we sought that kitten. With our cellar doors and windows locked, there could have been no egress. The peripatetic furnace man, who tended a row of houses on the street, was called in. Barrels and trunks were moved, dark corners explored.

Several days later, Mama's sharp olfactory nerve put her on the scent. I might never have known what happened except for the fact that I came in from school just in time to see the furnace man remove the lifeless little body from a ceiling rafter, where she must have taken anguished refuge and starved rather than venture out.

Mama cried. I didn't. I was a lump of total misery, the frightened-to-death kitten lived with me for weeks. I also knew something secret and, I supposed, rather terrible about myself. The kitten hurt worse than the dying of a little girl named Edna.

She had been cared for and loved and helped in every possible way. My kitten had died alone and so terribly afraid and nobody had cared—except me.

Mama said: Don't say anything about the kitten to your father. It will upset him. It must have been a wild and dangerous cat, anyway, to act that way just because I said "scat."

Mama's contrition went on for days.

Finally, to everyone's amazement, she bought me a canary in a round gilt cage. But it scattered seed and Mama forgot and was irate again, and Papa said: Fannie, don't you see you upset your mother by having the little bird?

It isn't a bird, it's a pig, said Mama, mopping beneath the cage. Your daughter likes the bird, but not enough to clean up after it. That's for her mother to do.

We gave little Lemon Drop to Mary Stutz, our dressmaker, before I had time to become too attached to it.

And at Mrs. Cleveland's, a delivery boy had once come into Mr. Cleveland's office trailed by a gray mop of a Skye terrier.

What is your dog's name? I asked.

He's not mine. Just followed me around all day. Lost, I guess.

The dog stood with one forepaw raised, his grape-sized eyes fixed on me.

Mr. Cleveland, couldn't you keep him? Mama wouldn't let me. But if you take him, I promise to do all the work, feed and bathe him.

Thus I acquired a kind of vicarious ownership of a spirited little fellow, an inveterate snapper at the heels of strangers and who was to present problems. But he was immediately taken into my heart and, fortunately, into Mr. Cleveland's.

He was never permitted above the basement, but I was constantly under rebuke for filching large portions of my own food from the table. Mama complained of dog hair over my clothing and Papa finally went to consult a doctor because of a sensation of a dog's hair in his throat.

That almost precipitated matters, except for the fact that technically the dog belonged to Mr. Cleveland. Nevertheless I lived in fear for Annie, named, in defiance of his sex, after Mr. Cleveland's deceased daughter Annie, mother of Harry. But with the connivance of Mr. Cleveland and Harry, and the tolerance of that dear soul, Mrs. Cleveland, Annie precariously remained.

This seemingly negligible experience of my first pet, furtive as it was, proved a memorable one for me. It released something hard and tight in me. I could retire with Annie to a dark storeroom, free to coddle and pronounce unrestrained endearments. The patient eyes of Annie, his tendency to cringe at sudden movements, indicating he had known cuffings, his warm grateful tongue licking my face simultaneously broke and warmed my heart.

Notwithstanding all my security, I felt the way Annie looked, chilly and alone inside, as when Papa kissed Mama, omitting me, or when they closed their door at night, or when I came out of Central High into a group of boys waiting to carry some girl's books, not mine, or even when I read a book or a piece of poetry, or thought something lovely and there was no one to tell about it. . . .

Now that Mr. Schuyler was gone—there was only Mr. Cleveland. In the coal bin I could make mention of what did not have to do with the definable, the physical. Hot, Cold, Happy, Depressed.

Not that Mr. Cleveland emerged from the mausoleum of himself, beyond long-winded vaporings and philosophical monologues which were largely mumbo jumbo interspersed with great and gleaming names—Plato, Aristotle, Darwin, Ingersoll, Luther, Eddy.

But once, when I had let slip an experience to him in a badly articulated way, he showed neither surprise nor amusement.

We had been reading *Hamlet* in class that day—"Lay hei' the earth: And from her fair and unpolluted flesh May violets spring . . ." What small and lovely flower would spring from my dead little sister? What tree from Mr. Schuyler?

I came home brimming and asked: Mr. Cleveland, when you read something wonderful, do the words make you feel like— I don't know what!

He puffed on his smelly meerschaum. A bucket of beauty, he replied, can make you headier than three buckets of beer.

I knew from then on that dirty fingernailed Mr. Cleveland and I enjoyed a kind of unspoken closeness.

Mama said: My daughter is no company for me. She comes home from school, rushes through her practicing, and is down there the rest of the afternoon with Mr. Cleveland.

Papa said: Why don't you and your mother go visiting together, Fannie?

Mama invariably flared at that: There you go again. I would be a fine one, wouldn't I, forcing myself on rich relatives. Boardinghouse trash is what you've made of us.

One night, to the consternation of all three of us, something happened after an outburst of this kind that made me feel as if someone had shot an arrow into me.

Suddenly Papa, seated in his straight chair, reading his newspaper through the familiar tirade, dropped his face into his hands and, shoulders heaving, began to sob:

I can't take it any more, Rose. I'm doing the best I can paying off one hundred cents on the dollar. Don't hound me! sobbed Papa into his hands, his breakdown unprecedented.

I wanted to throw myself into his arms, I wanted to hug his head with the new gray in it. I wanted—and didn't. . . .

I just stood by, with my throat hurting. Not so Mama.

Sam, she cried, running to him and encompassing him with her arms. My darling—the best man who ever lived—I didn't mean it, my darling. I'll save with you and scrimp with you and help you. What else means anything but you? Oh, my darling, forgive me—Fannie, come to your father.

I walked over and he reached around us both with his strong arms and we cried; and now it was Papa, so gentle, so forgiving, who began to soothe Mama.

It's all right, Rose. Now, now, everything is all right.

I crept from the room. They were so together.

Papa said: Fannie, just as sure as fate, we are going to have trouble with that dog. I understand from your mother that he snaps at every delivery boy.

At the mention of jeopardy to Annie, terror flew into me. No, no, I'll watch him.

Mark my words, Sam, said Mama, if you don't put your foot down on the matter of that dog, we're going to have trouble. If I so much as go down to the storeroom he shows his teeth at me.

He's smiling at you, Mama.

But now Annie had sunk her teeth into the trouser leg of the corner tailor, and he had brought the garment and placed it before Papa, while I stood by trembling for my pet.

Papa said: This dog belongs to no one in particular, Mr. Weintraub.

Oh no, you don't, Mr. Hurst. The butcher delivery boy told me he belongs to your girl and it was to her he gave him personally.

I certainly regret this incident, Mr. Weintraub, and will replace the trousers.

Oh no, you don't. My nerves are worth more than a pair of pants or maybe you only plan to give me one leg of them in damage.

Mama, more belligerent, spoke up and, as Papa said later, ruined what might have been an amiable adjustment.

The dog didn't bite you. Those are old worn pants, anyhow, and it looks to me as if you made the tear larger yourself.

You can't talk to me that way, lady. For that you'll settle bigger than you think. I'll sue the pants off you the way your dog bit them off me and gave me a nervous breakdown on top. I've a doctor's certificate to prove it.

As he slammed out, Papa turned to Mama. Well, Rose, I hope you're satisfied. I could have handled the situation if you had kept out of it.

If I had kept out of it and let you be *schlemiel* enough to pay that cheat for new pants when he put that hole there himself . . .

Now it will probably cost us many times that much.

That's the thanks I get. You can't have elegant ways with a fellow like him.

Your inelegant ones have ruined everything.

Mama began to cry in dismay: I begged that child. Fannie, I said, we will get in trouble with that dog.

I stood by, trembling: Annie didn't bite. She is just playful.

She bites a man's pants off, and she's playful. I begged: Fannie, don't keep that dog. He's got fleas. I itch since he's here. And now, who bears the brunt? I do. Abuse from your father.

Don't carry on, Rose. The milk is spilled.

You spilled it.

The important thing now, Fannie, said Papa sadly but sternly, is that the dog must go. I'll call the Society.

Papa—please . . .

The dog must go.

Papa, please—please. And prompted by misery beyond my control, I dropped to my knees and put my arms around him: I'll tie him up when I am at school and the minute I come home I'll never let him out of my sight. He'll never do it again, Papa. He's a good dog, you can see it by his eyes. I'll save and pay back for the pants. I'll do anything you want, only don't make me give up Annie, Papa. I love him so. I do love that little dog so.

But Papa stood sad but adamant: I'm sorry, child, he said, lifting me to my feet, but you'll see it is for the best.

You've ruined my life more than anything that has ever happened to me. That little dog has no home and no friends. He trusts me. Mama, if you love me don't make me part with him. I just love him so and want him so and need him so.

Papa's voice had thunder in it.

Not another word out of you. The matter is settled.

Now I could feel Mama's resistance crumbling.

Sam, shall we give him one more chance?

The dog goes, Rose. He'll bite others. . . .

I'll pay the old cheat off out of my own money and give the dog one more chance. Sam?

I've had my say, Rose.

But your own child! With you it's always the other fellow before your own flesh and blood. I say, give her one more chance with her dog.

Papa—please . . .

I won the contest that night, but the very next day my poor Annie sank his teeth into the trouser cuff of the postman. Realizing that I was beaten, I retired to hide my head under my pillow while the Society came and took my beloved Annie away.

Papa did not go into bankruptcy. With what must have been heroic machinations, which I am certain he did not reveal to my worrisome mother, he managed somehow to retrieve himself with honor; and from then on moved ahead to steady if conservative success.

We are back on Cates Avenue, the polyglot atmosphere of Mrs. Cleveland's boardinghouse a thing of the past.

I am concluding my four years at Central High, at the peak of a series of superficial successes.

In the areas of extracurricular activities I moved in a blaze of glory. Captain of the girls' basketball team. Ranking member of the girls' tennis team. Actually I cared little for athletics, but the spotlight beat down hard upon them. President of Literary Society. Assistant editor of High School News. Member Dramatic Club.

I was one of those pupils outstanding in practically every department except the educational.

I was a good "front girl." When Prince George of Germany came to visit our school on a tour of the country, I was chosen to speak a few words of greeting and present him with a citation. My name was conspicuous in the High School News and occasionally it appeared in the St. Louis daily newspapers.

Mama's greatest pride was in my varous appearances with the Dramatic Club. I must have been rather a bulky heroine. As a matter of fact, my most successful roles were the full-blown ones: Lady Gay Spanker and Lady Teazle. Not content with the makeshift costumes of amateurs or those rented from costume companies, Mama, well known in local department stores and using her prerogatives as a charge customer, would order gowns, hats, and even furs sent home on approval.

At cruel variance with the remainder of the cast, and unbeknownst to Papa, who would have disapproved of such procedures, my costumes were outstanding, Mama rushing about from store to store on approval purchases, more than rewarded by the applause which invariably greeted my resplendent appearance.

One night, after a performance of a local woman's dramatization of Thackeray's *Vanity Fair* in which I had played the role of Becky Sharp, Mama, Papa, and I, accompanied by my favorite classmate, Frances Windhorst, started home, all of us with the exception of Papa laden with boxes of dresses and hats which were to be returned to the department stores the following day.

I suspected that Papa's failure to make some provision for our transportation other than streetcar was not going to pass unnoticed, but hoped Mama would not steam up to it in the presence of Frances.

But, trudging ahead, clutching his umbrella, Papa apparently was not even aware of his omission as the laden female trio of us struggled with our burdens.

Suddenly Mama called out: Sam, can't I carry your umbrella for you? Give it to me.

With automatic obedience Papa turned, handed it over to Mama, who clutched it with what part of a hand she could manage, and resumed his trot ahead of us.

How glad I am, boomed Mama, that I married a southern gentleman.

At that, the laughter we could no longer contain burst forth.

Papa regarded us with a puzzled smile, as he always did when Mama provoked mirth.

I wonder if he anticipated that before he went to sleep that night Mama, reacting from our mirth, would explode into sound and fury.

I did.

In the questionnaire passed around my senior year in Central High I wrote yes after the query: Do you intend to go to college or university? What college or university? Only prestige names occurred to me. I wrote in three. Bryn Mawr, Wellesley, Smith.

Actually, I had not faced the matter, but as graduation approached the hour for decision was imminent.

Mama recoiled. Why college? You have a good education. What do you want to be? An old-maid schoolteacher like Tillie Strauss?

Papa said: Rose, if Fannie wants to continue learning, we should be in favor of it. Knowledge is power.

You'll sing a different tune when you hear what it costs to send a girl to college. And for what? If she wants to learn, she can learn at home.

Perhaps your mother is right. Study in the home.

Oh no, Papa.

That Washington University out there is an old maids' nest.

I want to go away to college.

Leave home?

All the girls do.

What do you think of that, Sam? She not only wants to go away from home, but our own Washington University, one of the finest in the country, isn't good enough.

Hold your horses, Rose. Let's talk this thing out.

My daughter wants to leave home to become another Tillie Strauss, instead of being a comfort to her parents after graduation like other children. I could cry my eyes out.

At long last, I compromised on the University of Missouri, noted for its school of journalism. Several weeks before graduation, Mama and I set out for Columbia, Missouri, to register in advance and arrange for living quarters.

Bertha Schaeffer, the daughter of our dentist and a second-year student there, guided us over the campus, assisted in the matter of registration, and, since freshmen could not live on the campus, led us to a quiet home on a side street of modest frame houses. Almost every one of them took student roomers. The double room which

Bertha's one-time landlady would only rent to two students was clean but depressing, and to be shared with its present occupant, a young lady from Peoria.

The fact that Bertha had lived there her freshman year was sufficient recommendation for Mama to pay an advance on the room months ahead of my arrival.

I had matriculated at the University of Missouri! I had a room engaged in a college town! Fannie Hurst. University of Missouri.

But Mama was a deterrent to dignity. Bertha, you will watch over my child, won't you? She's never been away from home. Do you think six sheets is enough? See that she sends her things home to be laundered and mended.

But on that walk back to the Columbia depot, not even the embarrassment of Mama's violent maternalism in public mattered. I was about to major in journalism at the University of Missouri.

The reaction began to set in as we rode in a shabby day coach through the thickening twilight of flat Missouri country. Isolated houses along the way began to show their lighted windows, the stretches of open field between darkening into vast loneliness. I could feel my high spirits plummet like lead.

Soon this same lonely kind of twilight would shut me into a strange world of strange people in that gray little house on that gray little street. That shoebox-shaped room with my future roommate's family photographs on her side of the dresser and her toothbrush in its holder on her side of the washstand. Mama?

Seated beside me, she was crying quietly into her handkerchief. As I spoke, she broke: Don't go, Fannie. Don't leave us. You're all we have—stay home, baby—with us. Go to Washington University if you must—do anything you want at home—but don't leave us.

I could scarcely breathe from emotion and relief at this opportunity to withdraw and yet save face.

Mama had saved me from a rapidly mounting impulse to turn to her with something like: I don't want to do this. I love you so. Mama, don't let me leave you.

Don't leave us, Fannie.

I won't, Mama—not for anything, I said with magnanimity.

Now came the suspenseful weeks. Would I be chosen to deliver a paper at commencement?

On the premise that I would, Mama began one shopping onslaught after another, even including fancy accessories for Aunt Jennie and Aunt Bettie to wear at the exercises.

Papa said: Rose, for pity's sake, don't be so ostentatious.

Mama said: You mind your business, Sam, and I'll mind mine, which is to see that my child doesn't graduate like a pauper. Besides, I am spending my own hard-earned savings.

Looking back, it seems incredible that I permitted Mama to overload me with finery so at variance with the remainder of the class. We graduated in dresses with trains. Mine was white net over taffeta, trimmed and trimmed in Valenciennes lace and Valenciennes lace. Weeks before the event, the frock hung from the chandelier in our sewing room, to be inspected and "ohed" over by the neighbors.

The class flower was the carnation, each girl to bring a dollar and a half to school for her bouquet.

Nothing of the sort for Mama. I was to carry a shower of three dozen giant carnations, especially ordered from a florist of her choosing.

Papa said: You'll make us all ridiculous, Rose.

Mama said: You don't deserve to have a daughter on the graduating program.

Mama, I haven't been chosen yet.

Nevertheless, there was open speculation that I would be. I proceeded on that premise, planning and plotting my paper. It was not to be about an event in history or a character analysis of Thomas Jefferson or the story of the Statue of Liberty and our debt to France. I preferred to write a paper about people who were not in history. People. The people in the streets and in little houses who were thick as ants and got stepped on like ants. I captured a wonderful title. "All the Little Human Ants." My fingers itched to begin. . . .

Then one morning I was summoned from the study hall to the office. The students buzzed. I was to be named!

But something told me that all was not well. Miss Hurst, the principal began coolly, we have unearthed a surprising situation. How many compositions have you written for members of English 4 that were handed in by other pupils under their own names?

I was stunned.

For almost the entire semester I had been writing compositions in exchange for ill-gotten help in algebra and chemistry from students facile in those departments.

I stood accused and guilty.

I wrote their compositions, I half explained, because it was difficult for them and easy for me.

Did it occur to you that here we operate under an honor system?

I guess it did. But I liked to write them—and did.

You realize that this is a matter for suspension, even expulsion. Do you expect to be graduated under these circumstances?

I thought of Mama and Papa and the graduation dress hanging from the chandelier. I thought of "All the Little Human Ants!" Except for horror of displaying emotion, I could have wept. I didn't think. I'll do anything if you'll let me graduate. My mother and father . . .

You didn't think. Well, last evening we held a special faculty meeting on the matter, and we did some thinking.

I stood numb.

Last week, Miss Hurst, you were unanimously chosen out of a class of three hundred and ten to deliver an original composition at the graduation exercises. You have forfeited your right to that honor. We will permit you and the recipients of your compositions to graduate, but all of you without distinction.

So it came to pass that a heavy-hearted, overdressed, flower-laden graduate sat in the last row of her class, while a mouse-colored little prodigy in physics, in his first long trousers, droned a thesis on Newton, Father of the Law of Gravity.

So far as I am concerned, time is a swift river, rising at my birth and riding me toward eternity. The years pile up, the arteries narrow, telephone-book print dims. The zenith of life comes, lo the span is more than half spent, the timetable shortens, and more and more of one's contemporaries begin to show up in the daily death notices.

Confusion that had to do with an annuity insurance policy once revealed the fact that the Hamilton, Ohio, birth records show confusion about my age. I am either two years younger or older than I reckoned.

I am pleased to give myself the benefit of the doubt and assume that my arteries are the two years younger. I confess, with embarrassment for my puniness, to answering at the voting polls: Over twenty-one. I omit the date of my birth in *Who's Who*. I even lie to doctors, although when explaining to one that I did not know my exact age, he replied: Never mind, we can tell.

Thus the college years glide timelessly through my memory. They are as remote as Mars, as close as yesterday.

Even with Papa's lip service of acquiescence, I think he secretly depended upon Mama, despite her capitulation, to divert me from my avowed intentions.

This she did as her emotional reactions subsided following our return from Columbia.

So far as she was concerned, I was crossing over, by way of college, into the barren wastelands of the Tillie Strausses, where femininity died on the vine, where no eligible man entered, where parents of erudite unmarried daughters buried their dead hopes.

Only a small percentage of young ladies, principally those with the ultimate purpose of teaching and self-support, were entering institutions of higher learning at that period.

But generally the bridge-of-sighs beyond a girl's graduation from finishing or secondary school was as brief a span as possible. Parents saw to it, to the limit of their financial abilities and often beyond, that daughters were placed promptly on the market.

During the period when my college plans still hung in the balance, Mama attempted to reach me with offers to move into a finer home, even build one, travel, follow the current fashion and take lessons in burnt wood, have a little Model T Ford car of my own, extend my piano education at the finest conservatory in town.

To add degrees to Mama's fever, Irene Wertheim, a featureless girl in my graduation class, became engaged to the son of the president of a mammoth burlap bag concern in East St. Louis. At Mama's urging, Aunt Jennie came to visit us. An obsessive matchmaker and advocate of early marriage, she dared be even more outspoken than Mama.

I am ashamed for the people in Hamilton. I brag about my brilliant niece and, meanwhile, the nieces of most of the women I know marry off, while you are still without even an admirer. Your mother tells me that Milton Jelenko, who is marrying that Wertheim girl, would have been glad to call on you if you had ever given him the opportunity. Your mother is right. Tillie Strauss is written all over you.

Now, *Gensbebla*, you and Rose leave Fannie to work it out her own way. There is no hurry about such things.

Sam doesn't talk that way, Jennie, when we're alone. That child and her father just aren't themselves before one another.

That was the way it went, up to the hour I became a freshman at Washington University.

Book Two

Labor to keep alive in your breast that little spark of celestial fire. . . .

Now, for the first time, it seems to me, I become intellectually awake, where before I had only dragged back my eyelids. I select courses close to my interest, based on my need to know, rather than for convenience.

Shades of the halls of learning began to close in my growing self. The university buildings were massive Gothic, the men of the faculty, in my fancy, Olympians who had temporarily descended to the lecture halls.

Interest in the outer world receded. After the day's lectures I lingered on the campus, in the library or on its great stone porch, filling composition books with vaporings. A course in the major Elizabethan poets drenched me in the reflected light of the era. My freshman year I submitted a masque in blank verse to *The Saturday Evening Post*. That same year I offered twice the required number of assigned "themes" to my English professor.

This struggle to capture the winged words that seemed to fly through my mind in flocks was almost as old as I was. It did not matter that once on paper they lost much of their iridescence—there was always the next clean page of the composition book.

As I examine those days under the microscope, I recapture the adult anguishes that went with them. Tormented, violently ambitious, jealous of the achievements of others, I slashed about in all directions at once.

I recall, when I was no more than five, Papa remarking to a business associate who was visiting our house: By the way, my little daughter has written some verse. Would you like to read it? Extracting a bit of paper from his waistcoat pocket, he watched anxiously the guest's face for reaction. So did I. It came promptly, in an m-m-m. Thus Papa's guest handed me my first rejection slip.

At this period of my freshman year, the march of the long envelope containing the returned manuscript with a rejection slip was uninterrupted. For years our faithful Willie had been marching upstairs mornings with the mail: Miss Fannie, here's another story come back, and each time, as every writer must know, that plop down into the bottomless pit.

Now I was also battering against the portals of the college weekly, *Student Life*, meanwhile almost automatically sending stories to *Reedy's Mirror*, an outstanding literary publication of the Middle West, the St. Louis *Post-Dispatch*, *Saturday Evening Post*, and the Munsey group of magazines.

Word got around during the first half of my second year that Neal Patterson, daughter of a Missouri state senator, a St. Louis girl who in her late twenties had made a name in the literary world, was returning to St. Louis to spend part of the winter with her parents and would attend courses at Washington University.

I had never seen, much less known, a writer. The prospect of encountering her on the campus excited and filled me with a jealous kind of anguish.

In due time Neal arrived, she was interviewed and photographs of her appeared in the newspapers. People said to me: Just keep at it and one day you may be a Neal Patterson.

Before her arrival, I wrote with accelerated speed, striving by way of daily themes to hurl myself before the attention of Mr. Starbuck, our young professor in English composition. I did succeed in attracting some notice from him but somewhere, despite my determination for leadership, I missed along the way.

I was not invited to join a sorority and it was many a month before I was to understand why. "The Potter's Wheel," an exclusive literary college group to which you were eligible only by qualification and invitation, passed me by; and I lost a race, for political reasons to be sure, for vice-presidency of the sophomore class. Probably one of the best-known girls on the campus, if not the best-known, where co-eds were in the enormous minority, I was more conspicuous than distinguished.

Mama continued to complain that I was wasting my time in college with girls who were destined to be old maids.

Papa said: Knowledge is power.

The coming of Neal Patterson began for me in the key of fantasia.

A little streetcar spur operated between the end of the main line, a few blocks from Cates Avenue, and the University, which at the time was about a mile beyond city limits.

One wintry morning, while waiting for the "dinky," a sporty little open roadster driven by a young woman in a long streaming "automobile veil" sped past me, then drew up suddenly and began to back.

Oh, she cried in disappointed inflection as she came closer, I thought for a moment you were my best friend, Ethel Barrymore. She is playing here next week.

I was a thickset sixteen. If she had said: I mistook you for Joan of Arc or Helen of Troy, I could not have been more surprised and, I must say, amused. I had seen so many photographs of the luminous Ethel Barrymore looking like no one in the world but Ethel Barrymore.

I'm Neal Patterson, pursued the girl in the car. Going out to the University? Want a lift?

She talked solo, every inch of the way. Ethel Barrymore was her bosom friend. One of the reasons, in fact, that she had returned to St. Louis earlier than she had planned. She was writing a play for her. Great names of the theater, Nat Goodwin, William Faversham, Marie Doro, Jane Cowl, fell from her lips as easily as loose coins from a purse. Marion Reedy, editor of the St. Louis *Mirror*, was also her "best friend." She was taking a course in

Shakespeare and one in advanced French—going to France for the summer—did I know Colette?

I rode beside her in a daze, hating her for all the things she was and I was not, blistering rather than basking in her reflected glory.

I knew in advance the adulation she was certain to receive on the campus from students and faculty alike. Her like was without precedent in our concentrated world. Her very existence was driving me further in my sullen determination to do something also. Be something. A writer—greater than—well, anyway, a writer . . .

And so it happened. Neal took the University by storm. She addressed us in chapel on the American drama and was immediately made honorary member of the Literary Society. Her presence in my English class doused me like a candle flame. Where before I had been the articulate one, most frequently selected to read my work aloud to the class, now I sat rigid and speechless before the worldliness, the flair, the professional status of Neal. A one-act play of hers, "Venus Out of Love," had been published in book form and frequently produced by amateur organizations. We read it aloud in class, the various characters assigned to students. I read my role from the lips out, burning inside because they were not my lines.

Neal for the most part seemed to have forgotten my existence. Then one day I met her downtown in Scrugg's, Vandervoort and Barney's Department Store, and she said: Walk up as far as Grand Avenue with me?

It was a considerable distance and on the way she regaled me with the romantic side of her life, of which I had heard provocative rumors.

More frustration. I tried to ease the impact by assuring myself that she was fabricating. Easy enough to tell us way out in St. Louis about her relationships with the great. But, nevertheless, her words did carry conviction. She showed me a photograph, in a locket, of one of the male idols of the theater. Read me excerpts from a letter from another, but kept the signature out of sight. You would know him. The whole world knows him.

On Pine Street, where the residences grew finer, she paused before an immense dwelling.

Do you know who lives here? I did not. It's the old Schrank mansion, she pursued, mentioning a name high in the social and industrial annals of St. Louis. Rod Schrank begged me to marry him for two years before he finally settled on the rebound for Marjorie Lippe.

It had to be true. She would not dare use local names that way. What did men see in her? She too was on the bulky side.

A sense of grievance against Mama and Papa rose in me. We did not know anybody who was anybody. We just ate and slept and ate and slept. Went nowhere, had no interesting friends, and all the while books were being written, songs were being sung, and pictures painted. Great people were doing great things. Neal's plays were being performed and she was being loved by men and going places while we "hucked."

Why couldn't my mother and father have been intellectual and out of the rut, instead of keeping me down in one with them?

I resented the things they were not, mostly, alas, the things which were secondary and which I had not the wisdom to recognize as such.

Neal commented: What Starbuck needs, referring to our English professor, is a good hot love affair. I give them to him on paper. He blushes when he reads my themes. You write pretty well too, Fannie. But what you also need is more "pash" in your pen. You are about as passionate as a yard of cotton wadding.

"Pash" meant to be like Sappho or Helen and launch a thousand ships. Mama and Papa felt deeply for one another, but in the cotton-wadding way—the way Neal said it was with me.

Other girls seemed to come into their inheritance of boy-meets-girl so easily. If, during my high school or college years, they had practiced premarital irregularities, it was beyond the periphery of my knowledge. There were those who "spooned" or let the boys touch or "fool" around with them. I knew what I knew, and it was plenty, from the unbridled hours of reading and piecing together scraps of sotto voce information from Mama's conversation with the ladies of the *Kaffeeklatsches*. Not infrequently I sat on the stairs eavesdropping . . . she had a miscarriage . . . he gallivants . . . she has it behind her ears . . . doctor says she can't have another . . . she blames him . . .

If I entered the room conversation halted abruptly.

The business of coming to life was evidently a shameful affair, going on behind the palm of the hand, behind the door of Mama's and Papa's bedroom, or, for all I knew, between the girls and boys at school. What were they experiencing that I was missing? I blamed my weight. I blamed Mama and Papa. Very occasionally I blamed myself, for holding back when I wanted to rush in. . . .

I was far from that day when either as person or writer I was to realize that I would always be more intimate with the anonymous public than with my closest friend—or to fully comprehend what Nietzsche describes as the "pathos of distance" between one individual and another.

Then, too, that freshman year I felt that if only I had it in me to project myself into the attention of instructors and professors I could somehow, some way, gain their interest in the very special being I believed myself to be.

Certain of the girls usually lingered after class in English composition to talk with Mr. Starbuck, Neal among them. I would have given much to do the same. Instead, I would leave the lecture room, head up, heart down, casting proud cold glances upon a procedure I longed to share. Someday I would show them! Show them what?

In the spare time inflicted by aloneness, I dug my pencil into paper and wrote, using up what Mama called a round-trip fortune in stamps and long self-addressed envelopes. East they went and westward they returned—"not up to our standard."

Once Mama, so bored by the proceedings, so eager to gratify my slightest whim, suggested: Fannie, offer to pay to have your story printed. I'll bet you that's what many of the writers who are in the magazines do. I'll give you the money.

Papa said: Rose, you should be ashamed to even make such a suggestion.

Mama said: Anything that costs money makes you ashamed. Fannie, do you want fifty dollars?

Oh, Mama, you're just terrible.

I wish I was dead, said Mama. What do I get out of it but abuse.

These ridiculous moments live on in heartache and regrets. Mama meant so well. She would have schemed to get me the moon had I expressed a wish for it. Yet time and time again I turned on her: Oh, Mama, please keep out of it.

Mama is gone now, but as the years pass, her warmth, her humor, her tempestuousnes linger on as if she had just passed through the room.

Fannie, take off your good clothes when you come home from school! Today, the adult me changes clothes immediately upon entering the house.

No woman who leaves a dish unwashed overnight is worth her salt. Still a cardinal sin in my eyes. Don't sit on the bed. I no more would!

With your kind of father, Mama used to say out of his hearing, you can afford to hold up your head with the best. I might have retorted, but did not: And with my kind of mother, all her this-and-that to the contrary notwithstanding.

People say: How much pleasure you must have given your parents. Wonderful that they lived to see it.

Yes, but how much more I might have given. In my middle-class world of that era it was no small thing for a daughter to break the pattern of fitting into the home for as short as possible an interlude between graduation and marriage.

Both Mama and Papa did live to enjoy some of the results of my nonconformity, but looking back, I marvel at my capacity for ruthlessness in leaving the home so concentrated on me. The fierceness of that concentration was doubtless part of the compulsion.

I left, hurting with the gentle resignation of my father and wetted with Mama's tears.

If only I had never heard the word "writer," sobbed Mama

ANATOMY OF ME

Ultimately I had two rather noncombustible beaux during college. Had them simultaneously, a far too friendly rivalry for my favor existing between them. In fact, to such a degree that it sometimes occurred to me they might be spoofing—which later proved to be an injustice. Together, they joked a great deal about rivalry for my favor. While I wanted it not at all, nevertheless it irked that neither of the boys ever attempted the "spooning" that I had reason to suspect went on between students. Although then, as now, co-eds were a bit déclassé, the boys almost making it credo to bring outside girls to university functions.

Steve Gleeson, tall, dark, too slender, destined to ultimately become a fairly well-known stage director, was already intoning "Please pass the butter" as if it were Shakespearean verse. A hard sinewed little grandmother managed to keep him well dressed. He had manners and mannerisms, elegance and slightly feminine graces.

Leon Firman, on the other hand, almost thirty years old when we were still in our teens, had worked eight years to earn his way into the civil engineering department of the University.

A squarely built fellow with good strong and unemphasized Semitic features, he was as realistic as Steve was visionary. The two fused into a friendship predicated on their dissimilarities. They got on famously. We all shared one another.

Mama, however, said: Both those boys are stuck on you. Is it for such you go to college? Why couldn't it be with a boy like Leslie Weiner, who is also in your class? No, you have to waste time on boys who haven't a rich father behind them. One a gentile, and one a kike!

Both these appellations rubbed me like sandpaper, even the former, which was proper usage. I doubt if the opprobium "kike" had retained much of its impact for Mama. It hopped about like a toad in the idiom of the German-Jewish community of our town. It connoted a race divided against itself. Similarly, light Negroes and dark Negroes. Touchables and untouchables.

"Kike" denoted the Jew originally out of Eastern Europe. Russian, Polish, Galician. The caste system held rigidly, German Jew segregated from Eastern Jew. The usage of "nigger" was still so general that it was only as a young adult (the University played no role in awakening this consciousness) that I began to be aware of its connotation.

Strangely, Papa's attitude toward the accepted status of "kike" was no different from Mama's. He seconded Mama by his silence.

Why don't you speak up, Sam? You say enough to me when we are alone.

I wouldn't get the reputation for spending much time with these fellows, Fannie. I have nothing against them, but it's high time a girl like you began to mingle more with "our people," but not of this fellow Leon's class.

Here it came, another abrasive. "Our people." *Unserer Leute*, as Mama and the Aunts said among themselves in German.

Nevertheless, Steve, Leon, and I held our trio through the remaining university years, the two of them continuing to vie for my favor. It was not unpleasant to realize finally that the rivalry was genuine, except that I remained as unaroused as the bric-a-brac bisque girl standing opposite her lad on our mantelpiece.

They wrote me long joint letters, unamorous, but together they analyzed me for pages and pages as aloof, cold, tantalizing, terribly poetic, terribly hurt somewhere inside, needing to be awakened, afraid to live the emotions I wrote about, afraid to let myself go.

I loved being "terribly hurt somewhere inside," whatever that meant, and what did they mean by the need to be awakened—let myself go—where? Into love?

Lacking the nimble wit to retort in kind, I threw a wide cordon of aloofness about me, and it worked.

Like myself, neither Steve nor Leon belonged to a Greek-letter society. We were "barbs," not because we entertained strong social views on discriminatory race and religious practices in fraternities. Like the University itself, we were undisturbed by such social issues.

But it was difficult to understand why Steve had not been invited to join one or the other of the fraternities, except perhaps because of his meager means. We never discussed any of this between ourselves, but the reason for Leon's and my exclusion was to become a source of bitterness.

However, leadership I once more attained, but, again, not the brand of my choice. I envied a large-boned, uncommunicative girl, Cornelia Coulter, who excelled in Greek and even before her graduation was assigned to an instructorship at Bryn Mawr. The chilly eye of this intellectual seemed to pass through me as if I were transparent. I felt a cheap and garish thing beside Coulter, who had chosen to linger back in the classic shades of Homer, Aeschylus, Virgil. I thought of a remark of the president of "The Potter's Wheel," the exclusive literary group I had not been invited to join. I would rather be a classic failure, she was purported to have said, than a popular success like Fannie Hurst.

Not that I fainted by the wayside at such indictments, although they stung. After all, I had a certain amount of compensation to keep me afloat. My growing leadership. The extravagant loyalty of my "best friend" Olna. Some small, class-acclaim for my writing. At least the boys on the campus whom I inordinately admired were not hostile: Hugh Ferriss, destined for international fame as architect; Orrick Johns, a gifted poet with a life span no longer than Shelley's and who was to walk on one leg and crutch through the dark ways of his life.

An undersized lad, Robert Prothero, greenish-pale as a lima bean, majoring in physics, slipped an envelope into my mailbox. Lines in prose to Fannie Hurst, who interests me. They were vacuous and not too lucid. I never acknowledged them, but I erased the signature and showed it to some of the girls in the cloakroom, hoping they would conclude they had come from Hugh or Orrick.

The word "pragmatism" was not yet in my vocabulary; but nevertheless it was being borne in upon me as I scratched away at my little writings that the meaning of life must reside in the soul of the artist as well as in the world about him. It must reside in me, in the faces of our neighbors on Cates Avenue, in the people on the streets, even when they seemed faceless . . . it was for me to take in and give out . . . the vast design of truth . . .

My instructors wrote notations on the margins of my themes. Fine character delineations. Rings true. Avoid purple patches. Excellent storytelling. You get into the heart.

Mama said: M-m-m-m.

Papa said: Goes to show, perseverance brings success.

Mama said with a straight face: Knowledge is power.

Papa, unplumbed, said: That's right.

Then one day in my junior year the English professor came into class with an air of excitement.

Without preamble he came out with the highest tribute he had to offer: A member of this class, he announced, has written a weekly theme so good I might have written it myself. Faces swung in my direction. Yes, Miss Hurst has not only done it again, this time she has outdone herself.

Later that day I crammed the longhand-written theme into an envelope and raced with it down to the office of *Reedy's Mirror*.

St. Louisans subscribed to this well-known weekly chiefly for its spicy columns and local news outside the pale of the ordinary newspaper. A smaller percentage read it for its literary merit, including Marion Reedy's brilliant editorial forays into diverse areas as farflung, erratic, and erotic as he was. First to publish Edgar Lee Masters' "Spoon River," Sara Teasdale, Zoë Akins, Orrick Johns, he was a sage who lived loosely and unwisely; but his tombstone, if he has one, must have a gleam to it.

The obscure office, high in a downtown office building, was locked the early afternoon I arrived. I dropped the long envelope through a slot in the door and, when I did not hear the inner thud, fell to my knees to peer through the door crack to see if it had landed.

The waiting weeks lengthened. Then one day my stalwart friend Olna flew across the campus toward me, waving *Reedy's Mirror*. Look, she gasped, have you seen this?

There it was, "Ain't Life Wonderful," by Fannie Hurst.

I wanted to run in all directions at once, and so I just stood. I wanted to embrace—everything. And so I just stood. . . .

After several years of piano lessons from Miss Lee, I was playing Chaminade's "Scarf Dance," a Hungarian Rhapsody, a Chopin Etude, and "Narcissus."

Mama said: Your father hates music, so don't practice when he is at home. Papa said feebly: Rose, how can you say such things? Go right on with your playing, Fannie. That's might pretty. Mama said: Sam Hurst, I know you like a book.

Next I turned to elocution. Between us, Mama and I ferreted out a three-named teacher, Mae Ames Deatheridge, a lady of Aubrey Beardsley slenderness, thyroidic eyes, and many scarves. She taught me voice placement and a rendition of "The Rosary" to music, and stoutly insisted that I was exceptional. Mama paid her one dollar an hour.

One day she announced that she had a gentleman friend who so admired talent that she would like to bring him to visit me.

That is how I met William G. Barr, six feet of mature and personable male who yearned. Born in Minnesota, little schooling, self-educated in a groping way, credit man for an East St. Louis lumber company, Mr. Barr reached hungrily for things of the intellect, most of which he was unable to digest. He belonged to his church literary society, attended symphony concerts, wore an Elk's head in his buttonhole, and striped trousers and Prince Albert coat on Sunday mornings.

He had strikingly mobile features and a salting of gray in his dark hair, which sixteen-year-old F.H. found exciting. Mr. Barr admitted to thirty, and Papa said he was fifty, if a day.

He called for the first time with Mae Ames Deatheridge, and following the visit she immediately telephoned to tell me that Mr. Barr thought I was the brightest girl he had ever met.

I was excited, not so much by Mr. Barr as by the unprecedented circumstance of a man, and an older one at that, signifying that degree of admiration.

He himself telephoned the following day to ask if he might escort me to a symphony concert at the Odeon.

On my own, I accepted.

Papa said: I am surprised you did not consult us first. Who is this man? What do we know about him? I am amazed that you would lend yourself to anything like this.

Mama said: Leave it to your father to throw cold water on anything that has to do with pleasure. What do you expect the man to do, Sam? Show his birth certificate? If you had your way, your daughter would sit home and mope herself into a Tillie Strauss. Well, you are not going to have your way if I have anything to say about it.

Papa sighed, rattled his newspaper, and resumed reading. I'm finished, he said.

As a matter of fact, after a few evenings Mr. Barr proved to be a colossal bore. Cliché after cliché, in the key of never having been said before, dropped from his sensuous lips, strangely set into a face of puritanical sternness. Yet his adultness, the flecks of gray in his hair, the man's hunger for the satisfactions of culture were new and in a mild way exciting to me.

He said it was a pleasure just to hear the way so young a girl used words. He said he learned from being in my company. He brought me books, most of which I had long since put behind me. Omar Khayyám. Mr. Barr liked to recite passages from *The Rubáiyát*. Longfellow. And next to the Bible, from which he quoted profusely, came Elbert Hubbard. He read aloud from the latter, his wide liver-colored lips revealing cared-for teeth.

I felt adult with him and very very dull. I judged he must be waiting for a first indication that a caress would not be amiss. My prissiness must have inhibited him. The room adjoining my alcove, in which Mama and Papa sat evenings, was directly above the parlor. We could hear them moving about and Mama's voice over the telephone. To my embarrassment, the plumbing sounds in our house were audible up and downstairs alike.

I begged Mama to ask Papa not to go into the bathroom when Steve or Leon or Mr. Barr was in the house. But to no avail. Papa was a great brusher of teeth, the rather dreadful audible way.

Often, while Mama and I stood in the lower hall, hatted and coated and waiting for Papa to join us for a walk or an errand, Mama, working into her tight kid gloves, would finally call up the stairs: Sam! Coming, Rose. Bring the bathroom with you, Sam, if you can't bear to tear yourself away.

Mr. Barr was no less settled and laughless in demeanor than Papa. He boarded with Mae Ames Deatheridge's sister-in-law and according to her was so meticulous that he scarcely seemed to inhabit his room. Mr. Barr did not drink or smoke.

Nevertheless, Papa said: I don't see where it comes in that a fellow like that should be calling on a young girl.

I know! You're against him because he's a *goy*. Well, I don't see the Jewish boys offering her so much attention.

Papa, what difference does it make what his religion is!

Papa regarded Mama darkly over his glasses: What did I tell you? Your daughter has been raised like a heathen, and now we are reaping the results. Even Mama looked taken aback.

She doesn't have to marry every man she knows. We simply can't afford to mingle with the rich Jews of this town. What is the child to do?

Fannie has years ahead for that sort of thing.

Dull as he was, I felt stubborn about Mr. Barr.

Mama wrote Aunt Jennie about all this and the *Gensbebla* came to St. Louis, packed with curiosity and interest.

Strangely, none of this irritated me. The first evening of her arrival, Mama and Aunt Jennie banished Papa to a rear room, turned out the lights, and stood behind the lace curtains to catch a glimpse of Mr. Barr as he came up the porch.

Papa said: You girls are crazy.

That's very well and good, Sam, said Aunt Jennie, who was bolder with Papa than anyone except Mama. It is your fault that Fannie doesn't associate with the best Jewish circles. You should have put your foot down years ago. If this nice *goy* is calling on her, it is better than having her sit here at home with no social life. She doesn't have to marry him.

I've nothing more to say, reiterated Papa, and retired to the back room with his newspaper.

When Mr. Barr arrived, and we were in the parlor, I could hear the banisters creak because Mama and Aunt Jennie were eavesdropping down the staircase. After his departure I stormed at Mama and Aunt Jennie not only for eavesdropping but, to my secret chagrin, because Mr. Barr had not been amorous.

However, Mama and Aunt Jennie declared they were unable to hear a word and Aunt Jennie was vociferous in her desire to know what he said—and what he did.

I remained cryptically silent.

I come all the way from Hamilton, lamented Aunt Jennie, and what does it get me!

Papa said to Mama, after Aunt Jennie had retired for the night: That *Gensbebla* hasn't got the sense she was born with.

Mama said: At least my family takes an interest in us. Your daughter could be elected President of the United States and that sister of yours would not send a telegram, much less take the train for St. Louis.

I felt ashamed that Mr. Barr had not even attempted to make love to me while Aunt Jennie was hanging over the balustrade. So much so that I lied defiantly.

Serves you both right for listening. He didn't even try to kiss me the way he usually does.

Was he ardent? pursued my incorrigibly romantic aunt.

Wouldn't you like to know, I retaliated with a dreary sense of wouldn't I like to know.

I did not want Mr. Barr to kiss me. His lips were heavy and brownish and moist.

But I did want to be wanted.

About this time, epitaphs from *Spoon River Anthology* by an author named Edgar Lee Masters began to appear occasionally in *Reedy's Mirror*.

Of all my undisciplined hodgepodge reading, first, second, and third rate, Edgar Lee Masters' *Spoon River* was to become a major literary experience; and this, mind you, following a period of extracurricular reading which included Hall Caine, Boccaccio's *The Decameron*, Maeterlinck, Smollet, Gertrude Atherton, Gilbert Chesterton, Norman Douglas, D'Annunzio, Upton Sinclair,

Mary Wilkins Freeman, Thomas Hardy, Arnold Bennett, Alice Hegan Rice, Olive Schreiner.

Spoon River brought my first intimations of the vineyards in which I, too, must labor. The vineyards of the common people. Masses of them. This was more of a visceral reaction than a conclusion. But indubitably, Masters had given me direction. A light had come out on the flat stretch between Chicago and St. Louis. The light was a stubby Chicago lawyer who, in the midst of law practice, was relating the fearful and wonderful story of the common man in terms of his headstones.

The saga of any man or woman's span of life moved before the reader in about twenty lines, the drama of human existence tamped down tightly into a form no larger than a sonnet or two.

Awe of Edgar Lee Masters' accomplishment has come down the years with me into today, a tour de force contemporaneously equaled only by Thornton Wilder's *Our Town*.

Masters jolted me into new aches and pains. What skills and wisdoms, I told and retold myself, must have stalked that brain of his so that people lived their lifetimes in his few lines. What skills and wisdoms needed to reside in the minds and souls of all good writers.

When we went to Hamilton our train passed through Indianapolis, a city irradiated, in my mind, by the fact that it was Booth Tarkington's home. Once when our train stopped there I wrote him a postcard something to this effect: Dear Booth Tarkington, Indianapolis will always be the most wonderful town in the world to me because you live there and write about people you make so real they live there, too. I think about you a great deal and wonder how you do it. He never replied. A lesson to me who all my subsequent life have answered every communication personally.

Wondering how they do it, I began an onslaught into biography and autobiography. St. Augustine, Cellini, Rousseau, da Vinci, George Moore.

It was difficult to realize that, even as Fannie Hurst on Cates Avenue, these authors were of the stuff that would suffer if you held a lighted cigarette against them. Men and women on their way to possible immortality should, like Olympians, have immunities from the way of all flesh. But their histories revealed that indigestion, jealousy, hunger, toothaches, loneliness plagued them as they plagued the ordinary people of Cates Avenue and those of Edgar Lee Masters' tombstones.

Reading biography was like entering a garden. But wandering deeply enough into the stories of their lives, you were likely to come upon areas as realistic as dumping grounds for old tires, stoves, discarded shoes, tin cans, and the litter of everyday living.

Everyone in Spoon River, from the lowliest to the first citizen, went to molder in his grave, tagged with the author's overall knowledge of their mere mortalness and their sublimity.

I wrote Masters letter after letter; none was ever sent.

Next I yearned to meet Reedy, who, I speculated, must have personal contact with Masters. But the days passed into weeks and still no acknowledgment from the editor who had published my piece in his *Mirror*.

Now, after the excitement of it had subsided somewhat, and the worn-ragged copies of the *Mirror* containing my story, which Mama and Papa had shown about, had gone the final rounds, Mama exploded: Don't magazines pay for what they print? Why doesn't that Reedy pay you?

It is we who should be willing to pay him for the honor he has bestowed on Fannie, said Papa.

He wouldn't print it if it wasn't good. I'm going to send him a bill.

Mama, if you do I'll never show my face in this town again.

Your mother doesn't mean all she says, Fannie.

No one respects what they get for nothing. Don't you ever send him anything again. The nerve!

What Mama and Papa did not know was that, since the publication of my first piece, I had been bombarding the Reedy office with subsequent offerings which were neither acknowledged nor returned.

The idea began to overhang that one of these days, if I could muster courage, it might be well for me to go personally to the

Reedy office and collect them. I lived with the thought for weeks, fascinated by the gossip surrounding Reedy and inhibited by my mental picture of the sage, sitting there in his lair, thinking both massive and lascivious thoughts.

Town talk concerning him penetrated the campus and even Cates Avenue. According to legend, naughty ladies and the cup that cheers were his pastimes. Mama said he was a nix-nux. I concluded he must be like François Villon.

Before Neal left our campus, leaving it gray, she had given the class a character sketch of Reedy. Speculation had it that he had fancied Neal herself.

Up there in his office, less than an hour away from where I lived, his mind burning like a live volcano, sat the controversial figure, like Teufelsdröckh in his tower, while I dwelt down among the people who never looked up or smelled the stars.

One day, following an impulse, I polished myself up and boarded a streetcar for *Reedy's Mirror*.

This time he was not only in but the open door revealed him practically reclining in a swivel chair, his feet high on an incredibly littered desk, his vast body seeming to run downhill in an avalanche of fat, mussed shirt crawling up out of his low-waisted trousers, a pair of cracked glasses low on his nose, dark graying hair pushed around on his head, eyeshade dangling from his neck like a bib.

Books, books, stacked on the floor, on chairs, overflowed the place.

I must have presented something of a spectacle myself, standing rapt in the dirty wintry light and gazing, I am sure beatifically, at the vast troglodyte deep in his cave of confusion. He slid his glasses higher on his nose and regarded me.

I am Fannie Hurst.

The ensuing douse was delivered with a smile.

And what am I supposed to say to that?

I wrote "Ain't Life Wonderful." You printed it.

Say, now, that was a good little piece. Sit down, he directed, sweeping sheaves of paper to the floor. What struck me was your keen observation. That gal in your story was so real you could have pinched her behind, he said, and laughed down the slanting front of him.

I had seldom if ever heard anything so grossly articulated.

Now, you just sit down on that pretty little fanny of your own, Fannie, and tell me about yourself.

It was also the first intimation I had ever had that all was not good in the pure application of my given name. I hesitated to be seated, which would indicate that I knew what he meant.

A wave of resentment toward Mama went over me. Mama and Papa had debated between Fannie and Beulah, and Mama had chosen in favor of the former. At least you did not sit on your beulah.

Reedy talked to me until dusk, without even a telephone call to interrupt. Read me excerpts from a book which lay open before him. Ovid's *The Art of Love*, luminous and lecherous-sounding to my Cates Avenue ears, erotica strangely in keeping with the red-light Olympus district in which dwelt this satirical fat man who laughed with his belly and talked like a cross between a scholar and a bum.

He told me of a talented St. Louis girl who, as he put it, needed to be bombed out of her virginity, of another who should have been sealed into hers.

Sara Teasdale he labeled a middle-western Sappho who bathed under a sheet. Most contemporary American writers, he declared, were wired with suppressed desires, but their sex life took place chiefly between book covers.

You are too young, he added, for me to talk this into you. Some lucky guy will one day kiss it into you and may I add, he continued, that you are exercising admirable restraint with me, or is it admirable?

This sort of talk was one thing on the pages of Flaubert or Lady Duff Gordon. But spoken, the words smoked. What could one say to this kaleidoscopic man who should have outraged you and somehow did not?

What could one retort to a man who said: I think you will

write one day, girl, if you let go. The question, as I look at you, is: Have you anything to let go?

I sensed double entendre of some sort and wondered what Neal would have said. Something brilliant and triple or quadruple entendre no doubt.

Well, I managed to retort, my mind doesn't bathe under a sheet. This seemed to amuse him, because he threw back his head and laughed, sobering suddenly.

Where do you live? Parents? Father's occupation? What stock?

Here it came.

Irish? Presbyterian? Catholic?

Since this is a clinical analysis, not a celebration of me, I am obliged to confess that my mind locked against what I knew I should or must reply.

We are American.

He did not pursue the subject. The suspicion flashed miserably over me that now he knew me for the snide person I was. But for the life of me I could not retract or supplement.

Had I known Reedy better I would have realized how transcendent his tolerance and compassion; I would have recognized the strange kind of spirituality that rode him with cloven hoofs, hurdling the untidy mishmash of the visible fat man who sprawled there amid tobacco and alcoholic fumes.

He talked of an H. L. Mencken, of a fellow named Theodore Dreiser, and then of the more familiar Bernard Shaw, Yeats, Hamlin Garland, Jack London, Amy Lowell, finally rising in dismissal.

Go home and write me some more shorts. Sweat for them and you may have something.

I have already sent you three, following the first.

They are not up to the Fannie Hurst first. Go home, you nice big healthy girl, and write like hell.

His parting words doused some of the new fire he had set going in me.

Nice big healthy girl! Hunk of a girl. Hunk of a brain . . .

It was during this week of my secret visit to Reedy that a poor little moment lived and died in our front parlor, all within its span of sixty seconds. Mr. Barr's romance.

During the dull first hour of his visit that evening, I could tell by the creaking of the banisters that Mama and Aunt Jennie were overhanging again, hoping to overhear. Finally came the sound of their tiptoeing back into the sitting room and the drone of their talk resuming.

All through what subsequently happened, a thought ran like a ridiculous thread through my mind. If only Mama and Aunt Jennie had remained at the banisters a bit longer, they would have heard with their own ears! Now they might think I had concocted it.

Mr. Barr proposed! It came not out of the blue but out of the dull gray of a typical Barr evening. Mr. Barr had written a paper on Abraham Lincoln, to be read before his church literary society.

An elementary exposition it proved to be, obviously gleaned from encyclopedia or textbook, which he read in the laborious fashion of a schoolboy declaiming, finishing with an eager bid for praise.

It isn't too bad, is it? Lincoln has always been one of my favorites.

I felt sorry for Mr. Barr. He was so hungry for learning, so drearily dull.

It is very good, Mr. Barr.

Will you come and hear me at the meeting? They tell me I am quite good before an audience.

Mama had lemonade and cookies on the table. We had the refreshment; and suddenly Mr. Barr, still in the throes of success, placed a hand over mine.

Miss Fannie, do you think you could like me?

Instantly I knew what he meant and simultaneously I felt a sort of horridness.

Then Mr. Barr proceeded, lifting my fingers one by one as he talked, and that was part of the horridness. I wanted to withdraw them but, again, crazily, something within me was enjoying it.

He went on to tell me about himself in a decent sort of way. Minnesota farm boy. Scotch Presbyterian descent. Orphaned at eleven. Cook's helper in a lumber camp at fourteen.

Mr. Barr wondered if I had noticed he was slightly deaf in one ear, owing to a blow from falling timber, otherwise sound as a nut. Mr. Barr was a great one for shortcuts to culture and correspondence courses in literature. Public speaking. Mr. Barr admired brains and needed a wife who would help him improve himself. Mr. Barr wondered if I liked him. Mr. Barr liked me. Mr. Barr's hand slid up my arm and he was very close. Repulsively close. Will you be my wife, Miss Fannie?

I confess it was a lollipop of a moment. Already, and I not quite seventeen, a grown man, not a college youngster, was paying me the highest honor a girl could covet. How many of the girls who received the bids to the dances and football games could say as much! Even though the denouement left much to be desired, I had my moment.

I saved myself just this side of the surrender moment by explaining that it could not be, my reason inspirational. My parents.

They think I am too old for you? I'm thirty-eight, young enough to appreciate a brilliant little wife. I can wait for them to soften. I can be patient.

It isn't all that. It would kill them. You see, we're Jewish.

If I had said we were head hunters, I think Mr. Barr could have been no more stunned. He turned almost automatically and said quite gently that he must be going. The poor gentleman, so unconscious of the horrendous facts, had been caught with his prejudices off guard.

No dramatics, no anything, except that he kissed my fingertips carefully, picked up his carefully placed hat and gloves, and closed the front door softly, as if not to leave the imprint of his departure on the silence.

Upstairs, Mama and Aunt Jennie were surprised by my early appearance.

ANATOMY OF ME

When I exploded the news, Papa said: I am glad you conducted yourself with dignity and dismissed him.

I don't say she should have accepted him, said Aunt Jennie, but a proposal is a feather in her cap.

The nerve, said Mama, he should know that we don't want a goy son-in-law any more than he wants us.

Late that night Aunt Jennie crept into my bed. Fannie, she said, you listen to your old aunt who has only your interest at heart. Get married young. Don't educate yourself into a bluestocking. The more you know, the less desirable you become to men. They want a homemaker, not a superior mind.

Aunt Jennie, you make me ashamed.

Naturally, we don't want you to marry a Mr. Barr, but one of your own people.

I hated the phrase "my own people." Who were my own people? All people.

Look at your Aunt Bettie, Fannie. She is worth ten of me. But what is her life as an old maid? A fifth wheel. Take my advice, even under the best conditions, an old maid is every woman's idea of what she does not want to be.

Thus ended my first romance, a dreary little thing, more than half dead before it was born.

My next piece, entitled "Home," which Marion Reedy published, followed about six rejections. It was originally written with the hope that Thyrsus, our university dramatic club, might produce it in the form of a one-act skit, with Steve and me in the roles of its two characters, husband and wife.

It did not happen. The director of Thyrsus, our assistant professor of English, considered the domestic drama of a wife champing at the restraints of marriage, and deciding to return to the theater, commonplace.

Steve suggested: Why not try Frank Tate of Keith's? He might put us on for a week. He did it for Neal when she started out.

I was struck by the daring of the idea. Frank Tate, manager of the Keith circuit theater, was a personage locally.

But Mama and Papa?

You're going to be in the professional world anyway one of these days. They may as well get used to the idea, urged Steve.

One noon, keeping it from even Steve, whom I did not want to know about it in the event my mission failed, I went down to see Mr. Tate. "Fannie Hurst, Washington University and Thyrsus," I wrote on a card. He received me after an hour's wait.

College years had somewhat modified my taste in dress, although what I wore could still have been sufficiently flamboyant for a theatrical man to appraise.

He placed the copy of *Reedy's Mirror*, which I had brought, unread upon his desk and listened. A man of quick judgment and action, it took him no time at all to realize that good, bad, or indifferent I might be local news like Neal Patterson and a possible draw. Local girl, prominent Washington University student, writes and acts in own play.

You say your father is a businessman?

President of the Standard Heel and Counter Company.

Cates Avenue? That is in the Cabanne district? And who is this fellow you have selected to play opposite you?

He is the most talented member of Thyrsus.

Dramatize your story and come back with it.

Even then I said nothing to Steve or my parents but, during the tedious interval of writing the adaptation, found myself half hoping my insane project would be rejected.

But upon reading my dramatization, Tate agreed to put us on, paying the two of us one hundred dollars for the week's engagement.

I warn you in advance, youngsters, you are in a tough spot. You follow George Beban in "The Sign of the Rose," a twenty-year-old success, season in and season out. Get to work and speed up your act by cutting it down five minutes. I'll put you on the week of October twenty-first, two performances daily, except Sundays. You're on your own from here on out.

Steve was like one possessed, the flames of his enthusiasm shooting out in all directions. I was stunned.

ANATOMY OF ME

How to break all this to Mama and Papa. Mama, I felt certain, could be managed. But Papa, to whom the theater meant only a licentious world of women in pink tights and divorce suits, was another matter.

However, with only three weeks for preparation, prompt action was imperative. I delayed as long as possible.

Then, one evening at the supper table, I let go my story.

There was a loud silence even from Mama. Papa laid down his knife and fork and pushed back from the table.

You are not serious?

But I am. It's the most wonderful opportunity a girl could have. Imagine a man like Frank Tate liking my work well enough to put it on the professional stage!

You mean to tell me that you are planning to go in a vaudeville show and make a spectacle of yourself for a man who means anything but good by you?

I knew we would live to rue the day she went to college for ideas that unfit her for her home, wailed Mama.

I forbid you, Fannie.

Your father is right to forbid you. An actress is all we need in the family. If you stay at home and mend your clothes and keep your dresser drawers in order, you'll have all the career you want. When I think of what I have sacrificed for that child. And for what! An actress!

Never mind, Rose, it won't happen.

It's your fault. You encouraged your daughter's highfalutin notions. I said no college from the start. High school is plenty for a girl. But no, knowledge is power. Well, you see what power it is. Your child is an out-of-hand stage nix-nux. I wish I was dead.

I have my own life to live, not yours! I don't want to live it the Cates Avenue way. Something in me won't let me.

That's the thanks we get, Sam. We are her enemies.

Tell your mother you are done with this nonsense.

But, Papa, we made a deal with Mr. Tate. We signed a paper.

You signed a paper!

Just a sort of letter, a little one, saying we are to be paid one hundred dollars for the week with some kind of dues and deductions.

You actually mean to say you signed a paper!

Yes, and if I have to give it up after all the trying, I just couldn't bear it. Mama, you try and make Papa see.

If you put your foot on that stage, Fannie, and humiliate me in a community where I have carefully built up good standing, I will sell my business and leave town.

Coming from Papa, this extravagant threat was thunderous. Food cloyed on our plates. I wanted to cry. Mama did.

I've had all I want from you for one evening, said Papa with the terrible sternness.

You're ruining my life. You've lived yours and I've a right to live mine. And here it came, the old cliché boiling on my lips: I didn't ask to be born. Now that I'm here, let me live.

Never that kind of life with my consent, interposed Papa.

I dropped my face into my hands and that was the straw that broke the camel's back.

I don't say it's my choice, said Mama in a tremulous voice that indicated the melt had set in, but, Sam, if the child has her heart set on it, let her get it out of her system. Most young girls are stage-struck. Shall we let her this once, Sam?

You're the darnedest woman, Rose. You will be the ruin of her.

Because I don't want her to have it the way I have it. She's seen enough to make her want to go on the stage or anywhere else to get a little out of life. Do I want my child to live a life of leather bellies? Fannie, you're right. Try to get some pleasure out of living.

I knew I had won.

After half a night of this, Papa took it with what grace he could muster, but my heart ached for him; and in moods of remorse Mama cried and said: This thing has aged your father.

He never referred to it again. I did not speak of the entire shattering experience, even during rehearsals, nor did he set foot in the theater.

I had won a Pyrrhic victory.

"Home," by Fannie Hurst, was produced on schedule, Miss Hurst, the author, in the role of Mrs. James Tompkins, Steve Gleeson as Mr. James Tompkins.

Preceding the event, there had been feature stories in the St. Louis *Post-Dispatch* and *Globe-Democrat* with our photographs, and Papa took to coming home evenings with certain pages torn out of his newspaper. I kept out of his way as much as possible, hugging my secret malaise.

Not only because of the unhappy situation at home, but panic had me. Why had I let myself in for this! The surer and more fluent Steve became in his acting, the heavier and bulkier I felt.

The highly realistic theme of "Home" had to do with a young married woman grown restive with her necktie-salesman husband and the disillusionments of domesticity. She is about to desert and resume a shabby theatrical career when a tragic circumstance of false accusation almost destroys her husband and simultaneously reveals to her the rare texture of the little necktie salesman, converting her to the rare values of him and home, in time to save the situation.

The role required shabby clothing, no glamour to conceal my shortcomings.

Mama said: Wear nice clothes, anyway. The audience won't stop to think where she got the money. If I had known you had to dress like a *schlomp*, I would have put my foot down. This whole business is aging your father.

We rehearsed only once in the theater, Mr. Tate keeping carefully out of range, although I was sure I discerned his dim face in the balcony. Our first performance was at Monday matinee.

On my way into Keith's Vaudeville Theatre, two hours beforehand, I spied friends and relatives, including Tillie Strauss and Hattie Heller, making for the Busy Bee Restaurant, where they would lunch before the matinee.

We were well rehearsed in our parts. Professor Starbuck had polished us up. Steve, I secretly feared, would walk off with the honors, although I had the heavier and more demanding role.

Mama had purchased twelve seats, first row, for friends and

neighbors, also preceding the performance with luncheon at the Busy Bee.

Our act went on following a pair of blackface comedians, six girls who rode one-wheel bicycles on high wires, and George Beban in his renowned "The Sign of the Rose."

Steve and I in makeup stood in the wings during the Beban sketch. The lines, read in a heavy Italian accent, came backstage without much effect. A wave of hope rose in me. If this was the alleged "great act," we had some chance. But then came the big heart jerk, when the old Italian, portrayed by Beban, stands with the lifeless body of his tubercular-ravaged little boy in his arms and sobs to the audience: Da leetla boy, he was so cold, he no could wait. . . .

The curtain fell on ladies with drenched handkerchiefs and wave after wave of applause recalling and recalling Beban and "da leetla boy" who was "so cold he no could wait. . . ."

Monkeys jittered in their backstage cages, awaiting their animal act, which followed us, ballet girls were toeing up and down, flexing. Steve also strode up and down, his lips moving. We were next.

In my shabby shirt and skirt, hair straggly, a kitchen apron tied about my middle, I stood trembling and waiting.

The orchestra struck the opening cymbals of our entrance music. Two girl pageboys carried out large placards and fitted them into frames on either side of the stage: Fannie Hurst and Steve Gleeson in "Home."

From the sparsely filled Monday afternoon house friendly hands spattered into applause.

We had had only one property rehearsal, and the vast stage, with what seemed new distances between stove, sink, chair, and window, threw my timing off somewhat. Steve, covering me where possible, went fluidly and unfalteringly into his role. There were no actual mishaps, our climax of tears and reconciliation came off not only as we had rehearsed it but under the stimulus of production somewhat better. As the curtain fell on our embrace, a thrill of success shot through me as we held the picture to the very last instant of the dropping curtain and, still clinched, stood waiting for the applause to demand another curtain.

But the brief spattering, even with what I knew to be the best efforts of Mama's claque, did not warrant optimism. I ran to my dressing room two flights up.

No sooner had I closed the door, wanting myself to myself, when Steve entered. It's a hit, he cried, snatching both my hands and whirling me around the room. Did you hear how I got every laugh out of my white-collar speech and every tear over my knee-scene in the confession? It's a hit, he cried, whirling and whirling me.

I, I, I. You may be a hit, I said dully. What about me, me, me?

Before he could reply, Mama, by some abracadabra of quick locomotion, entered.

I faced her, stricken. But Mama, with no time for perceptiveness, came at me head on.

Your father was right. I've nearly broken up my home for this. Your father was right. Believe me, Fannie, I'm your mother —the last one to see bad in anything you do—but you were terrible!

Oh, Mrs. Hurst! cried Steve.

You can talk, said Mama bitterly. You're a good actor who made her look even worse. Fannie, don't go on that stage any more. Would I tell you if it wasn't for your own good? Get out of this.

I can't, Mama.

I'll go to Mr. Tate.

Mrs. Hurst, Fannie and I are under contract. We can be sued. Besides, Fannie will get better. This is a first performance.

There is no better in this for her!

Numb to the soul and yearning to follow Mama's advice, I joined with Steve in arguing the futility of even attempting to extricate myself from ignominy.

Oh, how right your father was. If only I had listened to him.

The local press, all things considered, was as kind as could be expected. The blaring notices anticipated by Mr. Tate were inch insertions: "Home," a skit by Fannie Hurst, Washington University junior, acted by the author herself and Steve Gleeson, also a Washington University student, suffered by cruel contrast to George Beban's perennially popular "Sign of the Rose." Both Miss Hurst's writing and acting leave much to be desired. Steve Gleeson was a redeeming feature. However, Miss Hurst revealed some talent for character delineation.

We played out our week, but I cut all lectures at college rather than face up to what I knew would be the forced felicitations of colleagues, and suffered through the strained mealtimes at home, with Papa silent and Mama always on the verge of tears.

The final day of our appearance, George Beban came up to me: Don't be discouraged. You did well enough, considering. When you go to New York, look up my friend William Dean of the Belasco office. Tell him I recommended you. A few lessons from Dean will do wonders for you. Take your script with you. It's not so bad.

New York!

Stinging with the humiliation of the double fiasco as playwright and actress, I threw myself into a climactic senior year, writing, this time with campus success, our class play, acting in it as well, and graduating with a collection of rejection slips from major magazines that could have papered my room on Cates Avenue.

Mama said: Sam, we have a young lady daughter. Now that she is a college graduate, we must buy a home.

Papa said: All right, Rose, if you think so, but with real estate values booming and business what it is, it's a bad time to invest.

It is never a good time in this family for anything but leather bellies. That's where the twenty-five hundred dollars my father left me went, and that's where your daughter's future will go, if I don't put my foot down.

Have it your way, said Papa feebly, but I suspected that despite his quiet acquiescence he would somehow circumvent this move.

Nevertheless, panic gripped me. Buy a home! On the contrary, I wanted to be free of one. I wanted to go to New York. To write—or, second best, take dramatic lessons from Mr. Dean. Mr. Beban had also given me the name of a great man for whom Mr. Dean was director—a Mr. Belasco. . . .

Now began the fanfare preceding college graduation. Leaving the Gothic beauty of the buildings, their classic shades, was a wrench. Regrettably, the faculty had not made an imprint of any particular depth, nor influenced my way of thought or my cultural appetites to any appreciable extent. That my intellectual curiosity was awakened at all, and has not closed an eye since, was largely due to exposure to a collegiate world that by its very nature dealt in the best ideas that had come down through the ages from the minds of men.

Otherwise, the break of graduation, largely because of the University's seemingly chilly indifference toward its graduates, was more or less complete.

Suddenly I was back on Cates Avenue, Steve off for graduate work at Harvard, Leon taking a certified public accountant position in Omaha.

Despite activities with Mama, shopping with her, attending matinee performances of our local stock company, writing longer hours and more intensively, the days began to stare at me.

Mama's unease was palpable. Why don't you learn to play piano duets with that nice Pearlie Eisman?

What have we in common!

I wish you had some of her common sense in common. That family eats every meal off of her china painting.

Sure as fate, I reasoned, the miasmic world of the Pearlie Eismans, and the sedative sense of security of my home would close in on me unless, like a man in a blizzard needing to fight off his sleepiness by flaying his arms, I kept alive in me the need to be off!

Every morning Mama saw to it that Willie had a row of pencils newly sharpened on my desk, plentiful typewriter paper stacked, and my favorite refreshment day or night, a bottle of mammoth green olives, alongside. All the while, as Mama so fondly tended, I could feel myself and my impulse to write withering on the vine, dying of the double-edged frustration of wanting release and at the same time, in the idiom of Mama, being tied to her apron strings.

Your father thinks it is a good idea for us to join the Unity Club this fall. We are going to ask Laz Scharff to put us up for membership.

Mama, I wouldn't go there if you gave it to me.

Mama exploded that night at dinner: Your daughter refuses to go to the Unity Club if we do join, so there's no need to throw away the money.

Papa went into his routine: You are making a great mistake in secluding yourself from the right Jewish people.

I wonder who she thinks she is, said Mama. You would think St. Louis is not good enough for her.

That isn't it, and you know it.

I'll tell you what she wants, Sam. She's afraid to tell you. She wants to go to New York and live away from us. That's what we sent her to college for . . . to get ideas.

It was frightening and I was glad that Mama had said it for me. I had been trying to for weeks.

She—what?

Yes, Papa. I want to be a writer.

She can't write at home, Sam. There is no pencil and paper here. No typewriting machine which we bought her. The only place she can write is New York.

Papa, don't you see, I'm old enough to be out in the world. . . .

We should have the only daughter in town who is a misfit. At a time when we could have her in the home, as we grow older, her home is no longer enough for her.

Now, Rose, don't say that. Fannie is a sensible girl.

Then don't try to make me fit in with the Unity Club crowd. They are all right, but they are not my kind and I am not theirs.

Who is your kind? That old Mr. Barr?

Rose!

Where does it come in that she can't write at home? Nothing

is expected of her, no housework like other girls. We don't deserve this, Sam.

Your mother is right. Is this what we have looked forward to? A daughter running around in a big and dangerous city a thousand miles away?

All right, then, I'll stay here and decay.

Sam, let her go. We'll have no peace if she stays. But I wouldn't want to have on me what she will have on her when she leaves us.

Papa gave one of his immense sighs: Perhaps your mother is right. So this is the harvest we have reaped!

Suddenly I wanted nothing so much as to remain at home. Indecision, my lifelong foe, began its harassments. Fighting for what I wanted, suddenly I did not want it. Then, again, the overpowering unrest.

Mama and Papa knew nothing of this. They were only aware that the warm nest of our home, their protective love, had become intolerable to me.

Just exactly what is your idea, once you get to New York?

I want to observe life, Papa.

Can't you observe life right here at home?

She wants to observe life! Did you ever hear of such a thing. We graduate our daughter from an expensive college so she can go off to New York and observe life.

Now wait, Rose. Let Fannie talk.

Mama, you don't understand.

You would think I am a half-wit. I don't understand what? I understand you are making life miserable for your father and me.

Just how do you want to observe life, Fannie?

By observing it the way Dickens did. Roaming the highways and byways of—life—I mean the big city—standing on its bridges the way he did in London—watching the world. . . .

Well, Sam, now you've got it. She wants to be like Dickens.

Fannie, there are bridges in St. Louis. Eads Bridge is one of the finest.

Oh, I don't mean only bridges. People. I need people, Papa, and I want them to need me. . . .

And we can't even get her to the Unity Club.

I don't mean that way, Mama. I mean the—masses . . . people who work in factories, coal mines.

What about your father's factory here at home?

An idea shot through me.

Why not become an operator in Papa's factory, write the story of my experience and send it to the *Post-Dispatch*?

Papa, would you let me work at the Standard Heel and Counter Company? Just to see and observe?

Mama had inadvertently let Papa in for something. His smile was forced and quizzical. I don't believe you will learn much. It is a dull existence for operators.

Let her, Sam!

It is dirty smelly work and inexperienced operators slow us down. Besides, they know you by sight down at the factory.

It doesn't have to be your factory, Sam. Get her into that North St. Louis one that does your overflow work. The Lutz Brothers.

Thus, within a month following graduation, I spent two weeks as Miss Rose Samuels in rows of girls, most of them Polish, pasting layers of men's heels together with a foul-smelling concoction which smeared you until you acquired the knack.

Since the majority of the girls were immigrants recently arrived, they spoke their language among themselves, thus isolating me as an outsider. I managed, however, to go to the homes of two or three of them after work, and ate my lunch with one who spoke English.

All in all, my foray added up to an aching spine from the long confining hours, glue-smelling hair, and a new and shocked awareness of low wages in a dust-filled loft of dirty windows, wretched plumbing, the girls usually returning to homes as squalid and deprived as their working quarters. Confusions were churning more and more within me as I slid between my own clean sheets at night and thought of the girls of the Lutz loft and their kind of sleeping quarters. Nothing more acute than an uneasiness was beginning to prick at me, but it was uncomfortable, as if there were crumbs in my bed.

At the conclusion of my second week I presented myself to one of the Lutz Brothers, who had been careful to observe my anonymity, thanked him, and bowed out, sadder and smellier.

Mama said: Wash that glue smell out of your hair. I only hope you got nothing worse down there.

Papa said: Now that you have this out of your system, do you feel better? I spoke to Tom Lutz. He said you conducted yourself very well and he admired your spirit. Now you've seen how the other half lives and should be grateful for your own good fortune.

Like that strange feeling of having been in a place before, when actually you are seeing it for the first time, I felt that somehow, some way, I had always known how the other half lives. . . .

It was nice to be home, but I felt a futility, as if I had tugged and tugged at a door only to find when it finally opened that it led nowhere. . . .

I decided to again contact Mr. Bovard, managing editor of the St. Louis *Post-Dispatch*, whose citadel I had once before vainly assailed, and ask him if the story of my experience as a factory worker would be acceptable.

I was once more unsuccessful, but this time the receptionist turned me over to the city editor. The *Post-Dispatch* had no place for such an article, but would I consent to being interviewed, for which the *Post-Dispatch* would pay me space rates. The situation moved more rapidly than my brain. Before I had time to assemble my wits, my silence was taken for acquiescence, and a reporter was before me, pad and pencil. I talked too quickly and too much. The story broke the following day: Fannie Hurst, recent graduate of Washington University, daughter of Mr. and Mrs. Samuel Hurst of the exclusive Cabanne district, works as bench operator in North St. Louis shoe factory to observe how other half lives . . . recently authored and played leading role in her own sketch at Keith's Vaudeville Theatre. Advocates reforms in working conditions of women . . .

Accompanying the story was a large photograph of me, taken at the *Post-Dispatch*.

Papa said: This certainly places me in an embarrassing position with the Lutz Brothers.

Mama, trying to keep down the pride in her voice, said over and over on the telephone: Naturally, we don't approve of the notoriety. Her father is having fits. But, as I say to Mr. Hurst, times have changed. Oh, that about her going to New York? Newspaper talk!

But in her heart, Mama must have known differently. No sooner was Operation Lutz Brothers over than our little household once more began to close in on me with its claustrophobic grip. This was not the usual summer vacation interlude. This was a cul-de-sac, with me staring at the closed end.

Mama said: This is a house of gloom. I wonder I have the courage to go on from day to day.

Remorse overtaking me, I would suggest the Suburban Summer Garden for a stock company matinee, for which she cared little, or a shopping tour, for which she cared.

But, inevitably, the arid stretches would return to defeat me.

Mrs. Pulliam, our next-door neighbor, used to open her screen door and say: The cat wants out. I wanted out!

As midsummer approached and the days droned, my broodiness increased to such an extent that one afternoon as I sat chin-cupped-in-hand, looking out on static Cates Avenue, Mama, who had also been sitting in the silence, suddenly picked up the telephone receiver and called Papa at his office: Sam, I want you to come home. Things have reached a point where I can't stand it any longer. Your daughter has not spoken twenty words since you left this morning. Buy her a ticket to New York on your way home. Or to any place she wants to go, or I'll lose my mind watching her mope.

I sat silent and wretched while Mama, poor darling, stomped about the room, finally picking up the telephone receiver again: Sam, there is no use your coming home until your usual time. Bad enough that one of us has to go through this.

ANATOMY OF ME

Papa did come home a little earlier than usual that evening, grave and concerned over what he knew awaited him. He had apparently concocted a strategy which he presented without preamble.

What we all need is a little trip. A place like Petosky, Michigan, or Atlantic City. That's where the Scharffs go, isn't it?

I had always shied from the idea of summer resorts so popular with our heat-ridden populace. But neither Mama nor I had ever been "East" and such a trip would at least mean propinquity to New York City, seeing an ocean for the first time, to say nothing of one of the country's renowned resorts.

Besides, I told myself to allay my irritating awareness that my parents were taking this trip through no desire of their own, the experience might help them realize how deep their rut.

For ensuing weeks, Mary Stutz, dressmaker tried and true, hummed away at the sewing machine in an upstairs back room, and wardrobe trunks stood waiting in the lower hall. Papa said: One would think we were going to Africa. Such ostentation is unbecoming. Mama said: You run your business, Sam, and I will run mine.

The whites of Willie's eyes bulged these days, as the heat and my finery began to mount.

I declare, Miss Fannie, you are sure going to bring home a beau with all that!

I protested: Mama, I don't need all these clothes for only two weeks.

They say if a girl expects to be dated at the Royal Palace Hotel she must dress for it, particularly since there are certain to be more girls than men.

Now and now only, I began to be aware. These clothes were sort of a pre-trousseau. Well, I was in it now and deeply, because it had been arranged that Aunt Jennie, Uncle Joe, and Aunt Bettie were to join us at the Royal Palace.

Simple as were Papa's habits and way of life, he traveled the luxurious way. The best transportation and hotels with, of course, the exception of tipping. Against this last, however, Mama had fortified herself.

I insist, Sam, that you tip properly, or I will stay at home. I think I am going to ask Joe to do it for all of us, and you can settle with him.

You know my sentiments, Rose. It's not the money. That fellow Joe tips like a drunken sailor.

We were off one blistering July day, Willie, box-laden, accompanying us to the Union Station.

What is in those shoeboxes, Willie? asked Papa.

That's fried chicken, Mr. Hurst, and a mason jar of potato salad, some olives for Miss Fannie, hard-boiled eggs . . . said Willie, suddenly interrupting herself and clapping her hand over her mouth: Mrs. Hurst told me not to say nothing.

Mama!

Never mind, Fannie, said Papa. We are all going into the dining car for our meals.

Three dollars for chicken that I can fix at home for less than half.

But, Mama, we look like immigrants.

Never mind, Fannie, if your mother won't join us, we will have to go into the dining car without her.

In the end, of course, we ate all our meals in our compartment, Papa finishing off the chicken until the bones shone.

I did not encounter the Atlantic Ocean, although our gigantic packing case of a wooden hotel faced it, until twenty-four hours after our arrival.

We arrived at dusk, were shown directly to our rooms, which did not face the water. They were small square affairs, smelling strongly of salt air, with wall hooks covered by a cretonne curtain for closet room. There was a bath between Mama and Papa's and Uncle Joe and Aunt Jennie's rooms, but only a stationary washstand in the one I shared with Aunt Bettie.

Mama said: My Willie's room at home is better than any of these. Papa said: Now, Rose, remember this is the height of the season and we were fortunate to get accommodations at all.

I had never shared a room before, and the prospect, even with Aunt Bettie, was depressing.

The relatives, who had previously visited the hotel, arrived a few hours after us.

Aunt Jennie said: It is better not to dress for dinner the first evening. They will know we are new arrivals and show us attention.

The lobby, when the five of us stepped out of the elevator, was crowded with men in white dinner jackets and women in floating sheers.

A girl with a tray of corsages stood in our direct path. Uncle Joe bought three and pinned them gallantly on us. Aunt Jennie said: Joe, you should only have bought one. For Fannie. It would look as if an admirer had sent it.

The enormous dining room teemed, the tables close and crowded. White-coated Negro waiters, shining with perspiration, snaked their way between them, holding high on the palm of one hand their crowded trays packed with table d'hôte orders.

As we stood new and hesitant at the entrance, a headwaiter came to steer us. As Uncle Joe asked for a window table, he withdrew a twenty-dollar bill from his wallet and tore it in two equal parts. Now, George, he said, handing the waiter one of the halves, you take good care of us and you get the other half when we leave.

Papa looked his aversion of the pretentious gesture, and I felt mine.

Our rooms may have been little more than flimsy-walled cubicles, but the dinner menu was long and loaded with rich German and Hungarian dishes. Marinated herring, chicken liver pâté, noodle soup, boiled chicken with matzo balls, gedempte rinderbraten, goulash, red cabbage, water ices and stewed fruit served with the meat course, strudel, pastries, pies. Breakfast and luncheon similarly overabundant.

Two weeks of it and, like the majority of the Royal Palace guests, we ordered from the top of the menu down as far as the dateline.

Mama complained a good deal: These stuffed green peppers are too greasy. These biscuits weigh a ton. Willie can give them cards and spades.

After a first-night dinner, bountifully criticized and eaten, we repaired to a quiet corner of the lobby, there to observe the Royal Palace swing into its night life.

Swarms of beautifully gowned, corsaged young girls milled about the lobby, pairing off with young men in white jackets and disappearing with them into the outer darkness. My heart sank.

Aunt Jennie's obsession began to operate at once.

During the day these girls see to it that they are dated for the evening. Only the wallflowers sit around with their parents. Mrs. Silvercross, from Dayton, is here somewhere. She knows everyone and will introduce you around.

If you think I am going to maneuver for a date!

Now, Jennie, interposed Mama, I hope you can see for yourself. We have wasted our money so she can sit around with us and be a wallflower.

Never mind, soothed Aunt Jennie, Fannie is no fool.

Papa said: Girls, I wouldn't prod Fannie if I were you. She is too young to think about the things you have in mind. Let her be and have a good time in her own way.

Atlantic City lost no time in turning into a spangled nightmare for me. The weather, most unusual so they said, turned sultry as our own St. Louis, the salt air so heavy it seemed that at any moment it might become a solid.

About two in the morning of that first night, our entire corridor of sleeping guests was awakened by a loud crash. Night-clad figures appeared in the hallways, anxious and questioning.

With Mama and Papa apparently an overload, the lightly slung double bed had collapsed with them to the floor, into a splintering of timbers.

As we burst into their bedroom and switched on the lights, the spectacle of the two of them on the slant, Papa in nightshirt and Mama in a kind of chemise, was too much. While Aunt Jennie, Aunt Bettie, and Uncle Joe were pulling them out of the debris of mattress and slats, I stood by, hysterical with laughter.

Mama turned on me furiously. My daughter doesn't even ask if we are hurt!

Papa, his modesty outraged, was struggling into his robe. That was a mighty frail bedstead, he said with solemnity.

Twenty-five dollars a week for it and I would not ask my Willie to sleep on it. My *schlemiel* husband is too elegant to protest. I've already had enough of Atlantic City. I'm ready for home tomorrow.

Hope rose within me.

Now, old lady, said Papa, you'll feel differently in the morning, but that certainly is a mighty frail bedstead.

Suddenly I was again in the throes of laughter, Mama joining with me this time while Papa looked bewildered.

I don't see anything funny, he said. We might have hurt ourselves.

I'm sorry, I said, and off went Mama and I into more gales of laughter.

Fourteen days of it. Forty-two overrich, oversized meals. Two weeks of hot brilliant sea air, the sea itself half obscured by a boardwalk of milling crowds: enormous waterfront hotels façaded with shops exuding salt-water taffy, auctioneer's shouts. Window exhibits ranging from rich furs, antiques, and jewelry to gimcracks, souvenirs, hamburgers, cotton candy, delicatessen arrays. Great piers jutted far out into the water, and with their blaze dimmed it. Mornings on the snowy beach, hordes of greased bathers shouted, plunged, rode the waves, and lay flat on their backs and let the sun dry their drenching.

My new bathing suit hung unwetted. Surprisingly Mama said: I don't blame you for not wanting to go down there in that mishmash.

Fourteen days of: You're smarter than any of them, and yet a wallflower.

If Sam hasn't the gumption, it wouldn't hurt you, Joe, to bring a few young men around, stormed Aunt Jennie.

But, Jennie, I did. That David fellow from Detroit wanted in the worst way to date her for a chair ride and dinner down at the Shelburne. These fellows just don't appeal to Fannie.

It's that college education did it.

Rose, you take the cake, said Papa, as if the cake were bitter.

I discovered a strip of deserted beach, where the sun shone and the moon shone into solitude, stirring some of the old impulses that seemed to have dried during these garish Atlantic City days and nights.

All of this majesty of ocean and moon and stars! People, even at the Royal Palace, must have majesty, too, somewhere behind their flesh and flash. Even all of us in that dreadful dining room with the sweating waiters weaving their way between packed tables with the upheld loads of foods . . . People could not wear what majesty they had, the way the moon and stars showed theirs. People were too caught up in a world of marriageable daughters, cancer, taxes, dreams, ambitions, frustrations, tragedy, success, joy, and failure. People . . .

Two such serene nights I eked out for myself. They were more compensatory than I realized at the time. I took them back to St. Louis with me.

Whatever confidence Papa may have had in the efficacy of the trip to Atlantic City, it must have been quickly dissipated following our return to St. Louis. Almost immediately, the old sense of vacuum engulfed me.

Long sweltering days, during which I wrote and rewrote, polishing phrases until they shone or shattered. Long static evenings on the front porch, after Papa had sprinkled the lawn, and Mama, inside helping Willie with the dishes, rattled them.

If I offered to assist, she said: I don't want you in the kitchen. There is plenty of time for you to learn such things after you are married. Mama's fallacy!

After dark, when the trees closed us into the humidity and the crickets began their abrasive "Hind-leg Blues," I usually retired to the reception hall and sat on the dark stairs. I would have preferred to go upstairs and read or write, but the unhappy truth is that this was my way of impressing Mama and Papa with the fact that they had an unhappy daughter tethered to a newel post.

How could I have thrown my pall of discontent over the lives of these two! But I did, suffering along the way, it is true, but going ruthlessly ahead through that summer of discontent; and the round-trip parade of the long envelopes became a vicious circle, and Mama reiterated: What that child spends for postage would keep an entire family. . . .

Mama lived through Papa and me to such an extent that her friends imitated her vocabulary, so heavily peppered with Fannie. Mr. Hurst. Fannie. Mr. Hurst. I loved her over and above the tortures she inflicted and her strange talent for killing the things she loved.

A heartbreaking incident lies in a red welt across my memory. As Papa lay almost at the end of his final illness, Mama, who had not been told the fact of his impending death, hovered unceasingly over the bed. Nurses succeeded in banishing her only for the briefest time, and then she usually crouched outside his door, waiting.

On his last day, fright and doubtless realization suddenly laid hold of her: Sam, she cried, my darling, why don't you talk or look at me? Give me your hand, darling. To my heartbreak, Papa turned his head to the wall and said—Go away, Rose. . . .

I wept that day as much for Mama as for Papa. Withal, she had deserved better. Papa must have known that, too, but he was so tired—so very tired—and he said it with his tiredness. I pray that Mama knew that too. But I am ahead of my story.

All through the remainder of that summer of Episode Atlantic City, Mama's resistance was unflagging. Wasting my time! Had it not been proved to me with that endless procession of stories going out and coming back? Where did it come in that I had to be a writer! A moping daughter who, because she cannot write, takes it out on her parents.

Toward September, my Uncle Kaufman, Mama's sporty younger brother, high-powered salesman for a wholesale soft-drink concern, sent us a picture postcard from the Chicago Beach Hotel, where he and his wife were vacationing.

On the spur of the moment, Mama, so harassed, without consulting either Papa or me, put through a telephone call to the Chicago Beach Hotel. Would my Uncle Kaufman and his wife, Selene, let me join them for a few days—get her out of herself? Fannie, here, your Uncle Kaufman wants to talk to you on the long-distance telephone.

Uncle Kaufman was persuasive, and Selene came to the telephone and added her urging. To my own surprise, I agreed to have them meet my train two days later.

The Chicago Beach Hotel, situated directly on Lake Michigan, was a year-round resort. Selene and Uncle Kaufman were a fast-moving young pair, occupying a handsome de luxe suite with a spare bedroom for me.

Papa disapproved of Uncle Kaufman, said he gambled in the stock market and one of these days would run into serious trouble. Then, what! But up to his rather premature death, Uncle Kaufman, so far as I recall, continued to thrive. No one in the family particularly approved of Selene, although the worst indictment the sisters-in-law could produce was that she had been considered "fast" as a young girl and now encouraged her husband's extravagance.

The guests, chiefly young couples and a plentiful assortment of young men and girls, were a cosmopolitan mix, and Southern cities, Mobile, Chattanooga, Dallas, Montgomery, appeared frequently on the register.

A pair of honeymooners from Wichita, Kansas, a Dr. and Mrs. Brokaw, and Jules Einhorn, a handsome young man of about twenty-six from St. Paul, mixing business for his father's vast tractor manufacturing plant with vacation, shared our dining-room table. Young Einhorn was quick-witted and gay. Selene and Uncle Kaufman, who loved to swim, jingle the slot machines, dance, play bridge and ping-pong, proved compatible to him and to the Brokaws. We were a group unto ourselves.

Selene, whom Uncle Kaufman had met when she was buyer

for a Cincinnati department store, had style and flair. I was promptly introduced around to the men, who found her company gay and enjoyable, as a niece from St. Louis who aspired to be a writer. This did not exactly enhance male interest in me.

Young Einhorn, however, not only because he belonged to our group and more or less automatically paired off with me, was interested. I once thought I would like to be an advertising writer, he explained. Guess I couldn't have wanted it very badly because when Dad commandeered me for the business, I jumped my last two years of college for it.

But, actually, Selene and Uncle Kaufman were his meat. Our party, as Papa would have put it, acted as if money grew on trees, which seemed to be the case with Jules. His car was low-slung and racy; he hired a cabin cruiser by the week. Uncle Kaufman won a hundred-dollar jackpot from the slot machine and gave it to the headwaiter. Selene wore a solitaire diamond ring that for its size and blue brilliancy had won a prize at the St. Louis World's Fair. It was all in chic contrast to Episode Atlantic City, around which, considerably later, I was to write a short story for *The Saturday Evening Post* entitled "Summer Resources," and destined to set St. Louis quite agog.

The last day but one of our sojourn, Jules said to me: How would you like me to come to St. Louis?

I thought that would be just fine. That is, I added, if I am there.

Where will you be?

In New York, I hope.

Well, don't go until after I come. I may stop off on my way back to Minneapolis next month. Let's correspond, he suggested, even if your letters will put mine in the shade.

That evening before dinner I walked in on Selene in the act of telephoning Mama: . . . Ask Sam. He will know the name. Einhorn and Company. The largest lumber concern in Minnesota. An only son. They say the home occupies a square block. Wish we could stay longer for Fannie's sake, but Kaufman has to get back. They're going to correspond. . . .

Jules did come to St. Louis, less than two weeks after my return. He took me by surprise, telephoning from the Jefferson Hotel that he was in town and asking if he might come out.

It was Willie's day out and lace curtains were down and drying on stretchers in our back yard. Slip covers still shrouded the furniture and there was warmed-over pot roast for supper.

A thousand tormenting eventualities flew through my mind as I talked to him and it became apparent that he expected to be invited to remain through dinner.

What would he think of our little home in contrast to the world of the Chicago Beach Hotel? Would Papa remember about the plumbing? If only Selene had not made everything sound so different than it actually was. To be sure, Papa was president of a shoe factory. But the way she had put it, you would have thought the Standard Heel and Counter Company was the Standard Oil Company.

On one occasion she had described our home in Jules' presence as a white stone dwelling on a beautiful and exclusive street. But the white stone was rock front with brick sides, and the beautiful and exclusive street was one of similarly modest homes, lent beauty, it is true, by its double row of maple trees. Selene spoke of our five-by-five Willie as if she were many, instead of a grotesque and darling woman-of-all-work, whose slippers slipitty-slopped and who never wore a uniform except when Mama had a *Kaffeeklatsch* or company for supper.

All this and more flashed through my ridiculous mind as Jules spoke over the telephone, yet I had no alternative but to invite him to dinner.

Mama's panic was immediate. It would happen on Willie's day out!

But by the time Jules arrived, she had managed a first-rate chicken dinner, our best linen, silver, and china in use, and the silver fern dish in the center.

Jules brought me a gift, far too handsome and personal, Papa thought, to be appropriate. A sterling silver toilet set, comb, brush, and mirror on a tray. For the first time a kind of apprehension smote me. Supose he really did like me. . . .

But it seemed to me I could read in his face the reactions of surprise and disappointment. He appeared elegant and out of place, just as I, in turn, must have appeared in my realistic background like Cinderella home from the ball.

He talked of travel in Europe, his father's horses, his brother-in-law's speedboats, and his mother's skill with roses which she cultivated in their hothouse.

Mama plied him with food, and Papa, as always with young men, seemed cold and unresponsive.

Mama kept boosting my stock, but in a peculiarly negative way. I hope your sisters are more orderly than Fannie. We go about picking up after her. But it is wonderful that her thoughts are on higher things. I tell Mr. Hurst, sometimes I wish we didn't have such a bright daughter.

So it went and so went my anguish.

Papa suddenly decided to peel his olives as if they were apples. For the first time in my memory, he pronounced "dessert" as if it were "desert." Mama kept explaining the absence of lace curtains at the windows. Mama knew a family in Minneapolis in the wholesale meat business, named Rauh. They apparently were not the right people to know. Papa, changing the subject, asked Jules his politics. Jules said he guessed he would call himself a liberal Democrat, and then I changed the subject, fearing the word "liberal" might evoke Papa's use of "anarchy." Jules hoped to go to Europe later in the year. Papa enlarged upon his favorite theme: See America First. Mama asked Jules if "living was high" in Minneapolis. Jules did not know. Is help expensive? Jules said: We have had the same maids and butler ever since I was a small boy. Mama said: Oh!

After dinner Jules and I sat down in the parlor and Mama and Papa went upstairs, Mama leaving the perennial cookies and lemonade on the table.

Jules only stayed until about nine-thirty. I felt depressed and made little effort to steer the conversation. He was a well-bred young fellow and said pleasant things, but I could sense his not liking our environment, so different from what he must have pictured.

He said he was leaving town early the following morning.

After that we exchanged two or three desultory letters and that was the end. Mama gave the silver toilet set to one of Papa's Mobile cousins as a wedding present.

Mama said: I didn't care much for him from the start. I think he had *richus*, which is terrible when it is against your own kind.

Years later I ran into Jules Einhorn in a city where I was lecturing. He was on the Mayor's Reception Committee and rated an outstanding and philanthropic citizen. He had a beautiful wife and was the father of four.

We exchanged a long amused glance.

That autumn I enrolled at the University for a graduate course on Chaucer and the Renaissance in England. I will learn the beginnings of English literature, if I am to be a writer. I again applied to the *Post-Dispatch* and was given a couple of assignments. I resumed dramatic lessons with Mae Ayres Deatheridge and bombarded *The Saturday Evening Post* with short stories until they log-jammed in that office and came back three at a time.

Then one day a Street and Smith magazine bought a story and paid me twenty-five dollars. It was printed twelve months later and my next half dozen rejected. Mama said: You could make a fine living out of that business.

As the situation at home continued precarious, with Mama given to fits of depression over my state, Papa came up with another plan: Fannie should see her own country. See America First is my slogan. You outline the entire trip, Fannie, and I will manage to get away for three weeks. Your mother and I will fit in with your itinerary. Take any section of the country you prefer.

I knew the section all right. The section that contained New York! But I did not propose to be diverted from my intention to invade the writing world and registered no interest in Papa's plan.

ANATOMY OF ME

Mama said: No more trips for me! What I went through in Atlantic City I wouldn't wish on my worst enemy.

Papa said: But, Rose, this is something educational.

You and Fannie go. I'll take the money and buy something for my home. That is education enough for me.

In the end, Papa and I took the trip without Mama. True to his word, he permitted me to outline every mile of it, and I used my advantage to the limit, reserving the right to shift at any time from our planned itinerary.

Papa did not want that trip any more than Mama, but he was valiant about it. Inwardly ashamed, I directed it in the direction of New York, allowing for a week's stopover there.

Papa said: I am not breaking my word. This is your trip. But wouldn't you like to see the Far West now that you have already been East?

But I stood my ground. Aunt Bettie came over from Hamilton to stay with Mama during our absence, and Papa and I departed on an itinerary I had concocted with the aid of the travel department of a downtown department store.

As a concession to Papa, it called for Pikes Peak, and then a turnabout for the eastward trek via Niagara Falls, Detroit, a day on the Canadian border, Amish Pennsylvania, New York!

All subject to my change of mind or heart en route.

Thus Papa and I started on what, alas, was to prove to be one of the major frustrations of my father's life.

As for me, except for the flash of a whim, I might have ridden past what was to be the meaning of my life.

Who has not, at one time or another, indulged in the conjectural game of what-if!

What if I had done this instead of that! What if I had not turned that particular corner, or taken that particular plane! What if I had not decided to study pharmaceutics? What if someone besides John had collided with me that Easter afternoon?

What if, on my See-America-First trip with Papa, I had not suddenly inquired, while thumbing through a timetable en route from Buffalo to Detroit: What is this next stop, Mount Clemens?

Mount Clemens, replied my father, is a famous watering place about twenty miles this side of Detroit. Americans don't have to run to Europe for mineral baths. Mighty fine ones right here.

It was a clear autumn day, the countryside flashing past the train windows.

Let's get off there, Papa. I've never seen a watering place.

It was my first use of my prerogative to change the itinerary and, true to his word, Papa did not demur. He called the porter for the Redbook of hotels and, bag and baggage, off we got at the Mount Clemens station.

According to the Redbook, the hotel we had selected was first-class and adjacent to the station. It proved to be a drab-looking structure but adequate. Our rooms were dull and smelled of the sulphurous waters, but Mount Clemens was waiting to be explored and I set out, Papa making for the sulphur baths.

It proved to be a pleasant stereotype of a small town. Situated on a river that became Lake St. Clair, the sulphur-laden air permeated the residential areas where the homes became finer and larger.

Beyond these tree-lined streets loomed suddenly the Park Hotel, a structure almost the size of the Royal Palace. It was set deeply into a wooded acreage, automobiles lined its curving drives, guests were scattered about its landscaped lawns or played tennis on turf courts. Here was the spa I had originally visualized. I walked into the spacious hotel lobby and conferred with the room clerk. Yes, the Park Hotel could take care of us.

When Papa emerged from his sulphur bath, his bags along with mine were repacked and the Park Hotel bus waiting at the door to transfer us to our new quarters.

What if—we had not made that move!

I first saw Jack in what might have been the stage setting for a romantic drama by one of those lady writers with three names.

Wandering about the hotel that first day of our arrival, exploring writing rooms, lounges, and solaria, I came upon a small, darkened parlor dominated by a grand piano, my future husband seated before it, his head highlighted by a floor lamp.

I stood unnoticed in the doorway. Had I known him then, I would have realized that he had stolen quietly into the remote room, while most of the guests were at the baths or taking siesta, in order not to be heard.

Something of his sensitivity must have been telegraphed to me. He played the Chopin Etude with that special lacelike quality of his, and I stole away just before he concluded.

It was not love at first sight. It was love before first full sight, because I caught only his silhouette, the nobility of his lowered head, the mobility of his hands.

I did not see him again for two days. Papa expressed surprise at my desire to remain on at the Park Hotel, where there were chiefly older people taking the "cure" and few recreations outside of tennis or boating on the St. Clair River, which flowed past the hotel and on out into Lake St. Clair.

Don't remain here on my account. I enjoy the baths, they are toning me up, but I don't believe there is much here for you.

I lied magnanimously. That's all right. The baths are what you need.

Meanwhile, what had become of *him?* Had he been a mirage? I returned again and again to the dim room with the grand piano, the floor lamp, and the potted palms. I ran my fingers over the keys. In later years he was to tell me that he could always tell when I had touched the keyboard of his piano, and, curiously, he could. I imagine what he meant was that my impact had made them shudder.

Perhaps he had been a one-day guest from Detroit, after the manner of Philadelphians on flying visits to Atlantic City. I scanned the hotel register for a possible clue.

An acquaintance of Mama's had seen our name on the register and sought us out.

Afflicted with a hip ailment, she had been taking the baths for several weeks and appeared to know most of the guests. Several times I stationed myself beside her wheel chair, not quite daring to ask her directly, but waiting.

Mr. Hurst, she said to Papa, I must commend your daughter. How many young girls would take the time to help an old woman while away the hours?

Papa said to me later: It goes to show that modest and considerate behavior is admired. Just you let the flighty girls go their way.

The second day brought its reward. The hotel, remarked Mama's friend, has been unusually quiet since you arrived. Mr. and Mrs. Thal from New Orleans, such lovely people, immensely rich, and their five children left yesterday. The eldest girl, about eighteen, was beautiful and the mother as young looking as the daughter. Did you ever hear a name like Renalda?

No, I had not. Well, it seemed Mrs. Thal had named her eldest after a girl in a novel, and she certainly acted like one. She is engaged to a man down in New Orleans, but her mother had to lock her in her room to keep her from making a complete fool of herself. She went just crazy about a guest in this hotel, who did not seem to know she was on earth.

My ears pointed.

A lovely young man, so handsome, and a splendid musician, here from New York with the pianist, Rafael Joseffy. If I were twenty-five years younger I would be crazy about him myself. They will be back tonight from a couple of days in Detroit, where Joseffy had a concert. Now, don't you be the next one, she concluded playfully, to have to be locked in your room.

I haunted the poor lady all that afternoon and evening, remaining at her side when she played bridge, joined her after dinner while Papa talked politics with a group of men.

Late in the evening, he walked into the lobby accompanied by a stubby elderly man with a shock of gray hair.

Tall, slim, and straight, the same soft elegance about him that had characterized his Chopin, he had none of the shaggy qualities of his companion, the great Maestro Joseffy. His dress was impeccable, his heavy black hair groomed, his head beautiful in the way that Greek runners and discus throwers were beautiful.

I was smitten to the extent of pain. Pain that he existed outside of my experience. For the first time an overwhelmingly disturbing thought assailed me. He might be married! Why else lock a girl in her room?

Mama's friend sang out: Well, it is about time you two returned from your gallivanting in Detroit. They stopped to exchange pleasantries and I was introduced. I had looked into eyes that for all the lovely years were to light my way, until they closed to this world. And still they light it.

The following morning I sat on the veranda trying to think it through. Papa had remarked at breakfast that it was time for us to be moving along. At best we would have only three or four days left for New York if we were to be back in St. Louis on schedule.

He would probably be in Mount Clemens all the while I would be in New York. It became all important to be in Mount Clemens.

I rocked furiously, I racked my brain furiously, I suffered furiously.

Mama's friend rode by in her wheel chair on her way to the baths and remarked that I had on such a pretty dress, too bad there were not more young men in the hotel to see it. I could not have been less interested in more young men.

Then he came along with Joseffy, so renowned and so hitherto unknown to me. We exchanged good mornings, and after they had passed me three or four times Mr. Joseffy stopped, mopped his brow, and dropped into a chair, his companion beside him.

Mr. Joseffy had a foreign accent. He was jolly and asked me where I came from. When I told him, he wanted to know if I had any Anheuser Busch beer with me and said he had played in the St. Louis Odeon.

Then Mr. Joseffy's attendant came to escort him to his sulphur bath. *He* stayed on.

I do not recall much of that first conversation. Jack has always teased that I did most of the talking. But the probability is I was struck dumb, even though the figure in the lamplight playing Chopin became a rather humorous young man in a checked sports coat, saying teasing things.

And how is your rheumatism this morning? he asked.

I haven't rheumatism.

Then what are you doing at Mount Clemens?

Have you rheumatism?

No.

I wanted to add: Have you a wife?

Gradually, I, with a burning inner intensity, and he, with apparent casualness, drew each other out. He was there as a teaching assistant, friend, and disciple of the great Joseffy. They were returning to New York the following week.

And my father and I will be leaving New York just before you return there.

Do you canoe? was his retort. I do, every afternoon. Would you like to come along today?

I was deathly afraid of canoes. But would I come along!

We met by arrangement at the little boat landing. He maneuvered me skillfully into the frail-looking shell. But I landed heavily, my lack of affinity for it obvious. His fine hands, not squat short-fingered typical piano hands, paddled us rhythmically, to conversation desultory and always a little teasing.

So you are a country girl?

St. Louis is one of the largest cities in the United States.

Come now, compared to New York there are only small towns in America.

He would not let me through the banter into personalities, but it was enough to sit back and regard him, taking in every detail. The cobweb linen handkerchief protruding from the pocket of his coat, which he had removed and placed in the bottom of the boat. The small elegant monogram on his shirt sleeve. The faultlessly arranged necktie. And again the hands! The unathletic, unmuscular yet powerful hands.

Along with the moving water, the short precious afternoon flowed out from under us, and while I babbled on of myself, my desire to write, my obsession—New York—I had made no penetration into the way of life or thoughts of this man.

It is true that by the time we drew up once more at the hotel dock I had learned that he shrank from public appearances necessitated by concertizing; that besides assisting Maestro Joseffy he had his own teaching studios; that he loved the theater and was a *first-nighter*, a phrase new to me; that he had never until now been more than two hundred miles out of New York; that he had been born within the shadow of the Czar's Palace in Moscow, where his father had been royal sculptor; and that he had come to the United States as a lad of sixteen.

He left me at the elevator with a light impersonal handshake.

Will I see you before we leave tomorrow?

In case we don't, he said, be a good country girl when you get to the big city. That was all there was to it.

I sat the remainder of the afternoon in my room. If only we were not leaving! My whole life seemed to me to depend on seeing more of him. As a matter of fact, it did!

I decided to ask Papa if we could remain over for another week. As I crossed the hall to his room, I met him coming toward mine.

He had received a wire from his foreman concerning affairs at the factory that made Papa feel it wise for him to cut our trip short by a day or two. That will leave us only a day and a night in New York. I am needed at the factory. You don't mind too much, do you?

No, I did not mind, I said as my heart sank to a new low. Perhaps, I reasoned as I packed my bags, it is better this way. It had already crossed my mind that I did not want Papa to meet him— yet. Papa shied from "foreigners" in general, but Moscow! I knew his views on émigrés from such Russian towns as Minsk and Kiev. Papa's own parents, to be sure, had been "foreigners." But they were German, Papa would have told you. I felt certain Moscow and music would be no small obstacles. Yes, perhaps it was just as well that we were leaving. . . .

I did not see him in the dining room during dinner, nor in the evening as, dressed in my best, I sat in the lobby. At about ten o'clock Papa suggested that we retire early in order to be up for the following day's journey.

I said good night to Papa at his door. When I was halfway undressed, I decided, since I was in no mood for sleep, to get back into my clothes and go down on the veranda for a while, not admitting why even to myself.

Guests retired early at the Park, the lobby rapidly emptying. There were long rows of unoccupied rockers on the veranda. I slipped into one of them.

A late stroller passed occasionally, some of the overhead lights blinked out. Lateness descended and, incredibly, after a while he came.

We rocked and talked until the last veranda light was dimmed and still nothing memorable was said, nor my hand touched. I attempted to steer the talk in the direction of girls. The one who had been locked in her room. His pupils. There must have been plenty of heart-burning where he was concerned.

The surmise was generally true, but how was I to know the complete simplicity and lack of vanity of this man? The quality of cleanness and, to use a word for want of better, his innocence.

Before we separated again to go our ways, I blurted through inhibitions: Shall we correspond? I am not much of a letter writer, he said, and I was to learn how true! But I could not bear to leave without even a thread of a lifeline. I will do most of the letter writing if you will send me postcards.

He gave me his card and my heart lifted as if by magic. Which it was. The magic of having met him.

During our fleeting twenty-four hours there, I saw little of the New York that for so long had beckoned me. Of course its gorgeous and bawdy tumult came at me with an onrush.

We had rooms in the heart of the tumult. From my window in the Hotel Astor I looked out on the anonymous masses I had not yet come to realize were the people who were to make up my social register. The unhyphenated Smiths and Joneses. The people who, if killed in a plane crash, were designated as "and others."

The people who made up the rivers of them down there on Broadway, flowing like slow molasses, yet full of heartbeat and fear and hope and power and—infinity. Those people down there who were composed of persons. People were persons!

There, burning in electric lights, a stone's throw from my window, was the New York Times. Hotel Knickerbocker! Rector's! Storied names as far back into my childhood as I could remember.

But now, over and above, this was the city where *he* lived and had his being. Doubtless he had been under this very roof, walked those streets down there. Out there, over the high rooftops, in what direction I knew not, was his home. I knew his card by heart. Jacques S. Danielson, 625 Lexington Avenue, New York City.

To my eyes it was an astonishing street on which to live. Shops frequently interrupted the march of identical brownstone residences, which were high-stooped narrow structures, four and five stories tall, some of them with "Vacancy" or "Room to Let" signs in the windows.

On this particular block 625 was the choice house. There were no rental signs, and starched curtains hung at all of its four stories of polished windows, and its old-fashioned door handle and bell were burnished. I stood on the opposite side of the street as long as I dared, feasting my eyes.

That must be his studio, on the first floor, where the windows shone with some of his immaculateness and the curtains hung in starched precision. There dwelt my love, I told myself who had never been caressed by manner or word from him!

Before we took the train for St. Louis, I wrote a postcard to Mount Clemens with my home address across the top:

My dear Mr. Danielson, I walked past where you live. Does that surprise you? Regards.

It would have surprised Papa.

It was about six months later that Mama and Papa between them must have decided on complete surrender.

One day Mama said to me, suddenly and without heat: Fannie, your father and I have decided that we not only want you to go to New York, but you have got to. Go and get it out of your system. We cannot stand it this way any longer.

I was stunned.

If you think you can set the world on fire with those stories of yours, which come back by the dozen, you go and do it. I may as well be paying your expenses there as spending money here for clothes you won't go any place to wear.

Mama, and you won't be—mad?

On the contrary, I'll be glad. This thing has aged me. I haven't the strength to live this way any longer. This is a house of mourning, said Mama, and began to cry. I wanted to take her in my arms, which I was ashamed to do, and tell her I would never, never leave her or behave badly again.

Get your clothes together. Tillie Strauss knows a woman in New York who takes out-of-town girls to live with her in her nice home. It will be better for all concerned. Things can't go on this way.

A wave of reaction washed over me. Unrest turned into scare. The world out there seemed an abyss into which I was being pushed.

In all the months, there had been at most a half dozen postcards from Mr. Danielson, simple, informal, half humorous, wholly unamorous. Here is one: Dear Miss Hurst, The fire bells are ringing and the engines rushing in the street. Could it be that you are in town setting it on fire? Regards, J.S.D. Another ended: I think of you often. With that one I slept.

But in a note received the day before the outburst from Mama he wrote: Joseffy and I are at work on some exercise compositions for the piano. He is anxious for me to go with him to his summer home in Switzerland, where we can work quietly on a big undertaking. When my classes end for the season, I may join the old gentleman for an indefinite time.

That thought mixed itself in with my multiple emotions. He would be out of New York! Europe. Indefinite time! Indefinite time!

Mama, of course, had inquired about these cards.

Oh, just a man I met in Mount Clemens.

It's like pulling teeth to get a word out of that child. What man?

You wouldn't know. A musician staying at the hotel with Rafael Joseffy.

Who?

You wouldn't know. A famous musician.

Is Joseffy the man who writes to you?

No, he was with him.

I asked who is the man who writes to you?

A musician too, Mama. A wonderful musician.

That's all we need. A musician. They don't earn salt. Leave it to you to find the men who don't. Did your father meet him?

No.

Funny.

We just met once or twice.

Mama softened. Who are his people?

How should I know?

Well, if I met a young man and corresponded with him I would know. Is he a New Yorker by birth?

Here it came!

No.

Where do they come from originally?

What difference does that make?

Kikes? The word that usually went through me like a knife drew blood this time.

I don't know and I don't care! All I know is his little finger is worth more than all the smug ones in this town put together.

Where was he born?

I don't know, I lied a little wildly.

I can see now why you didn't want your father to meet him.

Mama, I only met this man a couple of times. He was with a great celebrity. Isn't that enough?

I don't see why I worry myself. If you don't want to take your parents into your confidence, all I can say is when you go to New York keep away from such. New York, they say, is filled with them—Russians and Galicians.

But apparently this incident made only a slight impression, because Mama went ahead with her new determination.

Tumultuous indecisions continued to sweep over me. The fleeting glimpse of New York, so dazzling, had nevertheless given me an idea of its immensity. Papa had felt that sense of aloneness in the crowds. This town certainly makes one feel insignificant, he had remarked as we stood on a street corner, looking upward at the buildings reaching for the sky.

What assurance had I that Jacques Danielson would have time for me in all that vastness? Or that editors would be any more receptive to my writings than they were a thousand miles away? Simultaneously, I wanted to go with the same old overwhelming urgency, and yet I wanted to stay with Mama and Papa, safe and sound on Cates Avenue. . . .

Likewise, Mama, during these weeks of preparation, sobbed as she packed my clothing. Once, in the act of cramming into my trunk more pairs of stockings than I would use in a year, she cried out suddenly, reaching her arms toward me: Baby, don't leave me. You're my life. Don't leave me and Papa. . . .

I won't, Mama, I cried. I love you so much. Take my things out. I'll stay with you and Papa always and ever.

Such unprecedented fireworks of emotion reduced us both to limpness. When Papa came home, we met him with assurances that things had resolved themselves; and then Papa, also on the verge of tears, used the strongest term of endearment I had ever heard from him.

Sweetheart, he said, this is the most sensible decision you have ever made. It will add years to your mother's life.

What had I done!

Compromise with me, Papa, I cried. Let me get it out of my system for a little while, and then I'll be satisfied, I feel sure, to do as you say. Just let me try it!

This time Mama, poor dear, flared into one of her most frightening states.

Sam, before you leave this house tomorrow, I want you to see that she has her ticket to New York. She goes, or I'll go to the lunatic asylum.

Looking back, I marvel at the ruthlessness which drove me on. For us on our tight little island of three, this tempest was not in a teapot. It was a holocaust. For two more weeks, while all about us Cates Avenue stood embalmed in its static quiet, that holocaust raged in the little house with the stone façade and the brick sides.

The day I departed for New York, with brand-new luggage and my cousin Lester Hurst in his Ford waiting at the door to take me to Union Station, Mama was crying so that Papa feared to risk the strain of train farewells and remained behind with her.

My baby, come home to me soon, screamed Mama after me, and the lace curtains of neighbors parted discreetly.

I rode beside Leslie through rain-streaked streets, admonishing and admonishing my cousin, and Papa's favorite nephew.

Leslie, be good to them—take care of them—go and see them often. . . .

Yeth, said kindly Leslie, who lisped, I'll come often to thee Aunt Rose and Uncle Tham. . . .

Book Three

MECCA

The Delphian vales, the Palestines
The Meccas of the mind.

I was on my own.

Through the long kaleidoscopic years ahead, I was to explore this fearful and wonderful mecca with a vigor and a sense of its stimulus that have not waned. For months of days I walked its streets, whisked through its subways, wandered its avenues and slums, a wisp on a tide that swung me high as aspiration, low as homesickness.

The home of Tillie Strauss' friend proved to be a brownstone house in a block-long row of them on West 102nd Street. Bare to austerity, the odor of institution and linoleum hung in my small cell of bed, chair, and chest. Miss Ell, extraordinary as her name, also sold insurance. A small brass sign above the doorbell, Miss Delafield Ell, Insurance, indicated that Miss Ell had a sideline. A tall lean woman with the unfortunate circumstance of one eye out, she bore a striking resemblance to a needle. I saw her on the three paydays during the three weeks I remained there.

My little room, two flights up, rear, chilled me like a wet bathing suit donned at dawn. I left it in the early mornings and returned at bedtime, the need to feel only transient there so strong that I read or wrote with my hat on, to make my departure from it seem more imminent.

Consequently, in an environment hostile to even the sharpening of a pencil or the unpacking of a writing tablet, I plunged into my exploratory days, not a human voice directed to me, except "Step lively," "Watch your step," "This is where you get off, miss."

In less than a week I had invaded the Public Library, Fifth Avenue, Central, Bronx, and Prospect parks, Hell's Kitchen, the Bowery, Chinatown, Brooklyn Heights, Staten Island ferry, Williamsburg, and Grant's Tomb.

New York tingled against my consciousness and against the balls of my feet.

To my alerted imagination, the big apartment buildings were hives of production, plays being written in them, novels aborning, bridges in the designing, artists at their easels.

But when I was back once more in that filing cabinet of a room, the elixirs of the day died down into solitude and nostalgia. I reasoned: I can go home to Mama and Papa any day I wish. . . . I am not alone. . . .

One night I awoke to a life-size dread. What if I should become ill in this strange chilly house? Who would care? Nobody. City hospital or the morgue for me. I rose and wrote out a slip of paper which I folded into my purse. I am Fannie Hurst. 5641 Cates Avenue. St. Louis, Missouri. In case of accident, please notify Mr. Samuel Hurst of that address.

But, again, once I emerged into the light of a bright day, it was as if a cork had blown off a magnum of champagne. New York fizzed around me, I exulted in the freedom of not being attached to Mama by the umbilical cord of a telephone and the need to call her every hour or two when away from home. Whoops, I was on my own! These murals and murals of faces riding the subway trains, jamming the elevators, the avenues, the lunchrooms, the slums were mines into which a writer must sink shaft. I cared about them. I felt about them. But there was that stubborn hiatus between the idea and the written word. The concept lively and boiling in my mind, the words coming in slow and painful trickle onto paper, there to torture with their inadequacies.

That monkey on my back has never relinquished hold in all the years. The urge to write versus the torturous process of getting it said.

These, indeed, were the months of no return, except manuscripts.

None of this in my letters home. It was during this period that I established the dangerous practice, that daily letter, which was to continue throughout my parents' lifetime, with frenzied long-distance calls from Mama on those occasions when Uncle Sam happened to slip a mail-delivery cog.

Following Mama's death, I was to come upon a trunkful of them. Here are excerpts from the very earliest, built on a minimum of fact.

Dear Mama and Papa, Your daughter is up with the dawn, thanks to her mother's training, and out walking long before the shops open. How can people say they would not live here if you gave it to them? It is wonderful to meet all the exciting young people who are here, just as I am, hunting fame and fortune.

This last, of course, to assuage home fears that I was alone in my fanciful quest.

. . . I am so busy making exciting contacts, meeting editors, writers. Have not even had time to register at the University. I am comfortably situated and Miss Ell is just what you would like. I am sorry I muss up your bank account by not cashing your checks. If only you would not keep sending them. I don't need them yet. The four hundred I left home with is not used up and I hope soon to be earning sufficient to pay my own way. Have made a fine start.

My sole alibi for these small lies is that they were white. Indeed, as time went on and my apprehensions deepened, I grew bolder, going so far as to invent editors of alleged prominence who were enthusiastic about my future . . . sending home unsigned feature articles clipped from the Sunday New York *Times* or *Tribune*, with the implication, if not direct statement, that they were written by me.

After these many weeks of exploring New York, I came to the decision that I must find living quarters more compatible to working. Following a disheartened search into rabbit warrens that smelled of sourness, I finally came upon a fairly bright looking place in the neighborhood of the Hotel Astor, led to it by a sign "Vacancies" backed by rose-colored window drapes.

For the same weekly sum I had been paying, it was brighter here, fancy to ornateness, and, instead of a bare cot, the bed was elaborate, wide, and covered with pink sateen. The landlady, dark in a Spanish way, made it plain there must be no going through the hallways in deshabille.

Here, too, were the long corridors of closed doors; but the odors were different, this time a combination of sultry perfumes and old beer. But once in my third-floor rear room, with its view of more rear rooms, I felt ready for the unpacking, hanging my creased dresses in a shallow wallpapered closet, and readying my table for the typewriter I intended to rent.

Dear Mama and Papa, Does my new address surprise you? Miss Ell suddenly decided to move to a larger and better house and here we are where my room is larger and has sun all morning. Papa, it is not far from the Astor Hotel and within walking distance of everything. Am now getting down to work in earnest. . . .

That letter crossed one from Mama, which saved a situation for me.

About the middle of my first week in residence at the new address, I returned home about five o'clock in the afternoon to find what appeared to be a moving van backed up before the door and a crowd of spectators surrounding the high stoop.

What is it? I asked fearfully of one of them.

Oh, just another raid on a "house." This neighborhood is a disgrace. If I had my way every prostitute in it would be jailed and these dives permanently closed. That would end the graft.

There were police standing about what proved to be a patrol car and, as I stared, a small battalion of more officers came down the stoop leading my landlady, who was covering her eyes with her hands against snapping cameras, four or five girls, obviously hurriedly attired, following.

ANATOMY OF ME

The crowd guffawed, one of the girls threw out an ugly epithet as the police piloted them, none too delicately, boosting them from their rears into what we in St. Louis used to call the "Black Maria."

The crowd dispersed. What was I to do? Pass on as if I did not belong and abandon my belongings? With the exception of the small amount in my handbag, my funds were locked in my trunk. So were stories ready to be sent out, photographs of Mama and Papa, and a packet of postcards from one Jacques Danielson. . . .

I rushed to the Hotel Astor, reserved a room, sat for a bit in the lobby to gather my wits, and, returning to the raided premises, made a dash into the house past the long rows of doors, most of them wide open now, rooms strewn with fineries of lace and chiffon, one terrifying occupant, a man, lying in what must have been a drunken stupor across one of the wide beds.

Without encountering even a chambermaid, I threw my belongings together, snatched the day's mail from the hall table, and tipped a taxicab driver opulently to transfer me, bag and baggage, to the hotel.

Once in my haven of room-and-bath at the Astor, I trembled the incident out of my system, rang for coffee, and threw myself across the bed to worry out what to write home of my second change of address. Mama's perceptions were lightning quick. I dared not risk flimsy pretenses.

However, a letter from her, which I had snatched from the hall table at the scene of the raid, saved the day for me. . . . Your father and I do not like the way you are moving around. Papa says your new address is in a bad neighborhood and the last place for a young girl. I am worried sick. What can that Miss Ell be thinking about? I was ready to come to New York, but who do you suppose I met at Moll's Market? Mrs. Harkins. They have moved back to St. Louis from Toledo. Her sister-in-law's sister, a deaconess, is an assistant superintendent in a wonderful place for girls in New York, called "The Three Arts Club." It is difficult to get in. There is always a waiting list. But Mrs. Harkins came to see me today and long-distanced Deaconess Mooney from here. You are to telephone her as soon as you receive this. It seems you have to be studying dramatic art or music, but you qualify since you played at Keith's. It is reasonable, costs no more with meals than you are paying without. Your father is having fits. So am I. Why don't you come home where you belong? If you won't, we expect you to move immediately to this club. Wire us. Do not return enclosed check. So much moving must cost a fortune in that town.

Providence and Mrs. Harkins had leaned in! I lost no time telephoning Deaconess Mooney. Yes, they were making an exception for Mrs. Harkins and admitting me at once to the only vacancy they could manage.

The address was immediately off Riverside Drive and the majestic flow of Hudson River.

The Three Arts Club consisted of what had once been two four-story apartment houses, now converted into one. Endowed by a group of wealthy women of social prestige, who were variously interested in music, painting, and the drama, it filled a need for out-of-town young women coming to New York to study.

Actually, it was far from my idea of the life of the freed spirit I had originally envisioned. But by now it represented a snug harbor, even though most of the rooms were shared by two occupants, you made your own bed, and if you remained out after 11 P.M. you were obliged to ring the bell, write your explanation on a formal slip and give it to the night porter.

Even before I was assigned to my room, the notices thumbtacked on the bulletin board in the little office had me agog.

Girls appearing in current productions will be served dinner at five-thirty, if so desired.

Girls who wish to practice in one of the soundproof piano rooms sign in at the desk before five o'clock of the previous day.

Students! Mr. Graham Degan will give the second of his series of illustrated talks on Manet, Monet, and Picasso on Monday, October third, at 8:30 o'clock, in the Marion Scott Lounge.

I was in the art world, all right, nor had I misrepresented myself to get into it. I not only intended to enroll at Columbia University for graduate courses, but also to contact the Mr. Dean at the

Belasco offices, as Mr. Beban had advised. Now I felt ready to begin these avocations as well as carry on my writing. Club stationery was available at the office. I purchased a supply. Three Arts Club. 340 West 85th Street. New York City.

I was in the art world indeed!

I shared a large double room with a desperately impecunious little stage-struck aspirant from Austin, Texas, seeking an engagement she was never to find, and returning to Austin about two months later to marry the boy back home.

Now I was organized. An extension course in Chaucer and the English Renaissance, two dramatic lessons a week with William Dean, four or five hours daily at my newly rented typewriter, an occasional balcony visit to the theater with one of the club girls.

What with my seven-dollar lessons from Mr. Dean, and the Columbia College tuition, a personal characteristic was beginning to stand me in good stead. I retrenched wherever possible in expenditures, but at no appreciable sacrifice. Personal comfort has never meant a great deal. My desire for adornment is considerable, but readily appeased.

Since fleshpots tempted me but little, if at all, reducing my expenditures to a minimum meant adjustments that did not matter too much.

It did not occur to me to purchase fewer clothes and thus keep their quality high. Instead, I bought two or three cheaper dresses for the price of one, the exhibitionist in me demanding frequent change. The result not too happy.

However, my lack of reverence for the man-made tenets of so-called "taste," as no doubt evidenced by this anatomy of me, has never wavered.

Mama continued to send the sporadic checks, which I in turn continued to return, always intimating without actually speaking the lie that newspaper stories were yielding me income.

Dear Mama and Papa, Thanks for the check, but I don't need it. Manage nicely on the journalism.

But now indeed I began to concentrate on the writing, tapping away with a blanket over the top of my typewriter to muffle its sound.

Sometimes in the evenings, the theatrical girls who were not working would forgather in our room and my little southern roommate would earn an extra bit "doing" their fingernails or shampoos.

During these sessions I usually would draw a screen around my work table and plug away, achieving the small miracle of concentration. Occasionally a girl or two would peer around the screen and regard me as if I were a specimen under glass. I knew some of their muffled giggles were for me.

As always, the writing came the blood-and-tears way, but, nevertheless, stories were pushing up from under the typewriter keys like seeds wanting to sprout. Stories born not out of direct experiences in my new world but as a result of a kind of seething and boiling they had set going. The crowded Lower East Side swarmed through my mind. Silhouettes of charwomen swabbing the deserted night floors of office buildings, interiors of tenements glimpsed from passing trains seemed to take form against my inner lids when my eyes were closed for sleep. People becoming persons.

My roommate, destined to return to her home town and her boyhood sweetheart and have five children within four years, was cast almost precisely that way in my mind some time before the big city had rejected her and the big dream had died and Mirabelle had returned home. Actually, I wrote her story, "The Reluctant Native," before she returned to Flowery Branch, where she now lives and has grandchildren.

I did not succeed in selling "The Reluctant Native," although it served a purpose more important.

Once again it was Mama on Cates Avenue who sat in the driver's seat. One of her friends, a Mrs. Sadie Kahn, wrote a New York relative to look up Fannie Hurst, a St. Louis girl living at the Three Arts Club, and let her meet some writers.

In due time, a Miss Claudia Lerner, a sophisticated young secretary in an advertising agency, came to see me. She in turn introduced me to a Miss Birdie Bernstein, who took time out of her business day to accompany a gawky overweight overdressed middle-western girl to the Flatiron Building offices of Mr. Robert H. Davis, managing editor of a string of Munsey-owned magazines.

Here I met my first New York editor, bluff, heavy-set, personable, with whom years of close friendship stretched ahead.

Miss Bernstein, who was on easy familiar terms with Mr. Davis, explained that I had written for Reedy's St. Louis *Mirror*. Mr. Davis knew Reedy, called him a magnificent lunatic. Mr. Davis said his brain was fuzzy that day from reading worthless manuscript after worthless manuscript, and called to high heaven for just one writer with what he called a gleam of gold in him. Mr. Davis begged Miss Bernstein to assure him that I was that one.

I had my latest short story, "The Reluctant Native," with me. He slapped it into a drawer and told me to return in a week.

I did, and was admitted at once. He swung around in his swivel chair, shirtsleeved and mussed.

I can't use your story, he said. It is static. But go home and write me another and let me see everything you do. Girl, you can write!

In about four or five weeks, writing in a laborious tempo I have scarcely increased through the years, I completed another short story. Mr. Davis read it in my presence, his jovial face straightening and tightening. Then, Papa-fashion, he looked up at me over his glasses: You should be ashamed of yourself, Fannie Hurst. Mama Katz is a classic. She walks right off the page. You've likewise made that kid Irving a brat with a neck so real I want to wring it. I swallowed a lot of tears over the kid and his mutt. And then what did you do! Essie, the cutie of your story, doesn't get her man. How the hell do you expect a lot of romance-starved women to swallow that one?

She couldn't marry George, I explained. She was true to herself.

Go home, pump a happy ending into Essie and George, and you're in.

But, Mr. Davis—I can't. . . .

Here came the Bob Davis split personality. Stories were so much merchandise to him. Give them what they want. Keep them happy. Our mission is to entertain, not educate. He built up the one-time strong chain of Munsey publications on that philosophy.

The other aspect of him was wired for delicate perceptions. He once walked me through four miles of Florence, Italy, seeking a certain shopwindow where he had seen and admired a tiny faïence cherub with a puckish face. It was this side of him that said to me: All right, if that is the way you feel, don't sell your soul for a mess of what-they-want pottage. Write me another, and try this one elsewhere.

I did, but it never sold.

But, in fairness, I must ask myself would I have held out for that fanciful phrase, "artistic integrity," had not a reassuring wad of folding money been securely pinned inside my blouse?

I like to think I would have.

To few is it given to walk the literary heights. But even valley folk can keep their sites high.

One day, remembering my letter from Marion Reedy to the editor of *The Delineator*, I presented it and was admitted to an inner office, where the man to whom my letter was addressed sat before a littered desk, a bootblack at his feet snapping a cloth across his shoes. A strange lantern of a face gave no sign of greeting: How's Reedy? Why do you want to write? Don't tell me. Come to my apartment tomorrow for breakfast at nine. He wrote an address on a card and handed it to me. It read: Theodore Dreiser, 204 West 17th Street. Apartment 4 C.

The name meant nothing to me. For that matter, neither did the following day's meeting which took place in an oldfashioned apartment over a bridge table of coffee and toast. His talk was strange, fragmentary, and unnotable. Later, of course, I was to become highly aware of him and know him better, but never to the extent of fully understanding the fearful and wonderful quality of this somber genius.

He asked me in a far-off tone to submit some of my work. I had two stories with me but could not bring myself to show them, nor did I ever follow up the interview. He seemed somehow to be regarding me without seeing me, focusing somewhere in an area between, rather than into, my eyes.

I told him as much, years later. He replied: You are wrong. I was thinking: Why does such a fresh-faced girl want to submit herself to the lonely tortures of writing, even if she has what it takes? I would like to pluck the stars out of her eyes.

Both he and Marion Reedy lived shabby, mixed up personal lives. Dreiser's ultimate place in the literary firmament is still hanging in the balance. Should he be ultimately destined to take his place among the Olympians, he will doubtless do so with that Dreiserian look of mockery in his chilly eyes.

As my capital began to show more and more shrinkage, I was forced to face the fact that sooner or later I must begin to accept checks from home, and thus admit that my fine front was false.

Doubling my efforts, I pounded sidewalks from editorial office to editorial office, more often than not getting no farther than the receptionist with whom I left my long envelopes.

One day I bombarded the Sunday magazine section of a metropolitan newspaper, where an editor challenged me from under an eye shade to go out and bring in a five-hundred-word human-interest story from the street.

But, suddenly and perversely, the streets of New York lost their magic as I wandered them, seeking. . . .

At the intersection of Forty-second Street and Sixth Avenue, I came upon the small glass showcase of an upstairs wig establishment. It displayed the wax head of a man. Rising and falling from his shiny bald dome, a toupee alternately transformed him from bald middle age to heavy-haired virile youth.

Here was my street incident! I wrote most of the five hundred words on a table in Child's Restaurant on a pad bought at a corner drugstore, moving on to coffee in two successive lunchrooms, rather than seem to linger unduly in any one. The vignette had to do with a balding bachelor, pausing before the on-again, off-again transformation scene of the toupee and the wax head. He hesitates, goes his way, returns, hesitates, then on sudden determination finally makes his way to the hair-goods parlor, leaving the reader with the wholesome inference that the happy street encounter will transform the aging little bachelor into a devastating Casanova.

But by the end of day I was not satisfied with the piece and took it home to work at through the evening and following morning.

The editor read it while I stood by, stamped and signed a pink slip which he handed to me with the sole comment: Present at cashier's desk, and turned back to his work.

I collected five dollars from the cashier and emerged to my sidewalk pounding.

My dramatic lessons were something of a farce. I realized, however, that somehow they afforded a connection with the star-dusted world of the doers.

In a rehearsal room above the Belasco Theater, Mr. Dean would pace up and down while I read excerpts or acted memorized scenes from old or classical plays. "Lysistrata." "Leah, the Forsaken." "Lady Windemere's Fan." "Trelawney of the Wells."

Mr. Dean was engaged at the time in assisting Mr. Belasco with an impending play for Lenore Ulric, and I doubt if he gave me even a third of his attention. His comments were vague, abstruse, even my poor efforts failing to stir his well-known irascibilities.

Often, when I had finished, he would continue to pace the floor, forehead knotted, apparently unaware of me and the fact that I had concluded.

He would utter sparse sentences. You are progressing. Watch your diaphragm. Place your hand against it, stand before your mirror and watch it rise and fall. Memorize the marked passages in this copy of *Macbeth* for your next lesson. Also, sit, stand, and walk according to the posture rules.

Apparently he did not pay me sufficient heed to take critical note of my generous proportions. But I seldom, if ever, allowed myself to dwell on the eventuality of putting this training to use. As a writer, it might help me. Beyond that I did not look.

In fact, as my funds continued to dip, I decided to discontinue the lessons.

One day I stopped by the Belasco offices to inform Mr. Dean that for the present at least I was obliged to defer further instruction.

At the time, David Warfield was playing his second year at the Belasco Theater. As I sat in the outer office, in the midst of a group of applicants for roles in the forthcoming Ulric play, the door opened and a narrow young man entered the waiting room, making a survey of those waiting.

His eyes finally rested on me.

This way, he said, assuming me to be one of the applicants.

I followed him, more or less in a daze, into an anteroom.

Have you seen Mr. Warfield in "The Music Master?" he inquired.

No.

There is a bit in the first act, he said, producing a one-page booklet bound in stiff blue paper. The young lady who has the role is about to enter a hospital for a major operation. Do you care to look at the part? Twenty-five a week, Rehearsal for your scene will be called at eleven o'clock tomorrow morning.

There were four single-line speeches:

Third Girl (*seats herself on overflowing suitcase, which promptly closes beneath her weight*): Oh, Master!

The following three speeches were exact replicas of the first: Oh, Master! Oh, Master! Oh, Master!

The stage direction, of course, told me why I was selected.

The scene demanded a girl with a figure that would enable her to sit on an overcrammed suitcase and thus close it, after two or three slim predecessors had been unsuccessful.

My impulse was to stalk out, rejecting the opportunity to try, but the impact of twenty-five dollars a week against a mind uneasy with the knowledge of dwindling funds had a staying effect.

I returned to the theater the following morning.

I got the part.

I was playing in a Broadway success! Well, if not exactly playing, appearing.

As one of three infatuated pupils of "The Music Master," I blurted out the three "Oh, Masters" and plumped myself on the suitcase. Laughter.

I had been playing for three weeks, six evening performances and two matinees, with only fleeting glimpses of Mr. Warfield and none at all of Mr. Belasco. For that matter, my contact with the entire company was slight, except for the two students who shared my brief scene and with whom I dressed in a trinket of a room, two flights up, to which we repaired immediately after our bits, there to await the conclusion of the play in order to take a full-cast curtain bow.

I had not succeeded in breaking down the barrier between myself and the two girls with whom I dressed, who chattered like magpies of heart interests!

Sometimes, during the long waits, I sat aside and tried to write. But the quarters were tight, the yak-yak between the girls constant. Besides, longhand seemed to log-jam my thoughts, so most of the time I read or pretended to. An incident recalls the books I carried into that little dressing room. From this vantage, they seem indicative of a torturous period of seeking. I came upon the two girls one day reading the names off my volumes with much clowning of pronunciation, Nietzsche, Tolstoy, Dostoevski, William Blake, and finally settling for William Blake as the only "local boy in the bunch."

The magic of the theater, except for the remote sounds of applause, the overture announcement of the callboy, the make-up smells, seemed far less here than behind the scenes of Keith's in St. Louis. I was never to see "The Music Master" from the front or hear Mr. Warfield, except for the brief moment of my scene with him. I had rehearsed with his understudy. I doubt if he was even aware of the substitution.

My status at the Three Arts, however, had noticeably improved. Following my engagement at the Belasco Theater, I was invited to a Sunday night cold collation in the room of a girl playing an important supporting role with Billie Burke in "The 'Mind-the-Paint' Girl" and her roommate, Stella, from Brattleboro, Vermont, a music student.

I cultivated Stella. Did she know, or know of, a Jacques S. Danielson, a famous teacher, at one time with New York Conservatory of Music and now associated with Rafael Joseffy?

N-n—o, but the name, she opined, was familiar. The aura of even this remote identification with the J.S.D., who seemed to have moved through my consciousness like a dream, drew me to her. But Stella, what with her practicing and almost nightly steady male visitor down in the lounge, had little time.

My daily letters home gave no hint of my new activities, except to assure Mama that I was not in need of money and as corroboration was able to enclose the toupee story, unsigned, but this time authentic. Five-dollar payment omitted.

Follow-ups to the toupee story had been rejected. Daytime tours of editors' offices, matinee days excepted, continued, as well as mailings to that mecca, *The Saturday Evening Post*.

Bob Davis reiterated: Keep at it. One of these days I'll be bidding for the rejects. Stick close to what you know best and write about it.

What did I know best? Well and good, but where were the words to put together the thoughts so deeply within you? The ideas so often came out broken, like an egg.

The wonder of words! Sounds that we shape. I lift a word from my English vocabulary. I admire it, as if it were an urn. The word "serene" is a lovely one, not alone for its connotation but for its feeling across the lips as you utter it. "Peace," on the other hand, is not as euphonious as its meaning. "Music," paradoxically, is harsh. But, ah, "love"—it falls gently from the lips but is loaded. . . .

Bob Davis once commented upon the temperature of my love scenes. They run high, honey, but they give off light without heat. Wait until you really know about it.

Know about love! I was knowing, all right. It shimmered beneath every day, like iridescent submarine life. And yet how true, it had no reality. It had brushed by with no more than a backward glance, a hasty postcard. Even these were dwindling. . . .

But, of course, I knew what Bob Davis actually meant. The things I knew best. It seemed to me that my intuitions sometimes preceded my actual knowledge. I was particularly aware of this after my foray into the lives of the girls at Lutz Brothers. I had the sensation of having known them beforehand. A small phenomenon, which I was to verify once more, after hiring myself out consecutively as salesgirl at Macy's department store, waitress at Child's Restaurant, and, years later, by accurately describing a French spa before I had seen it.

Meanwhile, my backstage existence during the second year of a successful run was a quiet routine affair, especially since we were not permitted to stand in the wings except while waiting for entrance cue. One evening, before going on stage, I glimpsed a face, third row orchestra extreme left, that gave me something of a shock.

I had not reckoned with the eventuality of someone from St. Louis happening to see me, but this man certainly resembled Mr. Dennison of Cates Avenue. I strained to see his companion, who was not Mrs. Dennison. Then I decided it was only a resemblance, and the incident went out of my mind.

A few nights later, as I was leaving the theater, a tall figure blocked my way.

Papa!

Aghast as I was, relief flooded me. Suddenly I felt secure. A backdrop had moved in behind me. I was no longer just a dot of water in a vast rushing stream. Papa was my substantiation.

Here in New York, I could not so much as cash a check without elaborate procedure! Even at the Three Arts Club they would not. One went to a corner place where they charged you and had you sign documents. In St. Louis, we were either known or identification was a simple matter. The average corner drugstore would accept your word. We had charge accounts in the department stores. My father was president of a business. People knew or believed who you were.

Papa in New York made me more than just someone nobody knew anything about.

Papa looked mussed and still carried his valise.

It had been Mr. Dennison!

Where Mama would have met me with tears, recriminations, and joyous reunion, Papa kissed me lightly, lifted his valise, and we walked away from the stage door, where he seemed so incongruous, as if we had met by appointment.

I am glad to find you in good health, Fannie. But I am worried about your mother. You can imagine how this thing upset her. She wanted to come too, but was in no condition.

My heart pounded. Is—Mama—really sick?

I am always afraid for her heart. She is heavy. We must get to a telephone and reassure her.

I trembled out of fright for Mama and dread of Papa, despite his gentleness.

We went to the Hotel Astor, where he registered. This time I was not the uncertain girl who, following the rooming-house raid, had signed the book timorously.

I accompanied Papa to his room and he immediately put through a call to Mama. In one tearful breath she was accusing, hysterical, raging, and tender: We had to hear it from a pillar of his church like Mr. Dennison, who calls us up to tell us he has seen our daughter on the stage. He didn't know we didn't know. And such a part as you were playing. A heavy girl on a suitcase. Lies, that's what you have been feeding us on. That is what you learned from your college education—to sit on a suitcase. I wish I was dead. I wouldn't want on my conscience what you are doing to your father. He has aged. Baby, come home with him. I need you. The house is dead without you. Lay out your father's nightshirt and see that he takes one pink and one white capsule before he goes to bed. The brown bottle of them is on the left side of his valise under his socks. I don't know how I am living though this. What does it matter, for the few years I have left? Tell your father when he gets off the train tomorrow to stop at that Market Street store run by colored people and bring me five pounds of hominy grits.

Papa took the receiver from me. Nothing to worry about, Rose. We will take the extra-fare train out of New York tomorrow noon. She is fine. We will talk that over when we get home. What? Grits! Good-by, Rose.

I put up little resistance. Papa was matter-of-fact.

There was a knock at the door. I opened it. A bellhop handed me a note addressed to Papa. I recall that I dug into my purse for a tip, mindful of Papa's old aversion. He read the note and, with a gesture of more than annoyance, handed it to me.

Dear Sir, We respectfully call to your attention a ruling of this hotel that male guests, unless occupying a parlor suite, are not permitted to receive ladies in their rooms.

Papa showed rare and red anger. This proves what kind of a town this is for a young lady alone. The management will hear from me.

Papa, you should be pleased that the hotel is so careful.

Come, I'll take you to your Three Arts Club. Tomorrow can't come too soon for me.

Papa, I can't walk out on a play without giving notice.

You will walk out on this one, he said quietly. Send a wire that your mother is ill. Which is true.

I will never be able to get another job. And the Three Arts! How can I leave so suddenly?

You have the same excuse.

The walls began to close around me.

I had editors to see!

You are going home.

You don't need to take me back to the Three Arts tonight. I go home alone every night.

I see. Through the New York streets alone at midnight. Come.

The old claustrophobia began. St. Louis suddenly became tomorrow's gray cell. New York, citadel of light, and something precious, anonymity in a crowd, was slipping away from me. . . .

Back home, the waters closed over, submerging me beneath the same old motionless surface of Cates Avenue. My laundress steals soap. There is too much starch in Fannie's petticoats. Miss Fannie, here's another story come back from New York.

Hay foot, straw foot.

Mama said: I should think your home would seem like a palace after the way your father described you lived in New York.

It did, in a way, but a palace of stale living and overpowering minutiae. Papa said: The faces of people in New York look as if they had been drawn through a wringer. And he concluded like a broken record: New York is all right to visit, but I wouldn't live there if you gave it to me.

It was true that many of those in the streams that moved through the streets of the metropolis looked as if, behind their masks, teeth were gritted.

But also behind these masks, who knew what great dreamers and doers were tussling with dramas, symphonies, novels?

Meanwhile, doubtless by collusion, the efforts of Mama and Papa to divert me were obvious. Hurtingly so.

Returning home one afternoon, I was overwhelmed to find tethered to my bed by a pink ribbon a fawnlike little Italian greyhound with a card attached to his brand-new collar which read: From Mama and Papa.

A few days previous, while walking with Mama, I had stopped to press my face against the plate-glass window of a dog shop to watch the antics of the tiny creature.

Mama was impatient to be on, but I lingered until she threatened to go her way without me.

That was all there was to the incident.

I realized all too well what Mama had to overcome in order to allow me the pet. For weeks I labored to train him to immaculate household habits, not always with complete success, but Mama exercised surprising restraint.

I named him "Wisp." Nights, after Mama and Papa had retired, I would steal down into the rear hall, lift him from his bed and carry him upstairs, returning him in the morning before Mama was up.

The little fellow more than compensated for all the difficulties attendant upon raising a young puppy in a household where doggie misdemeanor was high hazard.

I was happy and guilty with my dog.

Poor Mama, she watched Wisp's every move with anxiety. So did I.

Even at this far-flung date, regrets sting me.

People say: Ah, but you gave your parents so much pleasure in the end.

Perhaps. But who knows as well as I how willingly they would have exchanged those compensations for the simpler ones. A son-in-law out of our design of life. One who would ultimately take over Papa's business. Me in an nearby home of my own . . . grandchildren . . .

This anatomy of me is serving the double purpose of revealing me to myself.

I understand now that despite the beating of my wings my filial instinct was deep and uncomplicated. At heart I was a conforming girl-child, beset with troublesome inborn gimmicks.

My cross-purposes with Mama and Papa harassed me as much as they did them. Nevertheless, when I returned to Cates Avenue I brought them all home again, alive and squirming.

The days dragged by. I registered at Washington University for two graduate courses: "Early Trilogy of American Poets: Lanier, Dickinson, Whitman" and "Greece and Its Pupil Rome." I wrote, sent, wrote, sent. Bob Davis took another story and when the check for thirty dollars arrived, Mama rushed with it to the neighbors and Papa said: Fannie, I am mighty proud. It is not the money, but the accomplishment.

Mama said: It is not the money, but it should have been more.

Papa said: You see, Fannie, you can write just as well at home.

I cannot, I contended hotly. That story was written out of the stimulation I got out of being on my own. If you and Mama ever read my writings, you would understand.

You never show them to us, Fannie.

That was true. I did not realize a then incipient characteristic that was to follow me through the years, almost a phobic dread of discussing, much less displaying, my writings.

Mama said: I suppose we are not intellectual enough.

Mama, don't say things like that.

Your mother doesn't mean all she says, Fannie.

About four weeks later, this was brought tragically home to me.

One afternoon I was seated on the stairs with my little Italian greyhound, Wisp, in my arms, talking what I suppose was soft nonsense to him. Mama in the kitchen must have called to me several times without my hearing, when suddenly she appeared in the hallway.

Didn't you hear me call you three times over?

I didn't.

You mean you didn't want to.

But I didn't.

Of course you didn't. The only creature in this house you have ears for is that dog. I can wear my lungs out calling and no answer, but let that dog so much as whimper and you are at his side.

But, Mama, I tell you I didn't hear you.

That dog has to go! The Saunders across the street want him anyhow. He's going.

If he goes, I go.

What did I tell you? You love your dog more than your family. That dog is going and you'll stay.

I won't, Mama. If Wisp goes, I go. I am no longer a child even if I am treated like one.

Mama started for the telephone but stopped as if for lack of strength.

Willie, she called to our maid, who always stood shrinking in corners during scenes such as this, go telephone Mr. Hurst to come home.

Now, Mrs. Hurst, you must take it easy. Miss Fannie didn't mean nothing by not hearing you.

That dog goes. I rue the day I bought him.

Now, Mrs. Hurst, that child just loves that dog.

What about me? What about her father, who works his fingers to the bone for her? That dog goes.

All right, Mama, I cried wildly, I mean what I say. I'm going, I cried, and, Wisp in my arms, I dashed blindly upstairs.

So seldom out of hand, my anger was red lightning. Wisp under one arm, I began to throw things together with the other. . . .

Willie, dear Willie, with her big square separate teeth and her squat square body, came after me: Now, Miss Fannie, you know your Mama don't mean nothing by what she says. Honey, when you ain't around, she most smothers that little old Wisp with loving and eating. . . .

I'm going, Willie. I can't stand it any more. I don't fit in here. Mama is always angry with me. . . .

Honey, you know you're the apple of this house's eye. It's them stories keep coming back gives you so much misery. Can't you let the story writing go, Miss Fannie, and settle back and be the way all the growing-up young ladies are? Just enjoying yourself? Lord-me, if I could ever just enjoy myself. Now, you put those things back, Miss Fannie. You know you ain't going to walk out and leave your folks, after the way you've been raised by the lovingest parents. . . .

The way I had been "raised." A parent-child relationship which could explode into a lacerating situation such as this was wrong somewhere, and yet beneath it all I loved the way I had been reared. Psychiatrically speaking, it was perhaps all wrong—but Willie was right—the lovingest parents. . . .

By now Mama's temper had also overboiled, dousing the flame beneath it. She was in my room and here it was all over again: Baby, I didn't mean it. You know I wouldn't harm a hair on that little dog's head. Fannie, I didn't mean it.

Mama, I know you didn't. I'm sorry, too . . . and so on and on.

We sat on the porch after that, while a soft sunset fell over our browning autumn lawn. Mama, in characteristic after-the-storm contrition, was all for having Wisp in her lap.

He did not fear Mama. But he knew what he knew about her psychology with regard to him and, in spite of her manifestations, wriggled away. Dashing from her lap, he ran down onto the lawn, me after him.

Let the little fellow be, Fannie, a bit of exercise will do him good. Nice doggie—don't leave the lawn.

I didn't want Wisp loose, he was lightning quick. But I was deeply sorry for Mama in her state of humility, so sorry I could have cried for her as she chatted in a high excited voice . . . so I let Wisp romp on the lawn and returned to the porch.

You go. Your father and I will come to New York in the spring to see you, soothed Mama. You had better have two new suits made. Are you sure the Three Arts Club is comfortable for you?

If only I could find a way to take Wisp with me, moved through my mind during Mama's mood of repentance.

Suddenly, our neighbor's cat, Hillary, walked onto our lawn. Like a streak, Wisp was after her.

Wisp, shrieked Mama, don't cross the street.

There were grinding brakes of a passing department-store delivery truck, then a terrible instant of silence. The driver jumped down and picked up the small sleek body. Hillary had made it, but Wisp was dead.

Mama cried, Mama screamed, and, to my further anguish, all but prostrated herself before me. I would rather she had castigated me.

I would have cut off my right hand to save him, Fannie. No matter what I may have said, I loved that little dog——Oh, Fannie, don't be mad at me.

Mama, I said through numbness, I'm not mad at you. It was an accident. You couldn't help it.

My child will hate me!

Don't say such things.

I'll buy you anything, Fannie. Ten dogs—I'll wire Uncle Gus to buy you the best dog in Ohio.

Mama, Mama, my regrets for all the pain I caused you crowd in on me in these after-years. Your virtues transcended your faults. Papa knew that and bent his neck to your storms. I had neither his sweet humility nor fortitude.

And here they come, the most futile words of tongue or pen. If only—I could live it over again.

I am back in New York and in my stride. This time I have a room to myself, tiny and without a view, at the Three Arts Club. My typewriter is on a table, a story in the writing. My clothes hang with a permanent look in the closet.

I set up a little household. Photographs of Mama and Papa on the chest of drawers (if only I had one of J.S.D.!). A bookshelf on which I artily place not necessarily my favorite books. Boccaccio. Tagore. *Short History of the Elizabethan Novel. Shropshire Lad. Walden. Monsieur Beaucaire.* I purchase a slender vase and allow myself an occasional calla lily.

About this matter of the lily. Over the years, people have been asking: Tell us why you always wear a calla lily. There must be a very special reason. You surround yourself in your home with vases of them. You wear jewelry in that design. Why? Because I like them is my reply, an answer so simple it is bathos. But there is some deeper reason. Yes, but too tenuous to attempt to translate except at the risk of seeming to attitudinize.

Ever since I can remember, the calla lily has been my flower. In St. Louis we seldom saw them except at Shaw's Botanical Gardens, at Easter and Christmas, and, of course, at funerals, this last imbedding into the flower an association with the odor of death.

We were not a household to do much about fresh flowers in the home. None grew in our yard, except a tall row of resplendent sunflowers along our back fence and red geraniums which Mama bought off the flower wagon every spring with the proviso that the peddler plant them in a row before the front porch.

In time I was to piece together my explanation to myself for my attraction to the calm calla lily. It suggests a certain inner serenity into which I have consciously learned, come stress, come storm, to retreat. When Mama flew into one of her tantrums: Be serene, my heart. "Serene" came to be a quiet little treasure of a word which I liked to feel upon my lips. Serene. The calla lily is the symbol of that serenity. It is not hortatory or pretentious, has neither the confusions nor tumult of the complicated chrysanthemum or even the floriferous rose. It speaks its beauty in one single petal. It is as serene as the bland faces of the Madonnas the fourteenth-century Italians loved to paint.

William Beebe, the eminent naturalist, once fell ill. I sent him flowers. When he recovered and I remarked upon his apparent state of vigorous health, he explained that he was afraid to fall ill again for fear I would send him more lilies with all their implications. . . .

In my room there stood, most of the time, the tall and stately calla lily.

A girl named Margaret Wilson comes to live at the Three Arts Club. She is a music student. We discover a common interest. We are both ardent admirers of a writer long well-known to American readers but, strangely, new to both of us. O. Henry. Like O. Henry, she too likes to explore what he called "Baghdad on the Hudson." She is especially interested in churches and cults. Together we discover the Holy Rollers in Harlem, a Catholic cathedral in Chinatown, St. Marks in the Bowery, the Negro synagogue in Harlem.

Margaret is anxious to hear Mischa Elman, due to appear as soloist with the Philharmonic Society Orchestra at Carnegie Hall When we arrive the evening of the concert, there is not even standing room available. As we turn from the box office, it is announced over the loudspeaker that two hundred extra seats have been placed on the stage at five dollars a piece. Margaret has no such moneys. I meet the difference, and we find ourselves seated, looking into a vast bowl of human faces, and also within view of what goes on in the wings.

In an atmosphere charged with that sense of expectancy which precedes performance, the stage chairs fill rapidly, the orchestra files in. The men are almost within reach of us, tuning and twisting stringed instruments. Finally, to applause, Josef Stransky, Conductor, take his place on the podium. Overture!

The audience subsides to the magic of beautiful sounds.

I had never seen, thus face to face, mass capitulation to beauty.

Toward the conclusion, there is movement in the wings. A troupe of eight, led by a pudgy young man in thick-lensed glasses, comes in single file. Bringing up the rear, an Old-Testament-looking woman, carrying what appears to be a well-wrapped infant, emerges from the gloom, followed by a stubby elderly man, also in high-powered glasses, and behind him three little girls, graduating from about twelve years of age down to six.

As the orchestra nears conclusion, the woman begins tenderly to unwrap her bundle, fold by fold by fold. From the innermost depths of the swaddlings, she draws forth a violin, passes it to the young man, who holds it close to his ear while he makes tiny sounds, braces himself after the final applause for the completed overture, and steps forward to the stage.

It is Mischa Elman, stubby little giant, whose violinistic ebullience overflows the golden cup of his genius, until his instrument weeps your tears or lifts you to exultation.

The picture of that family, back there in the chiaroscuro of the wings, made deep tattoo into my mind—the procession of them suggesting from pogrom to the fulfillment that is America!

Seated on the platform, Elman's exultant violin levitating me, I felt I could write the story of that immigrant family, through every tortured inch of the mental and physical anguishes that had prodded them on their way . . . these Elmans and those like them who came to us stricken, yet bearing gifts.

If only I could have written it then, while the genius poured from that little fellow.

Come tomorrow, my written words on paper would not carry the load of what I felt. They would fall feebly to their knees like bony work horses unable to pull the load.

As we emerged, Margaret and I, each from our own music-borne experience, Margaret encountered a friend of her family. Jeffry Saffire. A food product, manufactured by two generations of Saffires and known the world over, bears his family name. One of a family of two children, he had inherited half of the large fortune their grandfather had accumulated from that homey product with its famous "V and V" guarantee. Vim and Vigor!

At thirty-four already an anthropologist of considerable status, he became voluble when Margaret explained that I was a writer, confessing himself to be a frustrated novelist.

He invited us to a famous Broadway restaurant, where the theatrical great and small assembled after performances. He seemed out of place in this setting of night people. I felt a fifth wheel with these two long-time friends, but was impressed by the achievements of this youngish and serious man in scholarly glasses.

When he delivered us to the Three Arts Club, where we were obliged to go through the humiliating procedure of ringing for the night man and signing the "late" slip, he said he hoped to see me again. The remark had that vague "someday" intonation, but the following morning he telephoned and asked what evening I would dine with him.

Any night Margaret prefers, I parried, hoping for the reply I received.

But I am asking you. I have already spoken to her and asked if she thought it would be presumptuous to invite you. She said: Speak for yourself, John, so I am speaking.

Shortly after, Margaret appeared, obviously pleased. You made a hit last night, and with Jeffry of all people. He is supposed to be woman-shy.

Be that as it may, I began to have an admirer whose erudition simultaneously delighted and dismayed me because of my own lack of it.

He wanted to read everything I had written. I offered him some of it with embarrassment. It transpired, incredibly enough, that he felt about my work as I felt about his scholarly achievement

His favorite eating place was the Harvard Club. We dined

there on ladies' nights, but after a while he was asking me out two or three times a week to various quiet and first-rate places.

I was impressed. Obviously Jeffry and I were getting along.

I was careful to weigh my words in my letters home.

Here is part of one I found stored away in the trunk: I have met an interesting man, a Jeffry Saffire, through the Margaret Wilson I wrote you about. He is a scientist and university assistant professor.

Mama wrote in reply: . . . Why don't you meet some businessmen? Is he a Jew? I cannot make out from Saffire. It sounds like it might be one of those changed Russian names.

I thought a great deal about Jeffry, but felt little. Nevertheless, flattered by his attentions, I was on tiptoe to impress him.

One evening in the Harvard Club, at a table adjoining ours, a fraternity dinner party was taking place.

What fraternity is it? I asked.

I wouldn't know, he replied shortly. I am not a fraternity man.

Although at the time I would not have admitted it, a feeling of closer identification with him moved into my mind. Then he in turn asked the leading question.

Are you a sorority girl?

I hated his asking me a question which was still difficult for me even to discuss. Are you Jewish? I hated his asking that, even more.

Yes.

I can't tell you how happy that makes me, he said.

What difference does it make? I told myself.

But inside me it was making a difference. All the difference in the world. Suddenly he had less to explain to me, and I had less to explain to him. We were knowing each other with our blood. In a strange way, I felt exultant. For the first time, pride of race, which my snide snobbery had so long denied me, stirred. I don't know what of this may have been telegraphed to him, but he leaned over intensely.

Fannie, he said, using my given name for the first time, I want to see much of you. I had better not go on, or I will say too much—too soon. Do you want to see more of me? Don't answer that now. I'm afraid of what it might be.

I was glad not to have to answer that.

We are in the first world war. One of the great holocausts of all time tore out of what to me seemed to be the blue, changing the shape of my world and yet, in the beginning, scarcely touching me personally or bestirring me to realizations.

But gradually the girls are bringing brothers, sweethearts, and even fathers in uniform to the Club as they pass through New York for debarkation. Flags and parades. Papa is doubtless talking with the neighboring menfolk about the war, but Mama's letters bear only casual reference. Eddie, Papa's foreman's son, has been drafted. He will look you up when he gets to New York.

I wondered about J.S.D. but not particularly with apprehension. Even with our involvement, war was not yet sufficiently real. From our long range, there was something almost festive. Flags. Uniforms. Parades. The men who came to the Three Arts in uniform exhibited only their readiness and desire to get "over there" and wipe up the mess.

Bells were ringing, and from my particular vantage of no direct involvement I was slow to know that they were sounding a dirge.

Ever so gradually, food shortages, food controls, casualty lists became the order of the day. Presently a proportion of Three Arts girls, namely those with the brothers or sweethearts, were doing volunteer service on the home front. In time I, too, was serving so many hours a week at the Red Cross. Already one of the girls, playing an ingénue role opposite Minnie Maddern Fiske, had lost a fiancé. Another, the brother whom I had met when he came to dine with her on his way overseas. Still another had a brother and a sister-in-law who were "caught" in Austria.

Then, actually, the war began to creep closer. Had J.S.D. and Mr. Joseffy been trapped overseas? Time and time again I had been tempted to telephone his studio and inquire, should anyone answer, about his return. Once I went so far as to call the number, but when a woman's voice replied I hung up the receiver, panicked. What if he had actually returned and would answer himself, or perhaps recognize my voice! My pride ran too high for the risk. True, I pass the Lexington Avenue address. The windowpanes shine. The shades are in their precise order. His sign is still there.

In all the months there had been no reply to my letter and two postcards, sent care of the Lexington Avenue address. Perhaps they had not been forwarded. For all I know, I reasoned, he is married. . . .

I carry that load at the bottom of my heart, trying to pretend it is not there, knowing it is always there.

The march of the manuscripts. Back they continued to come. My thirty-fourth from *The Saturday Evening Post* contained for the second time in the long series a handwritten notation: "Good try." These two words rubbed out thirty-two previous sinkages.

Bob Davis of Munsey's magazines kept my courage alive. He was buying, at the Munsey price, some of my rejects, although he knew I was showing them elsewhere first. His attitude was generous: Go to it. I know I won't be able to hold you long. You are certain to get into the big time.

By way of a long rigmarole of strategies, with the secret cooperation of management, I again decided to go out after firsthand experiences, and finally succeeded in obtaining an unpaid position as waitress in a midtown Child's Restaurant.

It was the era of the white-tile décor of the famous popular-priced chain, ten cents a portion for wheatcakes and maple syrup, five-cent coffee. Seven A.M. until four, over tile floors for my unaccustomed feet, all other daytime activities necessarily suspended. After a briefing course, along with a dozen or so apprentices, I was allotted my uniform, headdress, and salesbook with carbon sheets, and put "on the floor." The aprons of the slender girls tied crisply around their slender waists. I felt thick.

This particular all-night Child's Restaurant was in the zone of New York's mammoth department stores. Twenty-four hours around the clock, it milled with hurry-eaters. During the day, women predominated, their tips ranging from five to ten cents, the men averaging more.

From both sides of the kitchen door the human hive buzzed with motley life. I could have gone on for longer than I was permitted, between the steamy jungle of the kitchen and the eat-and-run jungle out front.

Jeffry came in for several dinners, took pains to make audible complaints about the service, and left anything from a penny to a brass check for tip. He insisted that my blue and white uniform was becoming, and I knew I looked broad. He said it was inspiring to know a girl who had what it takes, whatever that meant.

As a matter of fact, it meant this much: He put into words for me a scratching unease I was beginning to feel about him.

Did he have what it takes?

Without his saying it in so many words, it seemed to me that he was in the throes of difficulties that had to do with his war eligibility. On two occasions he asked me if I had any connections. Of course I had not. My suspicions told me that Jeffry wanted to evade soldiering for a desk job in Washington. And yet, for the life of me, I could not be certain. I had no real claim to my opinion, and again and again I threw my assumption out, but back it came. Besides, all young men did not want to fight. What preparation had American boys for the kill? But I did not even want to attempt to get at the facts, for fear of what I might discover.

And I did not want it to matter as much as it did.

Foolish and premature of me to have written home about him. Mama, upon inquiry, had learned that he was one of two sons of a family of wealth and connections: These are the kind of people you should meet. Your father and I are not getting any younger. What have we to look forward to, except knowing that when our time comes you are well provided for. . . .

Despite Jeffry's preoccupation with his own subjects and a mind which did not reach out far beyond them, intimation of the scholar did still hang over him and quickened my pulse.

But by now I wanted not to like him. This draft business would not let me be. I began trumping up indictments against him.

He was informed, but seemed to have little capacity for caring, one way or another, about what he knew. He spoke of beauty, but not of feeling it. Books, people, events, history, poverty, and now his country were far on the outside of him. A blind child, a lean dog, a casualty list glanced off him. In a sense, I glanced off him too.

His visits to Child's Restaurant and waiting around for me to come off duty did not have to do with any interest of his in that level of life. His coming was also interference with possible opportunities for following my co-workers into their after-work way of life. Even regardless of Jeffry, this was not simple. To be sure, I was part of their locker-room patter. They regarded me with neither particular interest nor suspicion. When questioned, I explained I was new to the town and the work. Some of the "girls" were married, many spoke the vernacular of Brooklyn, the Bronx, or Erin. Getting into their homes and lives was a matter of timing and tact.

The daily grind of people who work with their hands and feet was an awakener. As opposed to the slow-moving foreign-language world of the Lutz Shoe Factory, both on the kitchen side of the door and on the customers' side Child's was vibrant. Politics, intrigue, feuds raged between the workers. Chefs were potentates and had their favorite waitresses for whom they dished out the choicest and quickest orders. Waitresses vied for the tables that caught the male clientele. My union card had been "arranged." The workers argued among themselves as to the advantages and disadvantages of organization. Unsavory epithets, vulgar humor, expletives were the day's patois. Balancing a handful of dishes over a floor which could be slippery, unless endlessly mopped, was a dread. At the close of the workday, you were an ache, walking.

And yet in a way I was closer to awareness that these people on the kitchen side of the door were my people. Somewhere in my consciousness they had been trying to get at me through the smug security of Cates Avenue. They were my anonymous friends. I needed to know them and care about them and write about them.

Some of them were rude to me, others ignored me, still others were unaware of my existence. But more of them were friendly than otherwise. I yearned to get at them through the greasy vapors. I envisioned them as more denied than they were. I felt guilty because of what they lacked. Jeffry, coming into this experience with his neat single track mind, was an intrusion. It was Jeffry who precipitated my dismissal from Child's.

The more experienced waitresses were kind enough in helping me gain some degree of dexterity in handling a row of dishes from palm to elbow and maintaining a balance that would prevent coffee from slopping into saucers, and soups from reaching the customer's shoulder instead of the table. Most greenhorns, they assured me, were like that.

One or two customers complained of the slopped-over foods and liquids, and one gentleman insisted that I remove the spot of gravy I had deposited on his shoulder.

The eye of the headwaitress was on me.

Then Jeffry, with heavy-handed humor which ill became him, complained within her hearing that most of his oyster stew, spilly food which he had intentionally ordered, had poured over into his coffee. My dismissal followed.

The following week, after a series of maneuvers, I was behind the ribbon counter of Hearns Department Store on Fourteenth Street.

This proved to be another Waterloo, but more rewarding than Operation Child's.

My second day behind the counter I was invited home to supper with a co-worker, Celia Moretti. Seven Morettis lived in a six-room apartment on Bleeker Street, the front room serving as dental office for one of the sons-in-law. Below the apartment was an Italian pastry shop run by Mr. and Mrs. Moretti. An assortment of Moretti children romped around.

We ate ravioli, veal stew, cheese, and fresh fruits in an overheated room dominated by lithographs of the Holy Virgin, the framed bones of a saint, family rosaries hung on a key rack, the name of the owner beneath each. Bead portieres between living room and kitchen tinkled every time one passed from room to room. Mrs. Moretti dined with a suckling child at her breast. Apparently Celia was in the habit of bringing friends home. The family talked over and around me.

This, I exulted, is seeing life! After supper, Celia, a sickly girl with an unclear complexion, told me of her love life with a kind of detail that kept me looking away from her and out the window while she talked. After displaying a welt on her arm where her father had struck her after she had remained out all of one night, she launched into an informed dissertation on the contraceptive ways of the romantic life, and suggested a blind date for me one evening with her and her current "friend."

Quick at the elementary arithmetic required at the ribbon counter, she did everything in her power to extricate me from my repeated arithmetical mistakes. But after a week of a desperately confused salesbook with my peculiar conclusions regarding six and one half yards of ribbon at nineteen cents a yard, I was not only out of pocket but out of job.

My Dickensian idea of inhaling plots and characters from the passing scene did not exactly pay off.

I had yet to learn that for some of us experience infiltrates by a kind of osmosis rather than by way of photographic transference. Browsing has its values, and subsequently I was to carry it on over a not inconsiderable portion of the earth, but not in a direct line to creative writing.

Most authors must be familiar with this type of person: I have a great real-life story for you. My own. If only I had the time I would write it myself. It will be the Great American Novel.

You explain: Sorry, but I am one of those from-the-inside-out writers. Can't use other people's material.

But my story is the exception. . . .

Sorry, but . . .

But when you hear my story . . .

It was bound to come. Jeffry invited me to his home for Saturday lunch: My father is home that day. I would like you to meet my folks.

I like myself little for the mental processes which followed.

In a frequently rejected story, I had used the situation of a young girl facing up for the first time to her fiancé's family.

Following Jeffry's invitation, I dug out the unpublished manuscript in order to prejudge how my actual experience was going to compare with the fictional experience of my character.

It was in that reprehensible and clinical spirit that I accepted Jeffry's invitation. I was interested in myself, interesting to myself, and not at all sure how I was going to react. Perhaps if I saw Jeffry in his home environment I might—well, anyway—I owed it to Mama's peace of mind, was the pretense I made to myself.

Actually, I did not want marriage. I sensed rather than knew that, despite Mama, Papa did not want me to marry. Never would want it. And then, in my consciousness, like a bit of dragging seaweed, floated my constant awareness of J.S.D.

Wounded pride, however, helped me concoct a philosophy outlawing these thoughts. Most girls went through that sort of thing. There was the one who had to be locked in her room. What would I have in common with his kind of background, or he with mine?

I had been an indifferent music student, although Mama had once dreamed of me as a concert pianist. Coloratura singing affected me so that I, too, could have howled like my dog Annie, who would bay in a kind of anguish at the sound of one of the boarders who had a soaring soprano voice.

In addition, I tried to reason, this Danielson is too old for me. Nor, in all probability, could he afford me. The Lexington Avenue house looked dour. Women would always spoil him, if they had not already. I would spoil him. Then this had to be seriously considered: What on earth could he and Mama and Papa possibly have to say to each other? I had no right to do this to my parents.

But why speculate on something that was not to be? He probably did not even remember me. He had an accent (a soft endearing one). Our "arts" would clash.

What did I want with either of them, him or Jeffry? Certainly not marriage. I thought of women with writing careers. Of course most of them, with exceptions such as the Brontës and Amy

Lowell, had married or "lived it up." There were George Eliot and Mrs. Browning, Mrs. Humphry Ward, Mrs. Elinor Glyn, Mrs. Edith Wharton, Mrs. Gertrude Atherton.

The union of a musical and a literary career! Jerk my thoughts away as I would, back they would snap. Why had he written me at all—if he could drop away as easily as this?

I went to Jeffry's for lunch.

The Saffires lived in a handsome stone house on East Ninetieth Street, in a zone of unusual quiet, although the street was hemmed in at each end by heavy-ridden avenues.

Reminder of a gone era, a carriage step and hitching post stood at the curb, one of the few remaining in the city.

We lunched in a fine, high-ceilinged room, under a lighted crystal chandelier. It was obvious that in the twilight gloom of this heavy house there would always need to be lights burning during the day.

But somehow, despite huge proportions, steep staircases, long hallways, ponderously high ceilings, and heavy furnishings of an about-to-vanish brownstone era, there pervaded a certain warmth.

But was it for this I had come to New York! Here I was in an atmosphere little different than that which encased Mama's "rich relatives." A combination of wealth and what Mama would have called plain-as-an-old-shoe way of life.

I remember with what surprise I once heard Mrs. Leonard Hellman remark as we sat at luncheon in her magnificent dining room in St. Louis: Rose, what do you do when your linen sheets begin to go? Mending doesn't help much, but it goes against me to tear them up for dustcloths.

Mama said: My cousin, Carrie Hellman, with all her money, is as plain as an old shoe.

The Saffires seemed that way. Despite the pomposity of Mr. Saffire, a heavy-set authoritative man with a protruding front, and the matriarchal wife who wore immense diamond earrings set in gold, the occasion had a reminiscent quality.

I was back home lunching at Mrs. Leonard Hellman's.

There was pot roast for dinner at the Saffires'. I had always objected when Mama served it to guests. Her invariable reply had been: If the Hellmans, who can buy and sell us, serve it for their guests, it is good enough for ours.

Again, after the fashion of Mama, Mrs. Saffire inquired of her husband if the meat was tender, explaining she had rebuked the butcher for last week's roast, which was not. Jeffry's married brother, Joseph, and his wife were also present. They too were of a familiar pattern. Older son in business with his father and obviously more in tune with his parents than Jeffry. A young wife harassed by mother-in-law interference.

The talk turned that day to a baby show currently taking place in Atlantic City.

My daughter-in-law, explained Mrs. Saffire, smiling too brightly at the junior Mrs. Saffire, doesn't believe in picking up the baby when it cries. She lets the little thing cry it out. I suppose all those highfalutin books the young mothers of today read are all right if you believe in fads, but neither of my boys can ever say I ignored their cries. . . .

She would also be my mother-in-law!

It was not difficult to arrive at the conclusion that the Saffires had done some Hurst research.

Your father, I understand you to say, Mr. Saffire asked rather than stated, is in the leather business?

Of course he did not understand me to say, since we had not referred to anything pertaining to Papa, and Mrs. Saffire did not help the situation by adding: Why, no, Mark, Aaron Lowe, your friend who lives in East St. Louis, wrote you that—I mean happened to write you that . . .

Poor Jeffry. He had the good judgment not to attempt to unmuddle the muddle. No doubt about it, the Saffires had been checking up on the Hursts.

This must be said for Jeffry: As he escorted me back to the Three Arts Club following lunch, he made no attempt to explain or cover up for his parents. We sat for a while in the little park on Riverside Drive that terraces down to the Hudson River's edge.

The talk was desultory, but the silences were not. Suddenly he spoke out of one of them: I do like you very much.

I too liked his nearness on the bench beside me, and I liked what he said with the little tremble in it.

But this thought moved through my mind: I wonder where Jack Danielson is now, and would he care, one way or another?

It was nice being admired by the young college professor, even if his first-rate but singletrack mind was so highly concentrated on his one particular subject.

More than once, elaborately impersonal, we had discussed the right of a woman to pursue her career after marriage. But, somehow, his assent had the sound of lip service. At the thought of his mother and the curve of her mouth as she remarked: My daughter-in-law doesn't believe in picking up the baby when it cries . . . No, I did not want marriage with Jeffry. But being admired to the verge of proposal of marriage can make even an overweight women feel quite beautiful.

I cogitated on a story that would develop the idea of a homely woman bowed down with a sense of inferiority, who becomes beautiful to herself when, at the tail end of her youth, romance belatedly catches up with her.

Jeffry interrupted my plot by asking: What are you thinking about?

You, I replied.

In a way, I was.

The following morning, when I came downstairs for my mail before starting the day's writing, the dreaded long envelope was not protruding from my box.

This morning there were two letters. Mama's and one bearing the engraved inscription: *The Saturday Evening Post*.

I stood fingering it for minutes, my heart pounding. I had never before received anything but a long envelope from *The Saturday Evening Post*—at least thirty-five of them. . . .

I opened Mama's letter first and read, trying to concentrate on it through the boiling excitement inside me. Then, still standing there in the small office, I opened the second letter!

Dear Miss Hurst, We think "Power and Horse Power" is great. We want to publish it and we hope many more by the same author. Our fiction editor, Mr. Churchill Williams, will come to New York within the week to see you and will telephone you the day you receive this. We look forward to meeting you in the near future.

There will never again be a moment like this, I cried to myself.

I did not realize that every subsequent acceptance over the years would see a rebirth of that thrill.

As I turned from the letter, our Deaconess walked into the little office. With an outburst uncharacteristic of me, I threw arms about her, lifting her from the floor.

Deaconess, *The Saturday Evening Post* has accepted a story!

She separated herself from me with a gentle thrust of both hands.

You are a writer!

I want to be, more than anything in the world! And now this makes me one.

That disqualifies you, Miss Hurst, said the Deaconess in a kind of cold and quiet anger, for residence in the Three Arts Club. You evidently entered under false pretenses as a dramatic artist.

I had made my colossal error, but not even the prospect of ejection from the club deflated me.

One climax followed another. The next day came a telephone call from the *Century Magazine*, warning me in advance that they were rejecting a submitted story but requesting me to call personally. The editor was interested in discussing possible future work from me.

A gray-haired woman interviewed me in the musty high-ceilinged *Century Magazine* office. Magnetic and humorous, she poked fun at what she termed my idiosyncrasies of style, laughed with and at many of my weaknesses, but concluded: You use words with stunning force. Your genius lies in portraiture.

I wish this story, "Sob Sister," were for us. It is absorbing, undisciplined, its style violent. We expect much from you in the near future. If our budget permitted, we would buy first option on everything you do. But since we cannot, we hope you will continue to submit to us, preferably first.

Life was a stunning affair! I could scarcely wait to get back to my typewriter. The great town swung joyously about me as I walked from the Seventeenth Street offices of the magazine.

After the procession of rejected manuscripts which, I estimated extravagantly, if placed end to end would have reached from St. Louis to New York, my sun seemed about to emerge from its long-time cloud bank. "Seemed," I reiterated, padding myself against the possible impact of more slapdowns.

Meanwhile, Mama's antennae must have been moving sensitively, deriving from my letters more than I meant to intimate by my too-casual references to Jeffry.

Be that as it may, comes a letter announcing her imminent arrival for "just a little visit," this followed by a telephone call from Mr. Churchill Williams, assistant editor, *The Saturday Evening Post*. I agreed to be in his New York office the following morning.

Bob Davis was my mentor. What do you think he wants to say to me? I asked.

If I had his budget, I know what I would say to you. Give me your all.

What if he asks me how much I want for the story?

Ask what you think fair.

One hundred dollars?

That's fair enough.

Churchill Williams piled excitement upon my excitement. *The Saturday Evening Post* not only wanted "Power and Horse Power," they too wanted first look at my future work. The *Post* would feel lost without its long procession of Hurst manuscripts. I was now "in the family." As we parted, Mr. Williams held my hand in a long shake and asked: What do you think your story is worth? I had the sum one hundred dollars ready on the tip of my tongue. But the words would not come. What I said was: I'll leave that to you—wanting to recall the words no sooner than they were spoken.

The check came for three hundred dollars.

I found a pleasant room for Mama in the neighborhood. She said it depressed her the moment she entered the front hall of the rooming house, but she was afraid to stay alone at a hotel.

Her visit froze my activities and threw me into a state of tension. She went straight to the point. She wanted to meet Jeffry.

He had us to dinner at the Waldorf-Astoria Hotel the second night following her arrival, and two evenings later at his home.

Even if not quite her dynamic self, Mama was a success. At first with Jeffry alone, and then at his home for dinner, she tightened into the subdued restraint she displayed to her "rich relatives."

Her face, ample but pretty, her figure too ample, were all right with Papa and me. I felt pride in Mama. She looked nice, well corseted into her Mary Stutz foulard dress, with the inevitable V-shaped insert of cream lace.

The Saffires apparently found it an easy matter to be relaxed and communicative with Mama, especially as her restraints began to thaw.

Presently, conversation was being batted about like a tennis ball by our elders, Jeffry and I talking self-consciously between ourselves. . . .

With my third ear I could catch drifts of: Fannie this. Mr. Hurst that. Jeffry this. Jeffry that. I prayerfully hoped Mama was warming up into her rosy prettiness and exhibiting her humor, her quick wit, to best advantage. Despite everything, my problem-child Mama remained my own dear darling. I wanted them to understand her.

All through dinner and afterward, in the large and lovely drawing room, it did seem obvious that Jeffry liked me very much.

I slept with Mama that night in her room. We talked late: Yes, it certainly is wonderful about *The Saturday Evening Post*, but what a fine upstanding fellow that Jeffry is.

ANATOMY OF ME

Century Magazine? Who reads it? How many people even know it exists. *The Saturday Evening Post* is different. What did you and Jeffry have to say to one another while we were talking about Papa's business? Wonderful people!

But for my restraining hand, Mama was for telephoning Papa, late as it was, to tell him about our evening. My letters home, she declared, had given them little inkling of the actual situation.

Please, let us talk things over first, before you discuss matters with Papa.

What is there to talk about! Now, you will live like a human being, in a family that stands for something in this town. I wouldn't be surprised if after he is settled down Jeffry goes into his father's business like his brother. He is a sensible fellow.

What about my writing? Besides, he hasn't even—asked me.

Mama stared at me, incredulous. You call this runaround existence a life for a girl? That boarding house for old maids! A story here and there. All right, *The Saturday Evening Post* is a big thing. But do you mean to say you hesitate between such a life and a home of your own, with say a little writing on the side? That is, concluded Mama witheringly, unless *The Saturday Evening Post* doesn't believe in marriage.

For little split seconds, doubts moved through me. Could I do both with a man like Jeffry? Too much of that heavy house, with the artificial lights burning all day, was built into him to make it seem plausibile. I recalled what he had said to me half facetiously, the day of my engagement with *Century Magazine*. What! Breaking your lunch date with me for that? Does that mean it is first things first with you? Jeffry had a way of speaking his serious words in jest.

And so we talked, Mama and I, far, far into the night, Mama alternating between anger, cajoling, holding up examples of what other girls had done for themselves. . . .

Mama dredged up the case of a Cates Avenue neighbor, Gertrude Schlessinger, who at seventeen, already singing minor roles with the Castle Square Opera Company, had abruptly forsaken a career to marry a distant relative of her father, an industrialist in Stuttgart, Germany, and had promptly borne him twins.

I said, Ugh, but I wondered. . . .

That reminds me, said Mama: I brought along a letter that came to the house the day I left. It is postmarked Stuttgart. Must be from Gertrude.

It was not until the following morning, while Mama was in telephone conversation with Mrs. Saffire arranging a luncheon appointment, that I remembered the letter.

Dear Fannie, I have thought of you a great deal during these many disturbed months, and wondered how and where you are. The Maestro returns to New York next month. They have put me to work over here playing accompaniments for the troops, so of course I am only too willing to remain as long as needed. It was by accident that I happened to be over here and was caught up in this kind of special civilian service. My age keeps me in that classification. I do not know where you are, I hope in New York. But I will send this letter to St. Louis, the only address I know. I will be pleased to hear from you when I return to my Lexington Avenue address, which I trust will be in the not too distant future. Sincerely, J.S.D.

The prosy little note, written on onionskin paper, is before me as I write. A puff of wind would blow it away. It shaped my destiny.

To think that I could ever have permitted indecisions to plague me. How could I have even considered the ideas Mama put forward?

I was never surer of myself than when Mama returned a few minutes later from her telephone conversation with Mrs. Saffire. Sure and unafraid.

Mama cried and wished she were dead. Mama telephoned Papa and told him to come to New York.

. . . all of a sudden she has turned against the entire idea. I cannot make her out. Sam, I was with him again last night. A prince of a young man. Such a family. Such a home. She is throwing away a lifetime. This *Saturday Evening Post* business may turn out to be the worst thing that could happen. She is throwing away everything for it. . . .

I took the receiver from Mama: Don't worry, Papa. Everything is all right. I have never been as sure of anything. I don't want any of it. Besides, he hasn't even asked me.

Papa said: Don't let your mother or anyone else pressure you into such a step. I admire you for taking a stand in time. My advice to you both is to come home. Put your mother back on the wire.

Whatever Papa said, Mama listened. It must have been sharp and concise, because the crackle of his voice sounded that way.

I know, as usual I am all wrong and your daughter is right. I'll be home day after tomorrow with or without her. Click.

Poor Mama. She could not have known how sorry I felt about her, or how eager I was to placate her, or how impatient I was for her to be on her way back to Papa, or that the letter she had brought with her, presumably from Gertrude Schlessinger, had precipitated my decision. . . .

Too cowardly to face Jeffry, I wrote him a tight little note of finality.

Far from pursuing the matter, he wrote me a grave reply, a civil, perfunctory note, as if politely regretting a dinner engagement I had not kept.

I tried so hard to placate Mama in the hours preceding her departure. But she would not placate. Theater? Dinner? Drive? Let me alone, I wasn't meant to enjoy life. Go back to what you are doing. Run around town after the editors. All I want is to go home. I wouldn't want to have on my conscience what you must have on yours.

Mama, please, won't you understand?

I understand that your father and I cannot expect to have pleasure out of our child.

Not even Mama's hyperbole could mitigate my sense of guilt. A letter about which Mama knew nothing, from a man about whom I knew little or nothing, had suddenly swept all before it. A small noncommittal note that did not even invite a reply.

I put Mama on her train, loading her with small gifts.

Mama, please don't go home angry with me.

I have too little to live for to be mad or glad.

Of course, when the train made its first jerk, her resistance gave way.

My baby—I only want what is for your good. Be good. Come home to us soon.

Curtains of tears hung between us as her train pulled out and I stood blindly waving. I loved her.

The Saturday Evening Post having paid on acceptance, Bob Davis cashed the check for me and sent to his bank for three brand-new one-hundred-dollar bills, one of which I sent to Mama and Papa. Mama wrote: I cried plenty when it came and wanted to frame it, but it is too much money to have on show in the house where it could be stolen. Your father couldn't finish his breakfast after he read your letter, with enclosure.

Papa wrote on Standard Heel and Counter stationery: . . . your mother and I count ourselves very fortunate in our daughter and are grateful for our blessings, which I hope you are too. That was certainly a fine-sized check which you shared with us. I know you will keep your modest demeanor and continue to win honors for your efforts. With regard to the matter which has been causing your mother distress, I cannot but laud your decision. There is plenty of time for you to contemplate so serious a step as marriage. From what I understand, these people are of Polish descent and while I hold no prejudices I have never been favorably impressed in that direction. . . .

Three rejected stories came home to me that same day, after I returned from a shopping tour for a flamboyant hat which cut into my folding money.

In the millinery shop, to the coos and caws of the saleslady, I had visualized myself in it at my first meeting with J.S.D., its plum-colored "willow plume" dripping to my shoulder.

Meanwhile, a printed notice was inserted in my mailbox informing me that "members no longer qualifying for residence in the Three Arts Club are expected to vacate their rooms within thirty days after receiving notice."

The war was still something "over there," but by now American minds, hearts, families, streets, big and little businesses had caught up with its apprehensions, griefs, and terrible hazards.

The Red Cross assigned me to three evenings a week rolling bandages. The work seemed inappropriate for my clumsy fingers. It seemed to me a feeble kind of service, until motion pictures were shown at the Red Cross headquarters and I saw, first-hand, the bleeding wounded.

Thoughts engendered by the insanity of war pestered me. Here I was, preparing pads of gauze to absorb the blood men were spilling for what would have amounted to murder in times of peace but in wars were acts of valor.

By the time these pads of gauze reached their grim destination, firm-fleshed young men would saturate them with their blood. In our way we, in our Red Cross Madison Avenue loft, folding and folding and cutting, were part of the organized murder, readying for it, preparing for the kill—adding to the craziness.

Time and time again, the overseer undid and helped redo my elementary tasks of cutting and folding. One evening I was informed a little too kindly that because of the wonderful production of volunteers they were now in a position to reduce the staff of workers. If my services were required later, they would call on me.

I felt ashamed and said I understood. I had not even been able to roll little pieces of gauze for my country. But I could write. Why not enlist to write?

I did not know where to turn except to Bob Davis. In my presence he telephoned an executive at the United Press: Fred, I have a smart girl here who can write. Can you use her or direct her to a wartime job? Good bet for whoever takes her on.

No, but she is a comer in fiction. Sells to *The Saturday Evening Post* and to yours truly. Nothing came of it.

My writing slowed, the weeks passed. Thursdays, publication day of *The Saturday Evening Post*, I hurried to the newsstand, only to find my story not published. My spirits slowed. Perhaps they had shelved it. That thought slowed me still more. During this same period, Theodore Dreiser, who had not left the editorial staff of *The Delineator*, as I had been erroneously informed, returned a story with this note: Someday you may be a helluva writer. At present you are not. I have the same complaint that bedevils you. Too many words on hand and I say them all. Two of our readers were for your story. Three of us were not. One of whom I beg to remain. Keep at it.

I did, but now the need to move loomed, and again it was Mama, operating from long range, who directed it. Part of her yellowing letter reads: A Miss Deborah Gobert and her sisters run a fashionable school for girls on West End Avenue. They also have an apartment nearby, where they take older girls from out of town who are studying or working in New York. Go and see them and say Mrs. Pauline Stroebel of St. Louis recommended them. It will be more expensive, but I will pay the difference. Your father is getting very tired of this knocking about New York, so it won't be for long. Now that I have told everybody about *The Saturday Evening Post*, it doesn't come out. Your father is in the same fix. Can't you tell them to print it?

Miss Gobert's apartment for older girls, situated on the top floor of an apartment house at the tip end of West Sixty-ninth Street, overhung the New York Central switching yards like a tessellated castle.

All night long, cattle in process of shipment bellowed in the abyss below. The girls with whom I shared the apartment seemed to sleep peacefully through it. After a week of dreadful nights, I too acquired immunity.

Life at Miss Gobert's was in keeping with the select school around the corner. We dined in candlelight, off lace tablecloths, on food sent around to us from the school. The double rooms were furnished in "bird's-eye maple" and cretonnes. My housemates were two girls from Baltimore, another from Wheeling, West Virginia, all daughters of well-placed families, intent on doing "busy work" and, as usual in that era, a source of disturbance to their parents.

The exception was my roommate, a darkly beautiful girl from Little Rock, Arkansas, a social worker in a welfare organization, who helped support her mother. Another from Baltimore, daughter of a department store magnate in that city, contributed her services to the same organization.

The older Gobert sister, a handsome, more than ample woman, with two married sisters who were her partners in enterprises which also included a summer camp for expensive girls, was a warmhearted woman whose plump face and blue eyes belied the frustrations which plagued her.

The girls at Miss Gobert's were impressed by the advent of a writer in their midst. One who not only had been published but was scheduled to appear in *The Saturday Evening Post*.

With my roommate absent during the day and several evenings a week, I could work without interruption so long as I had the "Do Not Disturb" sign on the door.

But the home atmosphere invited intimacy. These girls, graduates of Goucher College, of Bryn Mawr, were more intellectually inclined than my associates at home or at the Three Arts Club. Two of them had been to Europe, one of them several times. Their manner of dressing bespoke more than words what was wrong with mine. Tailor-made suits, blouses with fine handiwork, small fur neckpieces in contrast to my immense pointed fox were almost uniformly their daytime attire. This conservatism also characterized Miss Gobert and her sisters, Mrs. Vera Zacharias and Mrs. Rebecca Barkhouse.

But my flair for the flamboyant was as difficult to douse as a forest fire. I doubt if it is doused now. I am that way, I reasoned to myself. Let them run with the herd.

The daughter of the department store magnate, whose quiet

clothes bore French and Fifth Avenue labels, tried diplomatically to take me under her wing.

Would you like to borrow my cashmere coat to wear tonight? It is warmer than your black and white checked one.

I knew what she meant and, despite my high resolve of independence, suffered inwardly. I was gauche, that is what I was. Overweight. Overdressed. I knew that they discussed me sotto voce, just as they had at the Three Arts Club. I knew there was laughter. But I also had reason to know that each of these privileged girls, with just enough scratching ambition to motivate them to leave sheltered homes, regarded my accomplishments, such as they were, with frustration and some admiration.

Miss Gobert and her sisters, animated, capable, and business wise, considered me an addition to their extracurricular enterprise. Miss Gobert, who seemed too elderly and matronly for "boy friends," nevertheless had them. One evening, when one in particular came to call, she knocked on my door and invited me into the sitting room to meet him, a New York assemblyman.

He was a squat, black-haired, sloe-eyed, fiery little fellow at comic variance with Miss Gobert: This is the young lady I have been telling you about: I want our future famous writer to meet another future celebrity. Mr. Fiorello La Guardia, this is Miss Fannie Hurst.

It was the beginning of a long friendship with a future three-time Mayor of New York City.

Vera Zacharias, who concerned herself chiefly with the social divertissements of the school, was popular with the girls. Indeed, too popular. A rather voluptuous woman of about thirty-eight, with seeking eyes, she was crazily miscast. Married to a gross, overbearing man of high integrity and fidelity, and herself lacking both these qualities, her two older sisters never relaxed watch over her.

"If I do say so myself," as Mama would have put it, I became the showpiece of the Gobert establishments. Vera took me over, maneuvering to have me at the school on one pretext or another when the girls' parents or visitors were expected, introducing me as a young writer from the Middle West whose work would soon be appearing all over the country.

In a way, I was responsible for this hyperbole, because in a burst of confidence I had retailed to Mrs. Zacharias my near and yet far relationship with various editors.

My few published stories were passed around. Mrs. Barkhouse, fifteen years Vera's senior, a magnificent matriarch of a stepmother to five grown children, and long-time widow of a distinguished Hungarian author, sent me a slender volume of her eldest stepson's poetry, *The Sun Rises in the East*, by Leonard Barkhouse, published by Yale University Press.

They were tender, unhappy, and nostalgic for what must have prompted him to study for the rabbinate, although he never followed in his father's footsteps, instead identifying himself with teaching. The scholarly head of the Barkhouse Academy for Boys, he was the center stone in a woman-family of small sparklers.

His photograph, rather self-consciously Shelleyesque, stood silver-framed on his mother's desk at the school. What I could not know at the time was that according to rumor she was in love with this man who was not her blood son, and who was thirty years younger.

Smitten also were his two stepaunts, Miss Gobert and Vera Zacharias, to say nothing of a finishing school full of girls.

In due time Vera began to insist that I must meet him. Brimming with high spirits, but tormented by a sense of guilt because of her love affair with a younger man, she caused her sisters anguish both for her and for possible jeopardy to the Gobert school and camp enterprises.

Her sisters welcomed her enthusiasm for me. I did not understand at the time it was because they hoped I might divert her from her dangerous interest in the young man, as she took me about with her to art exhibits, theaters, concerts.

It was some time before I came to realize that this going about was cover-up to conceal from her sisters and husband the fact that most of our cultural expeditions terminated in "accidental" encounters with the gentleman in the case, a nervous young man with quivering nostrils. Whether we encountered him in the Metropolitan Museum, in front of a drugstore, or coming out of theater, Vera would invariably exclaim: What a coincidence! Fancy running into you!

J.B. was vastly her intellectual superior, and responsible for many of her cultural interests. As the innocent fifth wheel in this arrangement, I learned a great deal from the sallow erudite fellow, who, somewhere in his thirties, had become misanthropic and oppressed with a sense of failure.

In no time at all, Vera was pouring out her heart to me. Infatuated with J.B., who unnerved, baffled, and fascinated her by his moody intricacies, she lived in turmoil and apprehension.

Incorrigibly romantic-minded, she evolved an idea which concerned me: I want Leonard Barkhouse to meet you. But he declares, and I am sure it is a pose, Save me from intellectual girls." I have an idea! I hope you are not above a practical joke. I will introduce you to him as a showgirl in a Broadway musical. Then, after he has begun to like you, we will tell him the truth.

My size, a showgirl!

Certainly, Ziegfeld uses big girls. All musicals do.

Apparently, I was not above Vera's brand of humor, because she finally coaxed me into the ruse. One of the girls at the Three Arts Club was playing a walk-on role in a musical comedy currently starring Elsie Janis. We arranged that following the performance I was to join her backstage and emerge from the stage door along with the members of the chorus.

Vera did not say as much, but when I suggested adding this and that to my wardrobe to make it more convincing, she advised me to do nothing at all, evidently feeling that my ordinary manner of dress was consistent with my role as Marjorie Tate, chorus girl.

This proved to be the case. In addition, my simulated role relaxed me. The stiff shyness which dogged me on social occasions, and still does, fell away. The stage door appointment was kept and Dr. Barkhouse and I promptly paired off, following Vera and J.B. in the direction of a restaurant for an after-theater bite.

Leonard Barkhouse had a leonine head, his hair curly and of a blond tinge that would have been a woman's glory and was a man's cross to bear.

For purposes of our so-called prank, I was a friend of a friend of Vera who had worn chandelier-size hats and infinitesimal leotards in many of Broadway's most lavish revues in the Ziegfeldian tradition of big girls.

I doubt if Barkhouse, living as he did under the wide wingspread of his mother and doting relatives, was any more worldly wise, except for book knowledge, than I. He was the flower of the flock and they tended him as such.

His heavy-handed attempt at twitting was doubtless in keeping with what he thought the occasion required.

I'm afraid the restaurant I have selected will seem a little prosy to you. I am not much for night clubs.

I had never been in one, but I let go some of the jargon according to my own peculiar idea of chorine vernacular.

You're a sweetie, he said, in what was probably his version of that vernacular, and pressed my arm.

Before we reached the restaurant he had already asked for my telephone number. I explained that it was difficult for me to receive calls where I roomed, because of an elderly landlady, three flights up, and one telephone in a lower hall.

He seemed interested but not sufficiently to ask me to call him.

At the quiet first-class restaurant, he sat beside me with a dignity that made his constant pressuring of my knee beneath the table hilarious.

Nevertheless, it was at this point that the fun began to sag. You did not betray a man thus caught in the machinations of a somewhat tasteless practical joke. It was obvious that the young Ph.D. was rarin' to go the way of all flesh with a chorine, and that he was enjoying to the hilt his acquaintance with Marjorie Tate.

He was interested in my beginnings and I fabricated as quickly as I had served up short orders at Child's Restaurant. I had no liking for alcohol, but declined a highball on the grounds that

I was temporarily "on the wagon" in restitution for having been hitting it too hard.

Barkhouse's knee pressed mine again, and he said: Well, we will have to do something about that.

He was for taking me home, but Vera urged me to spend the night with her. He insisted that four would crowd a taxicab and he would escort me there separately.

I understand. You two are going off dancing, or something. The key will be under the mat, Marjorie.

That cue was sufficient for Barkhouse. But instead of a nightspot, he ordered the taxi driver to take us around the park, and lost no time in proceeding with what he must have thought the occasion required.

This was difficult in a two-edged way. I hated being pawed. Moreover, something unsportsmanlike in the entire proceedings made me squirm. I was even tempted to reveal all, but there was the specter of betraying Vera. She had her plans.

You are an extremely interesting young girl, Marjorie, he said, holding me closely.

I am nothing of the sort, I protested, pressing backward from him. I ran out on school and an orphan asylum when I was fifteen. If you school people depended on my kind, you'd starve to death.

That isn't important. Deliver me from a female highbrow.

You'll take them female and let the highbrow go?

He laughed at my brassy attempt at humor and made the same old tiresome pass all over again: You are alive. You are a natural. May I come to see your show tomorrow night and meet you afterward? I want to see a great deal of you. I was dumfounded by the level of my retort to that one:

It will cost you two dollars and fifty cents, first row orchestra, to see more of me in tights, I replied.

I arrived at Vera's two hours later, considerably rumpled.

I was all for terminating the situation, but Vera pleaded with me not to ruin her little joke. Trust Leonard's sense of humor to rise to the occasion, she insisted. Her family dinner party for two evenings hence had already been arranged. I was to be present and introduced to him in my own guise. Please, she urged, see him between now and then, as often as he wishes.

It was obvious, even to me, that Vera was secretly angling to bring together two people she considered significantly compatible.

I prevailed upon Barkhouse not to come to the performance the following evening, but to wait until I could procure him a first-row seat. We met afterward, the procedure virtually repeated. Restaurant, drive around the park three times, only this time I was beginning to be more than casually disturbed by the dilemma growing out of the clumsy joke.

In an irrational way, I, who had never had an amorous word from J.S.D., regarded myself as pledged. I was being disloyal, even in this make-believe situation. This man was apparently liking Marjorie Tate in a manner that had no precedent in his somewhat limited experience. To be sure, he would not in all probability be hurt by it. Experience was teaching me that my knights fell away without tragic ado.

Nevertheless, the second evening he pawed less and set about for facts. What of my background? I elaborated on my lack of knowledge of my parents, enlarged upon my childhood in a Keokuk, Iowa, orphan asylum, my itinerant trouping with a passing road company. Was I free of romantic involvements? What did I want out of life? He did not ask my own faith but went so far as to query would I go over to the faith of a man I cared enough about to marry, even if he happened to be a Jew who had once studied for the rabbinate?

I sidestepped that one: I have never given it any thought. Would I then give it some thought? Yes. Did I think a man of thirty-eight was too old for a girl in her early twenties? No. Would I enjoy being the wife of a man financially well placed? Did a career mean as much to me as a home, husband, and children?

Something instantaneous was happening to this dreamy aesthetic man. Strangely, despite his effeteness, he liked my appearance. Greek goddesses, he maintained, were healthy, firm-fleshed women, goddesslike by virtue of their vitality. You are like one of them. Someday I will help you know more about them.

I think I stretched this one a little too far. Are there Greek goddesses around nowadays? I queried with seriousness. He regarded me for a startled instant and replied: None, except you.

I was relieved that the following night Vera was to put an end to a practical joke which was proving impractical. What else would it end? A flowering instant in the heart of a poet? I did not flatter myself that it was more than an instant.

Miss Gobert shared my concern: Vera would not have perpetrated this absurdity if my sister, his stepmother, were not out of town on camp business. His pride will be hurt and I don't blame him. She did not add, as she might have: I am surprised Fannie, that you would lend yourself to it. So was I, and mortified.

I was for retreating from the dinner, but the family decided it was best to go through with it in the hope that Leonard would see humor in it.

By design, I appeared last, walking into Vera's living room with my hair done smoothly as usual, in contrast to the Marjorie Tate frizzle, my manner also unfrizzled.

Leonard, this is the St. Louis girl I have been telling you about. Miss Fannie Hurst, my stepnephew, Dr. Barkhouse.

It seemed to me I could see the flood of delayed perceptions flow into his eyes.

The family stood eager for a burst of fun, while I waited, I suppose, for come-what-will.

Dr. Barkhouse did what none of us had foreseen. His rather softly outlined jaws came together with a little clamp.

If this is the family's idea of humor, I leave you to laugh it out among yourselves, he said, and strode from the room before anyone had recovered sufficiently to go after him.

Miss Gobert regarded her sister icily. Well, are you satisfied?

He's a bad sport, cried Vera. I am glad I showed him up for one.

I stood mute and inglorious. The family rallied around my discomfort. You are not to blame. Don't feel upset.

Early in my relationship with this high-strung family, I was being inducted into life as these educators lived it among themselves, behind the curtain of high decorum befitting the heads of expensive schools and camps for adolescing boys and girls.

What the family did not know was the extent to which Leonard had unwittingly gone in this ruse. That much he was spared, although I imagine he could never be quite sure who knew what.

He'll forget it, insisted Vera. Marjorie Tate is dead, long live Fannie Hurst.

Dr. Barkhouse neither forgot nor came around laughing.

I decided I was miscast at the Goberts' but could not bring myself to change living quarters again. First, now that I was settled in an environment that satisfied Mama and Papa, there was less pressure on me to return home. Besides, I liked these people, felt at home with them. Effervescent Vera, frustrated in her marriage, wretched in her love affair, seeking, banging herself against the restrictive walls of husband and family, yet unable or unwilling to leave, was a study in herself.

A red-headed young fellow from San Francisco, Gilbert Mallin, about to have a musical comedy produced on Broadway, and a young artist from Richmond, Virginia, were frequent Sunday evening guests at the Goberts', when we all gathered for cold cuts and chafing-dish concoctions. The electric little man whom I had met there, Mr. La Guardia, had promised to take me on explorations into places where I had no entree.

By way of Mama, of all people, I seemed to have stumbled on what appeared to me to be the artistic and vital New York I had been seeking.

In amusing reverse, the Gobert family regarded me, along with the playwright, the artist, and the rising young politician, as an asset in creating an "interesting atmosphere" about the Gobert system of schools and camps.

Upon her return to New York, I met the eldest Gobert sister, Mrs. Barkhouse, mother of Leonard, who had not been told of her son's escapade. A magnificent matriarch, obviously the dominant member of the Gobert dynasty, a force in local politics and philanthropies, she was the bell-sheep of a closely knit family. Her considerable wealth had not come from the school enterprises but from the small long-view investments of a rabbi's widow left with a brood of small children.

In the years ahead, G. B. Stern was to write a family saga, *The Matriarch*, purportedly inspired by the extraordinary Goberts.

Here even my negligible literary accomplishments were noteworthy. I was quite a frog in the small puddle in which I found myself.

Fortunately, this misconception sent me almost fanatically to my typewriter. I must work. I must read, shut myself away, and justify their blown-up version of me before they found me out for themselves.

I overheard Vera explain to a visitor: She shuts herself up in her room for hours and days without a sound, and then, all of a sudden, tap goes that typewriter as if something is driving her.

Something was. Something still is. The writer must be his own compulsion. He punches no time clock. He is his own slave driver in that lonely world in which he spends the greater part of his life.

Perhaps that rare bird, Genius, scarce as the whooping crane, parts easily with his thoughts. But for the run of the mill of us, we lay the lash upon ourselves.

Vera was right. Between the climax of *The Saturday Evening Post* acceptance and the descent back into the familiar death valley of rejection slips, I was writing as if something were driving me.

I imagine my teeth must have gritted while I slept. I was writing against time, against the possible disillusionment of this new little world I had managed to impress, against the realization that I could not indefinitely allay the restlessness of my parents for my return to Cates Avenue, against the realization that when a certain someone returned from overseas I would still be the nonentity he had met at Mount Clemens. And, above all, the growing fear that these tumultuous urges might be little more than a noise in the head, a pressing against the walls of the mind.

Even now, with the greater part of my life lived, these apprehensions still ride me. . . .

In the twenties of flaming youth, I, who was not conscious that they were to become historically "fabulous," wrote not of flaming youth but of old age which shrivels the body and, palsied, comes bearing the gift of wisdoms. I wrote and ultimately sold the story of a great-grandmother, wondering all the while whence I knew the distress of the old woman grieving beside a grandson's grave at Amiens. Another which mystified me, "Get Ready the Wreaths," subsequently a *Saturday Evening Post* story, was of a pair of Russian-born male twins and their early lives in a village called Minsk. I had never to my knowledge known anyone from Minsk, nor had I at the time delved into Russian literature. A woman living in New York's ghetto wrote me that I had resurrected both the happiness and horrors of her girlhood so vividly she had wept the night through after reading my story. How did I know so much about Minsk, down to the very street on which she had lived? Had I been there? Was I Russian?

Subconsciously, somewhere along the road I probably heard of Minsk, read of Minsk, saw pictures of Minsk, or as a child dropped off to sleep while my elders talked of Minsk, carrying Minsk into my dreams.

In any event, many are the times I have ventured to describe a place I have never seen and wait to verify it afterward, usually with few if any revisions of my preconceived version.

In *Back Street* I wrote a detailed description of the French spa, Aix-les-Bains. To be sure, I was already familiar with various European watering resorts, and for purposes of my story could have chosen one of those. But for some perverse reason, Aix-les-Bains it had to be, so I wrote out of my imagination. Upon completion of the book, I took a special trip there in order to verify the facts. After careful survey of Aix-les-Bains, I did not change a line.

In like manner, it so often seemed to me that I had known, somewhere, somehow, and long before, these multifarious moving masses that flow like sludge through the streets of the most heterogeneous metropolis in the world. Where? When?

An example in reverse involves a factual article entitled "No Food with My Meals," written at a later period, after I had started on the road to diet, and bought by Ray Long, editor of *Cosmopolitan Magazine*. Then he came asking me to insert bread into my list of nonfattening foods. His advertising staff insisted the magazine would lose important flour advertisers if he published an article eliminating bread in the diet. I explained to Mr. Long that a diet allowance of more than one thin slice of bread a day would invalidate my article, but I offered to take it back. In the end he decided to publish it unchanged and lost no accounts.

Ray Long stands in my memory as a man who rose and also fell by his own convictions. But more of him anon.

It was during this period that the first of what was to be an extraordinary series of letters arrived from Dr. Barkhouse. The strange tortures of Leonard Barkhouse! Now the late Leonard Barkhouse.

Dear Fannie-Tate-Marjorie-Hurst, I am back in my prison of invisible bars (he refers to his obsessive stepmother). To have encountered someone as special and young and vital as I am dull, prematurely aged, and tired is more than I had a right to expect. For almost the first time in my adult life, I felt excitement in my blood again after meeting you, and the desire to be fleet. Never mind what you did to me, what you are doing to me, what you probably will continue to do to me, I will see to it that I never see you again. What you have done I despise, but it was born out of an exuberance of one who can never wither in spirit as I have withered. Don't think I don't love you. I love what you did for me those few brief ridiculous hours, despite the insult and cheapness of what followed. I cannot believe that further cheapness would lead you to betray that I am writing to you and will continue to write you. This I shall do from time to time, as the humiliation that I should have been the butt of your monkeyshines lessens. But only if you do not reply. Your tolerance of my letters will be indicated by your silence. If you answer them, I shall disappear in a wisp of smoke, which is doubtless what I have already done in your esteem.

These letters, arriving at uneven intervals, took on a rainbow variation of poetic flight, slanting more and more toward moods of melancholy, frustration, and souring philosophy, perhaps even to his premature death.

During these years he was writing a biography of Michel de Montaigne, philosopher, which his death left two thirds completed. Apparently, the long shadow across the history of his race lay also across his mind. His scholarship was enormous and his broodiness something to dread. It was not unusual for me to hold his letters for days before submitting to their dual fascination and depression.

Nevertheless, coming as they did from a man of his erudition, they gave me almost a sense of personal achievement, impelling me to drive myself harder and faster.

Vera said: I feel sorry for that poor old typewriter of yours. Mama wrote: Don't be stuck in the mud, the little while longer you will be in New York. The Goberts are nice people. Mingle with their friends and get something out of it. I warn you, your father is approaching the end of his patience and I as usual am the one to bear the brunt.

This from home put even more pressure upon me. Small irrelevancies hung like low clouds in my mind. Mental pictures flashed. Papa on a Sunday afternoon, asleep after heavy midday dinner in his straight chair, his newspaper covering his face. Mama and the ladies over an afternoon *Kaffeeklatsch*. The whirring of crickets in the black silence after ten o'clock at night, when Cates Avenue had retired and Mama and Papa had closed their door and I sat looking out into the blackness, wondering about the people on our street—the monotonous days behind and ahead of them and me. Mrs. Massey across the street, who did everything the same hour every day, so that we could tell the o'clock by her movements. She hated her husband—told Mama so—and there they were, lying side by side in the black monotony of Cates Avenue—there I would be, only lying by nobody's side, and looking into the blackness and wondering. . . .

I thought, above all, of the long miles of rails between the still house on Cates Avenue and the high-stooped one on Lexington Avenue.

Little wonder Vera said: I feel sorry for your typewriter. How you race.

I was racing against return!

World events high as Himalayas had formed around me during this period. Yet I write primarily of one grain of sand, of a life, mine, being lived. That is my purpose. Not the anatomy of my times or my world, that has been done, is being done, and will be done over and over again, but the anatomy of the processes of the human being I know best, or should, because I have lived with her all my life, just as I will die with her and with her go into my eternity.

Thus, with a world war and the twenties raging around me, I was young, hungry, and egocentric. To a degree I was wanting everything. Me. Me. Me.

I was walking these days, not with world consciousness, not with deeply stirred social consciousness, but with old women in black wigs, machine-stitched down the middle, whom I encountered sitting on stoops in New York's ghetto. I was walking with the slum's shouting children, born or imported into a hurdy-gurdy world which was to separate them by language and cultures from their bearded and shawled parents behind the pushcarts.

I had not sufficient vision at the time to alert myself to the significance of this boiling mixture of races, cultures, colors. Out of this amalgam had come, and was to come, not the Americanized but the American people.

The impact of my desegregation from Cates Avenue threw me into another form of segregation. The world events swirled, but for weeks on end I walked within the boundaries of New York's Lower East Side, among a new people in the making. America was being carried forward in those black-windowed tenements, in Chinatown streets the shape of a crooked finger, in little Italy. The fat wide-kneed women with babies in the sag between those knees, the haggling men, the dark Easterners, the polyglot Europeans were fighting for their futures against the dour background.

Meanwhile, Mama's daily letters brought me her news, chiefly of engagements or marriages among those I knew or knew about. Always with the alarmed undertone of why-not-you?

Why not me, indeed? The consuming fact was, I had work to do. Who said that I had work to do? Not my parents. Not my circumstances. The monkey on my back said I had work to do. But why the consuming passion, the crazy compulsion?

I thought sometimes wishfully of the pursuit of marriage and children, of Mama and Papa fulfilled and being carried forward by me. Then of the alternative, sweating it out by the slow torture of creating life by way of the printed page.

Would I choose the same if I had my life to live over again?
Yes.

When I break it down into its component parts—the unending frustrations of the creative writer, his chronic state of reaching, frequently with an arm too short to touch his objectives, the harassments, the inner sense of failure—the grass does occasionally seem greener in what appear to be the more peaceful pastures of the woman who answers at the voting polls: Housewife.

The artist walks a lonely road whose end is ever beyond the horizon. The writer drops each book as a milestone, then dips pen once more into himself and sets out again toward that treacherous mirage—out there.

Not even success, popular or precious, is sufficient. The mirage still dances. The writer flogs himself toward the ever-receding light. . . .

Back there in Miss Gobert's apartment overlooking the cattle cars, I was flogging myself, while Mama's letters were saying: Irma Roth announced her engagement today to Fred Blum from Moberly, Missouri. Excellent match. He is in his father's wholesale grocery business. She is eleven months younger than you. Sometimes I feel so blue I could cry my eyes out. Love and kisses, Mama.

A few weeks later, this from Mama: . . . I feel the time has come for you to know. Your father is not well. He has shortness of breath and tires very easily. The doctor watches him for fear of a heart attack. Papa does not say much anymore about your return, but just the same you are helping make him into an old man. He has decided to retire from the business and when he does that you may know he is not well. If anything happens to him, that will be the end of me. What I will do with him around the house all day, I do not know. He is selling his two-thirds interest in the business to Sanborn, who already owns one third. It will be one of those pay-out arrangements. Now I have told you and you can decide for yourself. The enclosed check is for your railroad fare, in case what you have earned is running low. Your father has fits if I suggest it, but if I had my say I would write those *Saturday Evening Post* people what I think about them for not publishing your story. We are ashamed for the people.

I returned to St. Louis shortly after. Except for loss of weight, Papa looked quite himself. But now he remained in bed considerably later than I could ever remember, and there were bottles and boxes of capsules on his night table.

Mama had met me at the station and cried all the way home and told me not to let on to Papa that his weakness and loss of weight indicated that forces not yet diagnosable were at work in him. The doctor did not say more than that, sobbed Mama, and I am afraid to ask. All I know is that your father is failing. Fannie, don't leave us, we may not have him for long. . . .

It so happened that Papa still had a few years ahead. Too few, of course, but as his doctor advised me on this visit home: Your father may live on for quite some time, even longer than some of us younger fellows. But I am afraid his happy years are over.

This last hit. My father's happy years that had never been happy enough were over.

I doubt if I realized even then what it was going to mean to my father, so active over the long years, to be suddenly cast into the sidelines, marooned in a small house with Mama and her world of minutiae. Face to face with what I know now was his realization that his days were numbered, he must have been distraught about Mama's future, for which he had provided financially, but for whom he could provide no emotional stability: Watch over your mother, was about all he ever intimated to me. I won't always be here.

Mama lived for five years after Papa's death, but in a manner of speaking it could be said she died the day he did.

I remained at home several months, long enough to realize that Papa's illness was slow-paced. Long before my return to New York his doctor had advised me to go: Your presence here, when your father knows your interests are in the East, will keep him apprehensive about his condition. This was true. Papa now actually urged me to return to New York, because doubtless he saw how sporadic my writing was, and my restlessness must have been out all over me.

I left the house only on errands or to consult the doctor. Mama and Papa had suddenly become my children, dependent on me to make decisions for them. Mama, for all her one-time high-handedness, was saying more and more frequently: I'll ask my daughter, she knows about such things.

Most of my spare time I spent before the typewriter, but chiefly with idle hands. "Power and Horse Power" had now finally appeared in print. The need to deliver in short order a follow-up story plagued me. Life was quickening but somehow I was not. *The Saturday Evening Post* forwarded me a batch of applause letters, two literary agents wanted appointments, the St. Louis *Post-Dispatch* interviewed me, and a front-page story not unlike the Neal Patterson spread appeared—Fannie Hurst, St. Louis girl, scores success.

Papa read and reread it and the letters, and Mama's exaggeration mounted. But even so, excitement in our house, compared to what it might have been, was mitigated by the slow, sure slippage of the man in the easy chair with the coverlet across his knees.

Our little house, so ordered, so spick, so span, was packed with Mama's apprehension. A dozen times a morning she was in and out of Papa's room, where he sat reading his newspaper or sleeping in his chair: Sam, don't you want a little custard? Sam, are you tired? Sam, let me feel your head, you look feverish. Sam, why do you sit that way, just staring? Does something hurt you? Sam,

Fannie will run to the drugstore and get you some of those milk tablets Mrs. Moss says are so good for that tired feeling. Sam, how do you feel?

Wretched at being trapped on Cates Avenue, I bent far backward with sense of guilt. People were beginning to appraise me to Mama and Papa as their "wonderful daughter." And over the telephone, when Mama thought I was well out of hearing, she would run on something like this:

In all your life, Mrs. Moss, you never saw such an attentive child. All her writing has stopped and you wouldn't believe how they are after her in New York for more stories. No, it seems she just can't think when she is on Cates Avenue. You know how it is with artists. But now her father's slightest wish is all she thinks about. If I do say so myself, she is a child in a thousand.

Oh yes, I was a child in a thousand. Caught in the paradox of loving these two, yet like a hunted animal eying every egress from their home. Mama and Papa must have sensed something of this. But they did not talk about it to the Mrs. Mosses.

Another letter came, this time bearing a blurred French postmark: Dear Fannie, All these months longer and yet here I am. But it is fine that I am able to do things for the boys while over here. It is surprising how many of them enjoy the best in music. The Maestro has taken over my more advanced pupils in New York, which is a great thing for them and I fear they will not be so happy at my return. When that will be, I do not know. I hope it will not be too long and that we will meet soon again, wherever you are.

Again, scarcely a letter to ignite a young lady.

I fought on with my guilt, showering Mama and Papa with attention as my desire to be on my way quickened.

Mama said: Your father's improvement began the day you returned.

Papa said: Your mother is a different woman now that you are home.

Aunt Jennie wrote: Rose, this is the time for you to join the club, no matter what Fannie says. All Hamilton is talking about her story, and the same must be true of St. Louis. We brag enough, Bettie overdoes it. I do not speak to Madelaine Lederman. She said it was a good story, she guessed, but without Fannie's name on it she would not have read it through. I always said she was an ignoramus. We are sick at heart over the Jeffry Saffire affair. What a catch. And now this writing may scare men off instead of attract them. What is she waiting for? She is not getting any younger. You already had Fannie at her age. I am saving my necklace of oriental pearls for her. They have been in a safe deposit so long and they lose their glow if not worn against flesh. . . .

Even Mama and Papa had a good laugh over this. Papa said: That *Gensbebla* is crazy. Mama said: Fannie should never have a worse enemy.

The exchange of notes with J.S.D., very widely spaced, continued desultory. The quotes are from both his and mine.

. . . hope to see you soon . . . let me know when your stories will appear and where? There is quite a variety of American magazines in the barracks. . . . How near the front do you get? . . . This season of the year makes me homesick for New York and my studio. . . . My father is ailing, but improving. . . . When will this terrible war end? . . . It will be good to return to America after the long time and resume teaching and the compositions Joseffy and I were working on when the war broke. . . .

When Mama remarked to a friend who was an organizer of local music events that I had a friend who was associated with the great Joseffy, she replied: My daughter went to school in Switzerland with his daughter, a very pretty girl, if one can judge by class pictures.

Joseffy had a daughter about my age! New miseries overtook me. What if . . .

I turned to my typewriter for the sedation of work for the two months longer I remained at home and, with accelerated intensity, began a short story that ultimately was to bring a telegram of acceptance and congratulations from *The Saturday Evening Post*.

Toward the conclusion of that long Interlude-St. Louis came a pedestrian little note in an onionskin foreign-postmarked envelope. But there was a postscript: You are such a darling.

Papa was now taking slow walks, going to the barber or bank, and Mama had resumed *Kaffeeklatsches*.

At long long last, with Mama's hardy perennial cry of anguish ringing in my ears and Papa's quiet face etched into my conscience, I returned to New York.

In the years to come I was to ride and ride those rails between St. Louis and New York.

This time, following my return to New York, the deluge! Acceptances from three major magazines within a week. Editors bidding against one another, my price quadrupling and then on up. Bids for more stories.

The false armistice came and went, and then the real.

Next thing I knew I was dining with J.S.D. once a week.

Meanwhile, the apartment for older girls, along with the school and camp, had proved too much for Miss Gobert and she had discontinued it.

One of the Baltimore girls, Dorothy Barney, a newly graduated interior decorator, and I rented an apartment in Greenwich Village. A long railroad one of six rooms. A walkup in a four-story structure with a tailor shop on the ground floor. The woman from whom we sublet it furnished, a writer of children's stories, leased it to us at low rental for a period of six months.

Pleasantly furnished after a miscellaneous fashion, it boasted mahogany highboy, mahogany gateleg table, convex American Eagle mirror, brass andirons, spool bedsteads, cane-seated rockers, oval-framed ancestor. Dorothy labeled it mongrel Early American.

My bedroom overlooked a barren back yard, ironically dominated by a tree of heaven which had somehow survived the soot. Beginning about June, the summer garden of an adjoining restaurant emitted sounds and smells. At one time or another, O. Henry and David Belasco had lived in our old structure. Would anyone ever say Fannie Hurst lived there? queried my ridiculous ego solemnly.

Dorothy was a dour girl, older than I, well off financially by way of an inheritance from her parents, but embittered by homeliness and loneliness.

She once told me, after what was probably a fit of resentment against me inspired by my rosy turn of events, that she alternately hated and liked me. I understood and was thenceforth careful to withhold bright circumstances calculated to increase her desolation, about which she did little but brood.

Like Papa, I was slow to resentment, would compromise to almost any extent to avoid conflict. I am not sure that this is good. We might have helped Mama and her tempers had we been less submissive to them. Likewise, I might have helped Dorothy had I reasoned rather than deferred, as I became more and more the victim of her moods.

But at the time success was moving in on me and it seemed to me I could afford to be magnanimous. Often, as I typed in my room and a telephone call came from an editor eager for a story, or a magazine arrived containing one with my name attached, I curbed the impulse to rush to Dorothy with the tidings.

Jack and I were not yet at the stage where we were telephoning each other frequently or seeing one another more than once or at most twice a week. When we met, usually at a small table d'hôte restaurant or, conforming to his love of elegance, occasionally at an expensive dining place, he could not know that the days and nights between our time together were interludes of waiting.

Had I understood him better at this time, I would have been spared much of the anguish of uncertainty. The world was opening up for me, and his care not to thrust himself between it and me, his insistent self-effacement through the years, was obsessive.

I would leave him after dinner with a sense of emptiness and defeat. Where did I stand?

Weeks passed, then the months, our periodic evenings uninterrupted, except on those occasions when the Maestro asked him to a musical function or to accompany Miss Joseffy to one. I never inquired further, but at the mention of her name joy ran out of my fingertips, just as it did when I reflected that day after day young ladies dropped into his studio for lessons, and he sat close beside them at the keyboard.

Through him I came indirectly to know about the "musical greats" and also to realize that I would be meeting them personally, except for Miss Joseffy, whom it was his custom to accompany to these functions and whose photograph, as I once saw it in a magazine, was more than disturbingly pretty—and slim.

He was a first-rate playmate, a combination of humor and the intimation of melancholy characteristic of the Russian people.

In a crazy kind of way, our relationship was what I wanted it to be. In another, a source of despair. I was happy, I was intoxicatingly in love but uncommitted. The *bête noire* of my life, up to this present, has been my inability to arrive at quick and sure decisions. In this relationship I had not been called upon to make one.

That it could not go on that way did not trouble me. Head over heels in the throes of writing, head over heels in love, heady with my young successes, sufficient unto the day . . .

From the point of view of worldly appraisal, it could be said that I was a successful writer in my early twenties.

The round-trip processions of my manuscripts had not only ceased, but I was being wooed by one first-rate magazine after another. Publishers offered contracts and advance monies on my first book. Inevitably, since in America even a budding author immediately becomes an accredited authority on practically everything from the venation of fern fronds to Shinto philosophy, I was invited to address organizations, cut ribbons for the opening of new bookstores, speak to short-story classes, before my own techniques were beyond the toddling stage.

Bob Davis, who remained my mentor, kept me to a straight and narrow path of awareness: It is one thing to achieve success and another to hold it. Once you have it, all your lifetime your job is going to demand all you have to give it. You can't short-change it. Success, at your age, is rare and dangerous. Don't take yourself at bandwagon evaluations. Look inward and like what you see.

Papa remained true to type: Don't allow all this to turn your head. Knowledge is power.

Marion Reedy said: Don't overread. Rub shoulders with people. Soak yourself in human nature. People are your talent. Write them and write them and keep away from authors and author-patter.

This last was an easy matter. I was in awe of authors. I still am. I know few. I have always known few.

Mama said: I guess your stories are worth it, or they wouldn't pay all that money for them. You'll soon be able to buy and sell your father.

In the days when we began to talk of our future together, Jack said: Whatever you want, I want. A conviction from which he was never to deviate.

In the inevitable regrets of aftermath, I find myself asking again and again: Without me, might he have gone on to the pianistic heights of which I and so many believed him capable? Could a more skillful woman have prodded him on? Was I too fearful of hounding him? Was I overprotective? Yet who knew his sensitivities as well as I? Only once did he ever explain to me, and that was back at our beginning, that a concert career would be the most acute anguish conceivable to him. Even to accompany his pupils at their annual recital was a form of torture. His beautiful tone and technique, which he tirelessly developed at home and in his studio, were never heard beyond those walls. I became keeper of a secret—my husband's outstanding virtuosity.

Rafael Joseffy once said a fanciful thing to me. Danielson's Chopin! He plays it as if it were finest lace.

It was ironic and paradoxical that a man of Jack's generosity was congenitally unable to share his talent with the world.

In the beginning, when I pressed him to conquer this handicap, his face would become crimson and he would beg me not to ask it of him, nor could he bear even to discuss it.

Of course it was selfishly better for me that he chose as he did. I had him so much more to myself. Even his music belonged privately to me. This indictment of my selfishness is softened only by the fact that Joseffy shared my conviction that with or without me Jack would never have gone on to the concert stage, which to him was a guillotine.

In those early years, three quiet and memorable men, Papa, Jack, and one whom I shall not mention, stood at my elbow. Three quiet and memorable men! And Mama, not so quiet.

I wonder if any given era shows its pattern to the generation living it. Historians look back, sometimes down their noses, evaluate and tag, but from the perspective of time. Stone Age. Golden Age. Gay Nineties. Mauve Decade. Fabulous Twenties.

If the twenties were fabulous, I was too busy living them to realize to what extent the decade was to be typed by the flapper, Scott Fitzgerald, bobbed hair, knee-high skirts, the black bottom, Prohibition, the speakeasy, depression and breadlines.

Meanwhile, men like John Dos Passos, Ernest Hemingway, Floyd Dell, Sinclair Lewis were serving up the ferment of their times.

I was in, but not exactly of, that era. The speakeasy world I knew by hearsay. All about us in Greenwich Village basement doors, come evening, began to open warily to those devotees of the bent elbow who gave the proper code ring of the bell. According to the tailor on the ground floor, a group of writers on our street, including an author who was to skyrocket to fame as a major interpreter of those twenties, came staggering down our street dawn after dawn, only to land crashingly among the milk bottles.

I was to meet most American top-line authors of that era, but with two or three exceptions we passed one another in the night. Some of them were more than my peers, and perhaps a sense of inferiority froze me. But even where I was not disturbed by any such feeling I did not seem to know how to fraternize.

To be sure, American writers are scattered far and wide over the face of the country, indeed over the world. But even in New York, where so many coagulate, camaraderie among themselves is not particularly characteristic.

Whatever of literary coteries may have existed in New York in those combustible twenties, I had no part in them. Ultimately I was to be asked to dine often with amusing and cultivated people. I could scatter pages with the names of the literati, great and near great, and with literary bon vivants like Charles Hanson Towne, Frank Crowninshield, Rutger Bleeker Jewett, Condé Nast, many of them not much more than acquaintances, a few of them close friends.

At a carefully preserved and reserved distance, I knew Edna St. Vincent Millay and Willa Cather, who, if they regarded me at all, must have thought of me as a mute. What ailed me was awe. The beautiful Scott Fitzgerald added a disorderly note to a dinner I gave for Zona Gale. Edgar Lee Masters, Rupert Hughes, and Rebecca West were there that night, and also William Beebe and Vilhjalmur Stefansson, the explorer.

But events such as this were rare. In the main, down to this present, I run with the anonymous public, hot and bothered about it most of the time, but happiest with my long-time friend, the crowd.

This world, absorbing me day and night, claiming my time and interest, leaving me footsore and often heartsore at the end of a day, was far removed from the alleged "fabulous" goings on of the decade and the revolution of manners and morals of the post-world-war-one period.

No question but what this generation was kicking up its high heels, demanding wider freedoms. These first manifestations—girls smoking, bobbing their hair, going in for bathtub gin and all-night automobile rides with their returned doughboys—were the concern of the moralists of the twenties, just as premarital relations and juvenile crime are the concern of today.

So far as Dorothy and I were concerned, our Waverly Place might have been Waverly Planet. All around us artists and writers forgathered in the basement restaurants and bars, and worked in the skylight studios, some of them already arrived or on their way. Floyd Dell, Edna St. Vincent Millay, Mary Heaton Vorse, Max

Bodenheim, Sadakichi Hartmann, Boardman Robinson, Alfred Kreymborg, George Bellows, Max Eastman.

But they were only part of the hearsay of our neighborhood. The café life of so-called Bohemia remained as legendary to me as if viewed from our front porch in St. Louis.

After I had moved from the neighborhood, Vilhjalmur Stefansson, who lived in the Village although he seemed strangely miscast there, took me several times to one of the well-known haunts, "Romany Marie's" basement restaurant, run by a picturesque Romanian woman. We sat at bare tables with monograms carved into them, ate ninety-cent table d'hôte dinners with a raffia-wrapped bottle of pale red wine thrown in, listened to a Village poet named Bobbie Edwards strum a guitar for gratuities, heard a great deal of arty patter from one table to another. Stef drank his fourth glass of weak tea, Romany Marie began to move from table to table reading palms, itinerant habitués, bearded young men and bob-haired girls sat endlessly at the bare tables lighted by a candle in a bottle, drinking beer or the pale innocuous wine, exchanging the patter of their professions or jobs, seldom more than groggy.

So much for the Bohemia I knew, or did not know.

I wonder what Jack and I talked about during our evenings together in restaurants. Not music. I did not reveal my limitations. Not books. Perhaps Jack, who was not a profound reader, also had his reasons for detouring around my subject. Alas, not *l'amour*. Both of us mutely heart-hungry for one another, we sat it out through the months. . . .

It did occur to me that part of the static situation between us might be due to financial considerations.

I wanted him to know, with a lack of realism that was always to be countered by his clear practicality, that it would not matter. We could make out! An attic with him . . . I envisioned sophomorically.

As a matter of fact, it need not have been an attic. Even without my growing earning capacity, his own was well beyond the average in a generally underpaid profession. Years before I met him, he had been the support of a father, a sister, and a brother-in-law, all fastidious people of no small demands, who had found adjustment to a new world difficult. Even then he had managed to accumulate limited real estate and security holdings.

Once, during one of the indeterminate occasions when Papa was protesting our marriage, Mama, so torn between us, exclaimed: Does it occur to you, Sam, that you did not have one third as much as this young man when you married me?

I would have liked to convey to Jack during those apprehensive early days that, come what might, no deprivation in my life could equal the deprivation of not having him in it. Romantic, immature, and out of a schoolgirl's book? Perhaps.

Papa wrote admonishingly: I advise you to send your earnings home and I will bank them for you. Remember, success has its day and while it lasts we tend to lose sight of the rainy day.

That rainy day! Papa and Mama, it seemed to me, had allowed themselves too little enjoyment of the sunny ones, which were obscured for them by the rainy days to come.

My wants have always been few, therefore Mama's contention was that I did not know the meaning of comfort. By that I suppose she must have meant I did not crave or miss the luxuries.

But when Papa began reminding me by mail of that "rainy day" which had been so inculcated into me, I began to want to want more.

I desired no part of their rainy-day consciousness, particularly in a postwar world which had seen security go up in gunsmoke.

In my safe-deposit box these many years later is a packet of elegantly engraved worthless documents, "securities" left me by my father, who had saved for them for that rainy day.

Regardless of security, I knew, or thought I knew, what I wanted, even if it meant a narrow room in that tall brown house on Lexington Avenue, or worse. Besides, with my own growing earning capacity, it would not be necessary.

Despite Mama's and her two sisters' familiar variations on the theme of a girl "marrying well," my romanticism continued to smack of delayed adolescence. A loaf of bread, a jug of water, not even wine if need be, and thou.

Nor did the special hazards of the woman who outearns her husband occur to me, although I was promptly to learn that in the case of a sensitive man this situation requires supersensitive handling.

My formula for the success I achieved in meeting this problem I offer to no one, because our situation was on the exception side of the rule. Also, it developed that my enormous ineptitude in business and finance was to prove an asset.

In the beginning, with no sense of this, but because of my undiluted trust, I turned over my affairs in their entirety to Jack, and for the long and wonderful years ahead for us was to leave them to his successful and unquestioned management.

Yet all this time preceding our marriage I remained on the sharp horns of a dilemma. How could I be certain marriage would not clip my wings? Besides, I had realistic reasons for shrinking from it. The marriage with which I was most familiar, Mama's and Papa's, was good enough as things go, but certainly unwanted by me.

Mama was characteristically sharp, analytical, and intuitive: You don't know your own mind. You are making monkeys of us all, including your Jack. You torture us until we consent and then all of a sudden, after I have exhausted myself working over your father, you find excuses to put things off.

But in those beginning days, when Jack and I were sitting, still impersonally, across our table d'hôte red-wine dinners, I was not yet in the deep waters of indecision.

Letters from home kept me troubled and uncertain: . . . it is true your father seems at times to be better . . . but doctor or no doctor, I know he is failing . . . come home. . . .

Occasionally, when a letter oppressed me more than usual, I would mention it to Jack. His reactions frightened me: While my father and older sister and brother were living, I never left them. I owed them everything. They came to America only for my sake. I was young and they did not like the look of future Russia.

Not a word of what my possible return to St. Louis would mean to him. He baffled me. I did not understand at the time that it was the way he was put together. He was thinking of Mama and Papa and wanting me to think and feel for them, but, as he was to tell me later, he was thinking even more of what my leaving New York would mean. . . .

It was blessed circumstance that one as unperspicacious as I had at least the vision to look into the deep quiet of this man and want him for my own. . . .

I received a letter from a Miss Sonya Levein, an editor of the *Metropolitan Magazine*, inviting me to lunch. I had read about her. Russian-born, young, and quite a beauty, she had hoisted herself out of the slums of New York. It was she who had enticed Theodore Roosevelt to become associate editor of the *Metropolitan Magazine*. Sinclair Lewis, whose *Main Street* was yet to come, was reputedly her suitor. From time to time my stories had made the round trip to her and back.

During the first fifteen minutes of our luncheon she offered me a contract for twelve short stories at three thousand dollars each: Think it over. Meanwhile, I want to take you back to the office and have you meet Carl Hovey, our editor-in-chief. He is as keen as I am about your work. I am acting as his envoy.

This was happening to me! In my mind I was already writing it to Mama and Papa as I followed Miss Levein in a daze. I was already telling Jack, fearful somewhere in the back of my mind that the figures might be as intimidating to him as they were to me.

Carl Hovey returned to the offices about five minutes after our arrival there, accompanied by Sinclair Lewis. It was obvious that both these men were avid for Sonya. I felt fifth-wheel, overweight and self-conscious.

You did not remain constrained for long with Lewis around. Prankish as a boy, he suddenly grabbed my hand and for some reason broke into Irish dialect:

God bless young talent, he said, there's nothing the equal of it. See to it, lass, you make them pay well for it.

Hovey, it transpired, had also been making Lewis a literary offer across a luncheon table. Lewis, irrepressible, knew neither restraint nor inhibition. Let's stand together, Fannie. Don't let a pair of slick editors seduce us. . . . How much did she offer you?

I had been offered three thousand dollars a short story for twelve of them and the author of the most talked about book in America, and for all I knew in Europe, was calling me Fannie and bracketing me as a fellow writer!

Dear Mama and Papa, I kept scribbling to myself, hold fast . . .

Jack, what do you think! Hold fast . . .

The immense talent of this lean redheaded fellow, in the field where I so humbly labored, filled me with awe.

Suddenly he slapped Hovey on the shoulder: Let's go out on the town tonight, the four of us. Your offer at its present figure doesn't interest me a dime's worth, but I'll buy you a dinner. What do you say, Fannie? We'll get him to feeling no pain and pry open that tight fist of his. . . . I know the right places. Eleven and a half West Forty-fifth Street at eight. Knock three times and ring once. When the little window in the door opens, just show your teeth.

Before I could even reply, he made ready to depart.

It was my evening with Jack.

For a split second I hesitated, but only for a split one.

I'm sorry—but I have another engagement.

Break it, he countered instantly.

I—can't. Thank you.

My loss, he said nonchalantly. Well, I guess the showdown between Hovey and me must come sooner or later. It did. Sonya married Hovey.

I stood silent and torn, while arrangements for the evening were concluded. Jack would have understood. He would have wanted me to go. He would postpone—but that would mean longer for me to wait.

I dined with him as usual at our little table, with the pink wine which we scarcely ever touched.

In retrospect, how glad I am that I chose as I did that day. It gave me one more evening with him, in the long sequence of them that lay ahead.

I did not realize it then, or, realizing, did not admit it, but I was having my cake and eating it too. The status quo I enjoyed with Jack was what I wanted. I knew his interests and his activities the evenings we were not together, and that I was playing a more and more important role in his way of life and thoughts. That kept me buoyed up, excited, and happy. Also, free to carry on the long hours of writing and the many other interests that were accruing.

Charles Hanson Towne, editor, man-about-town, bon vivant, had taken me under his wing. Through him I was meeting some of the literary lights, almost all of them considerably older than I, some few my contemporaries, none younger. Henry and Agnes Leach, the John O'Hara Cosgroves, Wallace Irwin, Mary Austin, Gertrude Atherton, Cosmo and Clayton Hamilton, Carl Van Vechten, Edna Millay, Elinor Wylie, John Farrar, Irvin Cobb, Kathleen and Charles Norris, Glenway Wescott, Christopher Morley.

For the most part they were passing panorama. Withdrawn and indrawn, I had little or no technique for following up a meeting with a person or personality who attracted me. I was shy of the "great," fearful of seeming sycophantic, terribly concerned when the stature of their work towered above mine. Thus I remained off the main stem of the "literary life" of the big city.

I was to know later that this so-called literary life was largely a mirage. American authors mingle less than those in European countries. Our literary coteries seem to lack proper coagulation. In the last few years the American chapter of the group formidably named "Penmen, Essayists and Novelists" has gained strength, but even now can scarcely be regarded as a potential literary force. The forty-year-old Authors' League of America stands by to advise and hold our wrists when we tend to sign recklessly on the dotted line for the contractual rights to the words sweated from our literary brows.

The Algonquin Hotel "Round Table," a loosely assembled group of pundits, wits, wags, versifiers, critics, and a minority of literary figures of stature, met daily for good cheer, good talk, and libation, and probably represented the intellectual focal point of the town.

Dorothy Parker, Alexander Woollcott, Heywood Broun, H. L. Mencken shone there. Out-of-town visitors came to lunch at the Algonquin, vying for tables in proximity to the mighty "Round" one, hoping to overhear the crackle of wit or the reverberation of the alleged Olympian thunder of the literati. The thunder, however, consisted largely of witticisms of local vintage, epigrams, and sophisticated patter, gone now with the wind of that day's repartee and reportage.

Mama wrote: Since you are meeting so many writers, how is it you never mention being at that hotel with the Indian name where they are all supposed to eat? Why don't *you* eat there? When Mrs. Pulliam and Polly were in New York, their relatives took them to that hotel to see the writers eat. They kept looking for you.

Heywood Broun, critic who towered in the twenties and was to die too early, corroded, one could imagine, by frustrations, said to me when I was being introduced to him by Charley Towne: Call me up at the office someday and I'll take you to the Algonquin for lunch.

I shied away. This was the glib, smiting-word-at-any-price set, for which I had no talent.

Ironically, the authors I most admire seem to be the ones I know least. Neither, I confess, am I sought out by them. There are certain writers in this category, presently living within one, ten, or twenty-five-mile reach, whom I read, think about, and admire. Yet it would never occur to me to seek them out.

Where are the great literary friendships of yesteryear? Wordsworth and Coleridge, Emerson and Carlyle, George Bernard Shaw and Sydney Webb.

Charles Hanson Towne, who himself wrote brightly and inconsequentially, was gregarious to a degree. With his multiple gifts as raconteur, mime, and humorist, he was court jester to the social and *Who's Who* worlds alike. As we moved into what was to be a long rich friendship, Charley was for taking me about. I dreaded these invitations and yet when I refused or offered an excuse I felt equally frustrated.

I was happier in the surging swarms. The lusty life of the heterogeneous city seemed to flow over and into me. The bluish dead-faced murals of people with the unseeing stares, sitting in rows in subways, were more eloquent, it seemed to me, than the processed epigrams of the wits of the Round Table could ever be. I had chosen my jungle or perhaps it had chosen me. Somewhere in there lurked for me some of the truths and the meanings or the meaninglessness of the way we are. . . .

Occasionally, as these conflicts hammered away, doubt moved into me. Would I, after all, be better off working in the flat quiet of Cates Avenue? Here in the metropolis I wanted everything and I wanted little. I felt torn and confused. Yet, despite the confusions, here was quick life all about me. Here I stepped out of my apartment into the pounding vitality of millions.

But breaking the millions down into the individual, into the one you sat beside at an impersonal gathering, was another matter. The big concept became a man with a throbbing Adam's apple, who nudged your knee beneath the table while he asked: Why should a big good looking girl like you bother to work for a living?

This would not have made sense to Charley Towne, who had graduated from copy-boy beginnings into the rarefied areas where a certain amount of erudition and bibulous camaraderie were open sesame.

One evening, years later, Charley telephoned me: By any chance are you free for dinner? I was.

Thank God! he exclaimed. Gertrude Atherton has just canceled our dinner engagement and I was afraid I was going to be alone.

Charley lived that way up to the end.

Strange that he should not have known how to be alone, because he had a strain of light, imaginative fantasy. One evening, strolling with him down the street on which I lived, a full moon of lovely pallor hung directly ahead over Central Park.

He stopped before an apartment house, and by white moonlight wrote fourteen lines on the back of an envelope, "To a Pale Nun," which was printed, reprinted, and included in anthologies.

After he had finished, he looked up and said: Emily Stevens lives in this house. I am glad I wrote it here. We must be standing beneath her fourteenth-story window now. I'll dedicate it to her.

For years he had been hopelessly in love with the beautiful unattainable star. He had never confided in me, but that evening, standing beneath her window, he did.

According to the next day's newspapers, it must have been at the very moment Charley was writing across the back of an envelope that, fourteen stories about him, Emily Stevens was committing the act of suicide that terminated her stormy and eventful life.

Charley's need to dine out the following evening and the following must have been imperative.

Now editors were crowding me. Bob Davis said: Keep your head. Do not tie up with any one magazine while they are bidding for you.

I wrote Marion Reedy. He replied in almost illegible longhand on a torn sheet of paper: Those New York editors get all the breaks. Spread your wares. Your faults lie in your style, but your style is good. You are nobody's disciple but your own. Keep free.

Jack said: Don't force.

The Saturday Evening Post was buying up stories it had once rejected. *Metropolitan*, of course, and *The Delineator*, although Mr. Dreiser was no longer editor, were offering contracts. Mr. Yard, editor-in-chief of *Century Magazine*, wanted a story, and *Red Book*, their bids soon silenced as the larger circulation periodicals began to compete.

It had no reality.

Papa wrote in his fine austere hand: You are a very young girl to be meeting with so much success. Needless to say, your mother and I are gratified. I consider it the finest thing that has happened in my lifetime. But I urge you to bear in mind that modesty and proper demeanor are needed now as never before. Remember, success does not necessarily last forever. Enjoy it, but build your character to meet life as it comes. Take care of your health, because not even success can take its place. People stop me on the street to congratulate me, and you can imagine your mother's pleasure in your daily letters. Your regularity is admirable. Your loving father.

In a strange way, Papa's rare communications came down like a clamp upon high spirits. What if, as Papa indicated, my new success should suddenly cease? When Jack kept saying: Don't force, was it because he knew that even hard work could not compensate for talent? What if it should happen that my arm was too short to reach the ring on the merry-go-round? There were one-book people. Flash-in-the-pan writers.

Nothing seemed to matter except grasping that ring.

To write was the be-all, end-all. Anything but happy, because Jack and I were no more to one another than just two people who looked excitedly and longingly across the barrier of a restaurant table, at the same time I wanted it that way! To hold everything that lovely yet frustrating way! Marriage was not for me, yet nothing short of marriage with Jack would be bearable.

Thus I teetered in a state of indecision that was to dog me in one form or another throughout my life.

This adventure of mine in sustained self-analysis must be important to me, or I cannot hope to make it seem important to anyone else. Thus my continuing state of indecision with regard to marriage to the man who seemed so indispensable to me was to baffle and make me un-understandable to myself as well as to those looking in upon the chemistry of me, fusing in its test tube.

Dear Fannie, No doubt you were surprised to receive my wire announcing your mother's sudden decision to visit you in New

York. For some time she has been concerned about the way you are living. The tailor shop you describe as below your apartment seems to cause her worry. I hope you will be able to keep her with you for at least a week. She needs the change and all is well here. I can imagine you were surprised to see Henry Hatfield. What happened was beyond my control. At the railway station, we discovered Henry was taking the same train to New York as your mother. I felt relieved that an old friend would be traveling with her. Suddenly, she suggested to Henry that they take a stateroom together. I had urged her to take one in the beginning, but she was unwilling to buy the two railroad tickets required for such accommodations. In the beginning Henry did not take her seriously, nor did I, but knowing your mother, he laughed and said: Fine, Rose, if it is all right with Sam. I will go to bed first, said your mother, ignoring my dislike of seeing her make herself small, and then you come in and get into the upper berth. Well, as you know, when your mother gets her head set there is no stopping her. I also felt it indiscreet for the looks of the thing. Naturally, once more I found it easier to give in than to argue. That is how your mother arrived in New York with Hatfield.

Poor Papa, I wish he could have reaped the fun out of it that Mama and Mr. Hatfield and I did.

Of course Mama was dismayed at what she found. To her, our old-fashioned railroad apartment over a tailor shop amounted to slum existence.

My daughter is not used to this from home, she explained to Dorothy, and I am sure you are not either. If this is the artistic way to live, I am glad I am not artistic.

But when Mama walked to the corner newsdealer and asked for ten copies of *The Saturday Evening Post*, as her daughter was in it, she made sure there were people to overhear.

Charley Towne, Churchill Williams of *The Saturday Evening Post*, and Bob Davis decided to entertain Mama with a luncheon at the old Brevoort at Washington Square. Her quick wit delighted them and, as usual, her stories about me were at my expense, causing me to squirm even while I feigned amusement.

I never knew Fannie to have system about anything except writing. She goes at that like clockwork, but always was a *schlomp* about the house. Her room looked like a cyclone had struck it after she went off to school. Bob Davis appropriated the word *schlomp*. He would telephone: I would like to speak to the *schlomp*.

I tell Fannie I wish she cared as much about me as she does about dogs.

No, there are no writers in either Mr. Hurst's or my family. I always say I can't spell, much less write.

I was torn between embarrassment and amazement at Mama's lack, with these men, of the inhibitions she displayed where her "rich relatives" were concerned.

This occasion is a great treat to me, she confided to them. It is doing more for me than those cocktails you men are drinking. You see, my husband is a wonderful person but not a man with whom you can laugh. As a child, Fannie stopped laughing when her father came home and so did I. Which is not to say Mr. Hurst was not good as gold, but gold is heavy.

At the conclusion of that luncheon, I was an open book, at least to three editors. A rather dull one.

The apartment in Waverly Place was a block away from a women's night court.

I visited it frequently, disturbed by the nightly haul of women off the streets, the men going unchallenged.

Hard-pressed as I was to keep Mama occupied during her visit, it would never have occurred to me to so much as mention my interest in this murky world or refer to my expeditions. But a chance remark from Dorothy set Mama's sensitive antennae waving. To my amazement, she expressed a desire to visit the court, to see, as she put it, how the other half lives.

It was not to be expected that the inequities involved in meting out punishment in this dual matter of prostitution were going to be apparent to Mama. I doubt if the phraseologies she was going to be exposed to in the courtroom had ever entered her experience. In addition there was the hazard that such a visit would only enhance her convictions concerning my New York environment.

But Mama was not to be sidetracked, and one evening Dorothy and Mama and I walked across to the women's night court.

Within the span of two hours, Mama heard words and phrases that had never crossed her lips dropped as a matter of course. Her expletives were constant. Never in my life! I wouldn't believe this if I wasn't hearing it! For two dollars, mind you—has she no shame?

Mama's virtue stuck out all over her: Only ten days in jail! She ought to be locked away permanently from all decent women. Walking the streets when she could be earning an honest living! Her reactions, alas, were typical of the secure woman whose compassion is buried beneath the hard veneer of untempted virtue. So many of the attitudes of Mama and Papa were reflected in that hard veneer. Little wonder that my own social consciousness was to awaken as languidly as a cat in the sun.

Negroes were all right in their place. They are happier where they are. I believe in giving an ex-convict his chance but I would never employ one. I wouldn't see an illegitimate child go hungry, but my own child doesn't have to associate with one.

When I ventured to suggest to Mama that the women hauled into night court had fallen low but what about the men, it takes two to make the bargain, she was aghast.

So you give them right? Well, if this is the kind of life you have to study in order to become a writer, the sooner you come home the better.

If this had only been Mama speaking! It was millions of her speaking.

As I feared, the trip to the courtroom convinced Mama that my environment was not only ugly but dangerous.

Part of the unconscious cruelty of virtue, however, was that Mama enjoyed it and made a pretext for returning to night court: I just want to make sure I can believe my eyes, or they won't believe me when I go back.

She would not relate it to Papa, that I knew. Wanting me home, she would still protect me from coming.

Then one evening we took her down to the great seethe of New York's Lower East Side. She had never seen the like before.

To think how people live! I have always said, she exclaimed in the key of enunciating a profound truth for the first time, one half of the world doesn't know how the other half lives!

The pushcart jungle of the Jewish ghetto brought out something atavistic in her of which she had not the slightest awareness. In all this dirt, she remarked, and among all these beards and shawls and *shidels,* there is something that—gives you the feeling that you have seen these people before. Mama had, back in yesterday's two thousand years.

Is there any excuse, she asked, looking up at the clotheslines flopping between tenements, for dirty wash on the line? At least water is plentiful down here among the poor.

Through some sort of mental lapse, she was delighted with the linguistic ability of the Italian children.

To think that little children can speak Italian so fluently! Don't touch anything, you might catch something. I never saw so many foreigners in my life.

On the way home, Mama said with elaborate casualness: By the way, speaking of foreigners, do you ever see anything of that Danielson you were so crazy about for a while?

Occasionally.

Funny you never mention him any more, or have me meet him.

I will.

Let sleeping dogs lie. I'm only glad you don't see him.

My meetings with Jack during this visit had been sporadic, our schedule shattered. He asked little or nothing about Mama, and I told him little or nothing. I shrank from asking him to face my family's disapproval, even if unspoken. Nor did I want to give Mama one more reason for pressuring my return to St. Louis.

But on the eve of her departure I telephoned and asked him to come and meet her. I knew too well he was intuitively aware of his status with my parents. I also knew how much I was asking and how his sensitive nature shrank from it. But I wanted this meeting to take place far from Papa's influence.

Actually, at this time there was nothing in our relationship to warrant my asking this of him, but I was driven by that inner something.

And so he came, and, as it was always to be through the years whenever he was in the presence of my parents, I was tense and on watch and not myself. I guarded against having him hurt and yet, by the very act of asking his presence where he sensed he was not welcome, I was hurting. . . .

But Mama, who knew me "like a book," realized nothing of this when Jack came to tea. Her general talk flowed volubly.

. . . wouldn't live in this town if you gave it to me—— What Fannie sees in it, compared to what she has at home, I don't know. . . .

Jack was playful and suggested to Mama that she take him back to St. Louis and leave me to the complicated maze of metropolitan life.

It was plain that Mama was taken with Jack, but eying him with caution.

What a handsome and distinguished man, she declared following his departure. Too bad he isn't American-born. How did he ever come to pick out music as his profession! You have to be a Paderewski to make a living out of it.

Jack sent Mama a corsage to the train. Mama repeated: Too bad he isn't American-born. I'll wager these orchids cost him a week's earnings. I'm grateful you're not stuck on him any more.

About this time we were mouthing the Coué philosophy that every day in every way we were getting better and better. Derby hats were not yet obsolete. Knee-high skirts and hip-low waists created a state of national shock. The dance emerged from under the enchantment of the Vernon Castle period and became sinuous. "Necking" was the new name for an old technique. An ancient institution known as the chaperon became extinct. The lending libraries had waiting lists for *Alice Adams, Miss Lulu Bett, Main Street,* and *If Winter Comes.*

But this is the touted twenties as seen looking backward over the shoulder. In the living, it was just my world. Life was like that.

When Mama and Papa and Aunt Jennie and Bettie called up the kind of world it was when they were young, it had little reality. I saw it chiefly as a kind of tintype. Family albums and black walnut whatnots. The bisque shepherd and shepherdess, relics of Grandma Koppel, that stood equidistant on our parlor mantelpiece.

To me, living through them, the American scene of the second decade of the century was the way things were. Mine not to reason why. Having been around not too long myself, I had no basis of comparison. Reading, of course, brought other eras, other times, other twenties close up. But they were not my reality.

So far as I was concerned, when Mama at forty said "in my day" she was speaking the remote idiom of the elderly. Mothers had not yet swung into the mass movement of vying with their daughters for youthful silhouettes. Mama would never have been mistaken for my sister. I would not have exchanged her! Far too heavy, in a baby-flesh, talcum-powder way, her broad shelf of bosom, guiltless of Greek uplift, had Mama-warmth.

My years of exposure to her darkness as well as her light have left me uncomplicated, unscarred. Worlds divided us but something deep and tribal united us. I rode her storm and stress and have bitterness about neither. Doubtless, fissures in my character are the result of my kind of upbringing, which did not boast too much rhyme or reason.

But not even from the horizontal of the psychiatrist's couch could I be brought to conclude that unconscious and deeply buried resentments toward either Mama or Papa are responsible for all the things I am or am not.

It is true I hated some of the first twenty years of my life. The going was lonely most of the time. But I loved Mama all of the time.

A chance acquaintance in an English railway carriage, a member of the peerage, once said to me in four unadorned words: I hate my mother. It was the first time I had heard such blasphemy uttered. Surely God would strike him dead. But God did not take action, and the lovely countryside through which we were riding kept smiling.

At this time I would not have admitted to what degree race heritage, which in the name of assimilation I chose to ignore, was the explanation for many of my attitudes. It was to take me almost half a lifetime of the Biblical three score and ten to evaluate properly the richness of that heritage.

All this was part of wanting to be in, as well as of, the twenties. I tried the externals. I bobbed my hair. I tried smoking. I sipped cocktails. I wanted to dance, but the dearth of dancing men in my life and my sense of overweight precluded this.

Neither the brief excursion into smoking nor the sipped cocktails took hold. I let them lapse and I was glad when my hair grew out and I could once more slick it back into the bun at the nape of my neck, where it has been ever since.

In review, it is interesting to note how little these phases of the twenties, which lent themselves so dramatically to fiction, were uppermost in my writing mind.

New York of that period, even after the rush of immigration deterred by a world war had slowed, was nevertheless still seething with the problems of assimilation sparked by previous immigration waves.

The schisms between the foreign parents and their American-born children were wide. Down in the boiling East Side, German-born, Russian, Irish, Jewish, Italian-born parents were rearing an Americanized, public-school-educated generation of children who spoke a language different from what they heard in their homes where their elders had not learned English.

The "fabulous twenties" cast little of their glitter over the scenes in which I spent so many hours. Here the sordid speakeasies and the forbidden "joints" of the slums functioned on a still lower level.

Here the grade of bathtub gin made beasts of the lost men of the Bowery, the boys and girls necked and smoked, drank and soaked their share of names into police blotters.

But there was another, less heralded, phase of life going on below Fourteenth Street. Night schools, Cooper Union, settlement houses, educational alliances were crowded with boys and girls who worked by day in factories, machine shops, behind counters, drove trucks, and at night studied law, vocations, arts, and sciences. These youngsters, whose youth was taking place in the mess and mass of streets where their parents manned pushcarts or tailored in sub-sidewalk shops, and whose family life was being lived in walkup, cold-water, jampacked tenements, were finding the urge to put their narrow margin of leisure to work.

I took Mama with me to visit the Rabinovitches on Monroe Street, a family I had come to know by way of sidewalk conversation with Mr. Rabinovitch, who sold used bric-a-brac, kitchen utensils, clocks, copperware, tools, doorknobs, towel racks, wire, and meat-grinding machines from a pushcart.

The family with four children had emigrated from Warsaw twenty years before. Mrs. Rabinovitch had one eye shot out in an anti-Jewish riot the month they fled, and had fallen down a flight of stairs with a baby in her arms. That child had received a brain injury and at twenty was living her days in a playpen. Against this scarred background, Rabinovitch had managed to educate two sons, one a practicing dentist with an office in the front room of the apartment, the other a rabbi in Elkhart, Indiana.

The evening we were there, the married daughter, chic and over-Americanized, who lived in the Bronx, and her husband "in fire insurance" were there. We had tea served in glasses and a table array of *lox* and *bagels*, sweet cakes, and a bowl of pollyseed from which everyone nibbled all evening as if on nuts.

What a combination, observed Mama, salmon and bird seed! One half of the world does not know how the other half lives. But it was a wonderful evening. Mrs. Rabinovitch took a fancy to

Mama and wrapped her up some of the pollyseed and sweet cakes to take with her on the train.

Mama declared she could see how New York was the place for me to obtain plots, as she put it.

A difficult fact to convey is that I did not associate writing with these forays. Fascination with the human scene, which concentrated on an island called Manhattan the meaning of America, was sufficient motivation. The great amalgam taking place and coagulating into the American scene.

To Mama, viewing it objectively, these people were denizens of that "other half"—foreigners who came to our country to stew in their own customs. Tea in glasses! *Bagels*—pretzels without salt! Mama did not for an instant associate her father, David Koppel of Baden Baden, Germany, arriving in America with a hundred dollars and the address of a cousin in Ohio, with the Rabinovitches on Monroe Street or the Cattonis on Mulberry Street.

When I reminded Mama of Grandma Koppel's feather beds, homemade candles, barnyard skills, and German accent, Mama said: That's different.

People often ask: How do you know these folks you write about so well? Mama took pains to explain: You may be sure she does not know them from home. Mr. Hurst and I always surrounded her with the best. Far beyond our means. To think, said Mama and began to cry during the evening with Jack, that a child like Fannie, with the home she has, should be living in that awful coop over a tailor shop.

Jack comforted her and of all things said: Never mind, one of these days she may change her mind and return to St. Louis. How little he cared, cried my misery. My return to St. Louis would mean nothing to him.

That evening, after I had put Mama on the train with a sense of relief and guilt, Jack and I met for dinner.

How had he reacted to Mama? Did he like me more or less

now that he had glimpsed my family? Could he see through to her soft core?

I was not to learn in so many words, but before our evening was over I was to know.

Why do you want to write? he asked me suddenly.

We had never talked a great deal along these lines, remaining by almost tacit agreement out of one another's domain and for the same reason. I was not musically interesting to a musician and knew it, and Jack read little if any fiction. I could answer this question of his readily enough, but why did he want to know?

I don't know that I want to write. It is just that I can't help writing.

Are you sure it is not because you have the gift for making money out of it?

If there was an indictment I did not merit, it was that one! Of course the gainful aspect was gratifying, as well as an indication that my work had value for editors. But I would have written on a shoestring, lived accordingly and gladly. The money aspect was secondary. In much the same manner I never had given more than transient thought to Jack's financial status.

Mama's reply to that would have been pat. Easy enough for you to talk. You've never had to worry where the money is coming from. We've done that for you.

The reason behind Jack's strange question was soon apparent. Your mother is a very realistic woman. It is as difficult for her to understand me musically as I imagine it was for her to accept your writing before it became profitable.

Every time in her meeting with Jack that Mama had referred to my secure background and comfortable environment, I had tensed. Apparently Jack had too. In various ways he had made it plain to me that even with his high rating as a teacher, music was rewarding but not financially so.

His large comfortable studio, his rather easy way of life were the result of a practicality folded into the artist, which in our years to come was to stand us in good stead.

His financial status concerned me less than ever now that I

was earning on my own. A circumstance, I should have realized, that would inhibit him more than ever. Had I thought this out, I might have been spared months of doubts and despair.

I am glad for a very special reason that I happen to be making a great deal of money.

You will become a famous writer. That will be your place, and I know mine.

You would look at it—that way?

You realize my work is not a field where men expect to earn great sums. I have a fair nest egg, considering my profession. But, as standards go, I am a poor man.

For the moment my restraints were down.

You mean to say you would let that make a difference—between us?

You are talking very young. Your parents are down-to-earth people, and they are right where you are concerned. We, on the other hand, are the kind who have lived easily. We were not stern about life. Your father is doubtless a very fine man, but stern about life. He is right to have only the best and highest ideals for you.

What about what I consider highest for me?

You actually think you could be happy with me?

Did I think I could be happy with him!

We will have very little, besides each other.

Very little! I would have the sun and the moon and the stars. This man, gentle, elegant, beautiful, an artist! I would have everything. . . .

And, strangely, through these sophomoric exudings of any girl in love, I spoke a perfect truth. With him, I was to have everything. . . .

The creative writer with that "strange compulsion" is foreordained to go through life in a state of chronic labor pains, for which no anesthetic has been found.

The very act of pen-in-hand or typewriter-under-it induces a state of cramp. The shooting pains begin, the ideas press, the mind heaves and hos. Delivery for some is brief, for others long and hard.

At least you suffer in private. Pain, like everything else connected with creative writing, is a private and lonely affair! I have knocked at the door of the experience of others. Almost universally, even for the humble among us, the survey adds up to blood and tears. Sweat and ink are part of the terrible dilemma of authorship.

Mama had a habit of standing in the doorway to my room while I was writing and finally commenting: You just sit. You don't write. If I had such a terrible time over something I did not have to do, I would quit.

Quit—if, like Ixion, you are tied to the wheel?

When I was about eleven and having my teeth straightened, I was obliged to sleep in a steel cap with rubber bands anchored to my front teeth, which created about a six-pound pressure against them. As I lay fevered and tossing, Mama would come into my room and beg me to remove the headpiece. But I endured it.

Mama insisted: Suppose your teeth do protrude a little bit! Likewise: Suppose you don't write. Will it matter to the world one way or another? When I see other girls at your age married and settled down, I could cry my eyes out.

Poor Mama's cried-out eyes. They were so brown and shining.

Mr. Yard of *Century Magazine* was urging me to try my hand at a novel. It will probably not be mediocre, but very good or very bad. You are not a middle-ground writer. In a way, I hope the first one will be bad. Successful first novels are dangerous. Too early success in any field is dangerous. Here came that threat again, this time from a wise old man. Old to me, he must then have been all of forty-three.

But, meanwhile, with success succeeding, I continued to sweat it out, short story after short story.

One of them, "Summer Resources," which appeared in *The Saturday Evening Post,* had St. Louis either hot under the collar or shaking with laughter.

I am ashamed to go on the street, wrote Mama. I met Birdie

Hoffheimer yesterday and when she saw me coming she turned down Clara Avenue to avoid speaking to me. Anybody can see you meant her. To do that to a woman who especially made goose grease to rub on your father's chest when he had bronchitis. Sit down at once and write a nice story about her. You should be paid even more for being nice.

Papa wrote: Your mother and I are surprised at the story you wrote, reflecting on the foibles of people at summer resorts. Naturally, everyone assumed you meant St. Louis people. I am sure it is an excellent story, but it places us in a very embarrassing position, and to my regret has caused quite a bit of criticism. I think you could mitigate some of this by returning to St. Louis and explaining, perhaps in an interview, that you meant no harm or ridicule to anyone.

It was on the strength of "Summer Resources" that Ray Long, who inaugurated the skyrocketing prices to authors who wrote for William Randolph Hearst-owned magazines, decided he wanted me exclusively for *Cosmopolitan Magazine*.

At the time, the *Post* was paying me twelve hundred dollars for a short story, the *Metropolitan* fourteen hundred, and Ray Long topped them both, advancing in due time to five thousand and, still later, on and on.

Thus it was that one brace of magazines soon became notable or notorious for controlling the highest-priced stable of writers in the world. Gertrude Atherton, Arnold Bennett, Sherwood Anderson, Willa Cather, Zona Gale, Ellen Glasgow, Aldous Huxley, Somerset Maugham, Scott Fitzgerald, Sinclair Lewis, Edna Ferber.

To the more mature writers, this price boom must have appeared more spectacular than it did to me. As the large checks came moving in, I did not realize that I too had moved in at just the moment the boom was in the making.

The money itself made little change in my way of life. I had few desires. There was no time for travel, nor inclination to leave New York.

In the years ahead, when the revenues came freely from stories, novels, motion pictures, translations, radio and television, lectures, my way of life so far as luxury living was concerned remained relatively unchanged. But inevitably our home grew in size as my library swelled into thousands of books and, for one reason and another, there came the need to expand as our lives expanded.

For years Jack and I traveled to farflung places of the world, collecting for a home which was never formally decorated but grew into a certain distinction by slow accumulation. This from Russia and Portugal, that from Cádiz, Bagdad, Athens.

Thus, before I knew it, I was being labeled the "highest-priced short-story writer in America," which, however, had the effect of bogging me down in mind and spirit.

A phrase from my undergraduate days, when a young college intellectual, indicting me for my popular success, had remarked: I would rather be a classical failure than a popular success, came back to torment me.

Fears and doubts smote me. Did my mass appeal prove lack of stature? Why the implication that one could not simultaneously be a popular and important author? I conjured up the case of Charles Dickens, I read the best-seller lists and flipped the tables of contents of the popular magazines where there were such names as Somerset Maugham, Willa Cather, Sinclair Lewis. . . .

It is noteworthy that as the legend of highest-priced short-story writer—and legend it was—gathered force, I had yet to encounter an editor who attempted in any way to control my writing, direct its course, or exact compromise. Except for occasional cuts in the name of space, stories were published as written. Whether realistic, romantic, tragic, buoyant, or grim, as the case might be, they were written without editors, masses, or classes in mind. They were written the way they were because, even had I so desired, I had not the skill to tailor them to fashion. They came that way because I felt them and saw them and lived them that way, and that was how it had to be.

I once sent a story to Ray Long entitled "Guilty." Part of his editorial genius was the ability to adjust to the temperament of each author. Many of them leaned on him as adviser and even collaborater. In my case, he recognized the lone wolf. I never discussed a story with him either before or during the writing.

When "Guilty" was completed, it was with some misgiving that I forwarded the manuscript. By way of having my little joke, I wrapped it in gay gift paper tied with ribbons and sent him what he termed one hell of a study in terror.

A woman, happily married to a fishmonger, develops during pregnancy an emotional horror of him and the odor of his shop which he brings home to her nightly. The hallucination that he himself has been transformed into a huge biped catfish lays such hold on her that one night as he enters their home, bringing her gifts, she meets him at the door and thrusts a knife through his heart.

If you had told me the story before you wrote it, said Ray Long, I would have warned you that I would not have touched it with a ten-foot pole. But now that I have read the blamed thing, I will publish it if it costs me my job. It almost did.

In the end, however, Mr. Long justified himself. There were protests and criticisms, but the story has repeatedly been cited and included in anthologies.

Going over into Ray Long's stable of high-priced authors was a risk. Magazine editors were banding together against *Cosmopolitan's* untoward price boosting. George Lorimer called it author-stealing and warned that capitulation to this formidable competitor would permanently disqualify writers for future publication in the *Post*.

I felt a sense of loyalty to the magazine that had first presented me to a vast reading public and, with Jack's tempered wisdom behind me, held out for a considerable time, until all competing magazines were finally forced to get in line with the soaring prices.

I wrote proudly home of Ray Long's offer and my reasons for hesitating. Mama replied special delivery: Have you lost your mind? Business is business. Papa wrote a little bitterly: You must do as you think best. My unsolicited advice is needless, since you have already acted. You doubtless have more competent advisers. But as a businessman of considerable experience, I would think very little of such high-handed methods as those of *The Saturday Evening Post*, threatening never to publish you again.

As a businessman. Of course, Papa was sensing Jack, who was not a businessman, in the background of my decisions. I would have given much for the opportunity to explain to him the combination of sound practical judgment and artist's sensitivity that characterized Jack, but Papa would not let me in.

Fortunately, these external excitements did not invade Waverly Place, where I fought my long daily battle of the words. Neither did acceleration come with the stimulus of demand for my work.

The casual reader who picks a novel off a book counter or unwraps the monthly ready-to-serve selection from his book club often reads spottily, jumps the descriptive passages, and has little conception of the slow contemplative hours that have gone into the page he has skimmed, or the long concentrations that have labored to bring forth the passages he has jumped.

There is no adequate definition for creative writing, any more than it is possible to describe pain or flavor or color.

One day, Mr. George Horace Lorimer, in New York for a few hours, invited me to lunch at the Brevoort Hotel. We were joined by his assistant editor, Churchill Williams, and an elderly woman who was introduced by all three names: Carrie Chapman Catt, who impressed or rather depressed me, chiefly because she reminded me of a one-time Latin teacher.

During the conversation, which she dominated, it developed that she was a leader in the woman's suffrage movement, which interested me so little that her name conveyed nothing to me.

Mama's indictment of Tillie Strauss had always been: She dresses like one of those suffragettes, ground-gripper shoes and hard hats.

Mrs. Catt was rather pleasantly gray and hung in a variety of silver chains. The crusading spirit was out all over her.

Straight as the crow flies, her attention focused on me: We need fresh young girls like you in the movement. Join up with us. You will find new and exciting material for stories. Make His Royal

Nibs Lorimer realize he has a new woman-world on his hands now that we have the vote.

I did not understand the zealot's eye. Every female was grist for Mrs. Catt's mill. She saw in me young material from an important area, the Midwest. She said so, frankly: We need your kind. Come and join some of the New Voters parades we are planning to hold. Diving into her briefcase, she produced a handful of pamphlets: Take these home, read them carefully and pass them around to your friends.

Hands off, said Lorimer. We can use a good straight article from you on "Where Do We Girls Go from Here," but we know where this girl is going from here!

Don't let His Royal Nibs trap you into his profile-to-profile school of fiction. It's dated.

Don't you believe it, Carrie. Time flies, but it will always remain sex o'clock.

I did not want to be identified with a suffrage parade and I had no intention of "joining up." I smiled and yessed and George Lorimer talked through Mrs. Catt's talk to the business of the day, which was the article from her, and a story from me.

But in a strange way I could not put this woman all the way out of my mind. I recalled a few St. Louis women who had been in the news from time to time for participation in Washington demonstrations of the militants. The wife of a prominent throat specialist had even gone to jail, fighting for the vote.

Like politics and world affairs, they were beyond the periphery of our little Cates Avenue world. But now, as it so often happens, having once encountered the name Carrie Chapman Catt, it kept recurring on all sides. A New York *Evening Mail* delivery wagon bore the placard: Read "New Woman in Town," in Saturday *Evening Mail,* by Carrie Chapman Catt.

But I could not reconcile myself to the idea of women resorting to disorders over the vote. Even Papa did not always vote. Politics, he said, was getting too dirty for him. But something to which I had never given thought was awake in my mind: I can help elect Presidents. I have a say-so in Government.

Then, one Saturday afternoon as I was walking down Fifth Avenue, I ran bang into one of the suffrage celebrations. Phalanxes of women swung up the street, their banners proclaiming!

Young, old, blond, dark, gray, fat—on they came. Then a solid cluster of men, grinning and a little sheepish, but their banners read: Welcome, Girls! Glad to Have You with Us. Then more women and more women with interludes of brass bands.

At an intersection, squads of women stood in formation, waiting to fall in line with the marchers. I turned into the side street, mingled with the wonderful anonymity that New York affords, listened to the soprano din. The older zealots were firm-faced dowagers who caricatured easily. But the younger had a long-stemmed casual quality. Modish bobs, simple sporty clothes, once more putting me in strange contrast to them.

These women spoke the language of lobbies, pressure groups, hearings, resolutions, chairmen, and delegations. Martial music blared over them. Next thing I knew, I was in formation, marching up the Avenue, and helping my neighbor clutch the pole of a banner which read: Move Over, Gentlemen. We Have Come to Stay.

I felt stimulated and embarrassed, particularly the latter when I avoided the eye of a young Mr. Ahler, assistant editor of *Argosy Magazine*, standing at a curb waiting for a break in the procession. I hoped he had not recognized me.

The woman with whom I shared the heavy pole was a brilliant-eyed, dark-haired mite who introduced herself, Marie Jenny Howe. Marching in the phalanx of men, I was later to discover, was her husband, Fred Howe, Commissioner of Immigration at Ellis Island. By happy chance they had read aloud one of my stories only the night before. It was thus I came to know a pair of fiery young liberals of the twenties, and it was Fred Howe who was to initiate me into the drama of the "tired, poor, huddled masses yearning to breathe free" who were still entering the United States by way of Ellis Island.

The day following the parade, I received a hand-delivered note from Mr. Ahler suggesting that I write a piece for his magazine entitled, "Gentlemen, Move Over."

I was not a flash-in-the-pan or at least not a one-or-two-story author. My name had already taken root in the masses. But a kind of snide snobbery still lived with me. This mass business bothered me. Rather be a classical failure than a popular success. The phrase out of my college days stuck crosswise in my memory like a bone in the throat. Did popular success necessarily mean kiss-of-death to artistic achievement? I made no conscious effort for popular appeal. That, in a way, was even more disturbing. It meant that if I did not write "down," I was myself down.

Still callow enough not to understand that I owed what warmth I had to my capacity for feeling and honestly caring about my anonymous friend, the public, my success, for a while at least, was actually a fly in the ointment.

I had come to my senses, however, long before the days when I could sit in the subway and see shopgirls and stenographers reading my stories in current magazines and know also that I was required college reading, included in textbooks, anthologies, and Best Short Story collections.

Guiltless of social ambitions, I ask myself in this adventure into self-psychiatry, how come I needed to pass through this phase of intellectual snideness?

Meanwhile, outside the solitary confinement of the six-hour writing day, life was a fast-moving affair. New and exciting faces that could, if so desired, make a name-dropping holiday of this journey into me.

Although the tremendous surge of European immigration had slowed, Ellis Island was still sorting, rejecting the specked or damaged immigrants, releasing those who qualified into that promised land across the harbor.

Fred Howe allowed me to mingle with the incomers, and I attempted to get through to them in my broken bits of their languages.

People said: What a wonderful way to get local color. Usually,

I said, yes. It did not seem necessary to try to explain that my prime interest, regardless of writing, was people.

Long and frequently tortuous could be the rigmarole required between arrival at quarantine and that moment when the newcomers walked down the slant of gangplank and onto mainland America!

Time and time again, while bewildered entrants, men, women, and children, awaited relatives, I gained admission into the picture. Sometimes the social workers and interpreters to whom I became known enlisted my services.

Once they were cleared, I occasionally accompanied the men and women "yearning to breathe free" to their new destinies, usually in the crowded tenements of relatives or friends.

A heavy-cheeked Slavic farm girl, who was met with a telegram from her fiancé informing her that a fall from a tractor would delay his arrival in New York, spent the night with me. She was clean and obviously outfitted in bridal finery that would very soon seem outlandish even to her. A bed was a novelty to her who knew only a pallet. I attended her wedding three days later. Her son is now a professor of husbandry at a western agricultural college. Her grandson, my godchild.

Anna Orlorfsky and her six-year-old son, who had never seen his father, arrived to join her longshoreman husband. Inexplicably, he was not on hand to meet her. I escorted her to his address with instructions to report back to the authorities on the situation. When we reached her husband's two rooms near the waterfront, a priest was performing last rites. He had been mortally injured that morning by a packing case plunging from its crane onto his back.

In a room that had been fitted out with a new double bed, a cot for a child, and a dish of fresh flowers, Anna kept tryst with her dead husband.

For a time, her destiny hung between deportation and adjustment with the United States Bureau of Immigration.

Ultimately, we solved it. She and Peter went to St. Louis, Anna to work as a domestic for my mother, Peter to attend public school. Mama, who said Anna was a *schlomp* in some ways but excellent with the rough work, "married her off" to a prosperous local butcher. Every Thanksgiving they send me a turkey. Peter, who now has five half brothers and sisters, fell into bad company and served a brief reformatory school sentence. He, too, is now married and over many years has held his position with an East St. Louis iron foundry.

Thus I watched the second blooming or the withering of many of these voluntary and involuntary adventurers into a new life, a process on which our country's history is predicated.

The settlement houses and the educational centers bulged at the seams with boys and girls who worked in factories and shops by day, studied and inched themselves up by night, among them future judges, musicians, educators, lawyers, diplomats, industrialists, composers, authors, artists, doctors, merchants.

I realized none of this. I only knew that despite the backwash of crime, the hordes of tired old people with prunelike eyes, the flabby-breasted women old at forty, the rickety-looking children, the life and the hope of these sodden streets tingled through the soles of my shoes, vibrated in the night classes and crowded reading rooms of East Side libraries!

Meanwhile, as I delayed and procrastinated, decision stood waiting. Personally, I was in a state of immense peace. I was the choice of the man of my choice. I knew that now. We talked of marriage and plans and future. His presence and everything he was and stood for made my paradise.

I had yet to learn that throughout our lives together it was never to be a matter of what he preferred, but the way I wanted it. How often I must have acted not realizing that.

But when we talked of the actual time of marriage, I had a vague and unready feeling. So long as I was secure as to his state of mind, there seemed so many things I needed to be and do first.

In addition, I had yet to return to St. Louis with the news. Mama wrote: You never mention what you do with your evenings, except go slumming, which your father considers dangerous.

Haven't you met any desirable young men yet? Now that you are making such a name for yourself, I should think you would have no difficulty. Believe me, you would be better off at home where you would be a somebody. Mr. and Mrs. Bamburger, the paper-bag Bamburgers, stopped us in the picture show last night and said we should be proud. He is President of the Kiwanis Club, and says when you come to St. Louis you must address them. They have two unmarried sons, both in the business. Of course, they will inherit it. But what good does that do, with you off in New York, slumming? Sometimes I could cry my eyes out, with all these congratulations.

I, too, could cry as I reread these letters. Mama, whose life was in me and for me, was being cheated. Try as she would, and did, to adjust to my marriage, and granting that Jack was a "fine fellow," I had not "done well." Neither Mama nor Papa was ever to understand that so far as I was concerned mine was an almost perfect marriage. When I told them so, repeatedly and with urgency, they said the equivalent of: Yes, of course.

Although he continued not to mention it, Jack, alas, kept on knowing about this chilly climate. Nor did I ever for an instant forget it. I tried to make up to him for it. I think I succeeded. Our interests may have been different, but our compatibilities seemed to know no end.

My growing surge of outside interests, the intensification of my writing were all accessory to the fact of him. He knew that, and in a sort of unspoken accord we drifted on, with me in my state of delayed adolescence thinking I could go on and on . . . having my cake and eating it too.

To be sure, I yearned for the scene-complete that went with marriage, but it seemed to me that even as conventional lovers my cup brimmed over.

It was during this period that Irma, one of the Baltimore girls with whom I had previously shared an apartment under the Gobert regime, conceived the idea of a five-week trip to Europe. A party of four would entitle her, a seasoned traveler, to a free trip as guide. Dorothy and a cousin of Vera's joined up.

The itinerary stretched from the tip of the Italian boot as far up as Scotland.

To me, Europe meant Jack's background. I wanted to see it, to know his beginnings and feel them. I wanted to be able to walk on the side of the world where he had been growing up while I was doing likewise in Missouri. I would have preferred that the itinerary include Asia, but my public school knowledge of geography was sufficiently vague to permit me to rest content with the European scene.

When I mentioned the trip to Jack, he was enthusiastically for it. Mama and Papa rather timorously agreed. We sailed on the *Vulcania* for Naples on a May day sparkling with spring.

I had never set foot on an ocean liner. The departure was a gala one of music, confetti, confusion, tears, smiles, messengers, flowers. I had a separately boxed corsage a day, ten in all, from Jack. More flowers and sweets and telegrams from editors and the Hamilton relatives, and a canoe made of roses from *Cosmopolitan Magazine*.

Trying to be glad, I stood on an upper deck, watching the widening, the receding, and the separation.

And even as I ached for what I was leaving, within our windowless, airless cabin three decks down, dissension had set in. So different from descriptions presented by Irma, it was only the beginning of typical accommodations that were in store for us.

The girls were stormy and indignant and Irma laughed it off and said: What did you expect for seven hundred dollars?

But my decision to leave the party and remain in Italy, sacrificing the sheaf of tickets that were to carry me up into Scotland, had nothing to do with our disappointing accommodations.

The trip across was not notable. We were ten at a dining-room table of middle-aged couples. But a nearby table for one was occupied by an arresting man who proved to be the celebrity on board.

Here I encounter one of the snags of circumlocution which autobiography so often imposes. For complicated reasons I shall call him Hugh McDonald. It was not his name. Suffice it to say, without revealing the department of endeavor in which he had achieved high distinction, he was a world figure and scholar. About forty-five, he was affable enough, but usually immersed in a book or journal propped before him as he dined.

On the final day of the trip, a passenger with whom I chanced to be chatting introduced us, identifying me as a "promising young writer." He looked interested, said the pleasant thing, and went on.

I did not see him again, not even at the disembarking, where I promptly forgot about him in the Neapolitan scene of Mediterranean splendor and squalor.

Our book of tourist tickets provided for two days in Naples and environs. True to form, we were established in a rather dingy second-class hotel, four in a room. The second day's itinerary included the incomparable Amalfi Drive, Blue Grotto, Sorrento, Capri, and at the top of the scenic climb, overlooking the Gulf of Salerno on one side and the Mediterranean on the other, the picture-card village of Ravella, perched high and close to blue, blue sky.

Here our hotel hung like a crag from a mountain, and it was here I made my decision. I was not liking the climate of angry bickering that Irma's handling of the trip was creating within our ranks. After a few hours in Ravella, I concluded that nothing in our future travels could surpass the allure of these scenes. Here let me linger for the remainder of my five weeks, sacrificing my booklet of tickets and delving into my letter of credit.

I cabled Mama and Papa and Jack noncommittal notice of change in my itinerary. The bombshell fell upon my little group. One of the girls was inclined to remain with me, but was dissuaded. Thus my companions began their journey on the day I practically ended mine.

My weeks in the hotel that, seventy years before, had been a monastery, its vineyards dropping in terraces from its high perch, were joyous abandon to beauty.

I opened my eyes and from my bed, a narrow hard one, I could look down upon a fishing village at the base of the vineyards, the old colors of its roofs like faded calico. A slightly curling sea. Horizon.

No yesterday, no tomorrow, only the iridescent present, realistically interrupted by meals of veal, spaghetti, Italian bread, red wine, and spumone. Elderly English ladies with dyed hair and old-fashioned jewelry, set with small dirty diamonds, sat about the musty sitting room, rickety Englishmen with stained goatees and window-glass monocles, German tourists inseparable from guidebooks and rucksacks, were part of the daily busloads of tourists.

Only I, of these birds of passage, had remained behind to explore through the long sweet summer days, to browse in the cobblestoned village of Ravella in its typical huddle around its cathedral, always feeling beneath me the soil of Jack's hemisphere. That he had never trod this part of it mattered not. A stupendous procession of men and civilizations had. Dante, Julius Caesar, Michelangelo had breathed this air. Crazy, sweet, uncoordinated fragments of imagination lent the days their magic. Reality fell farther and farther away. The pages of my history books and the world's yesterdays came alive and dwelt with me in the stockstill village of Ravella.

The third or fourth evening of this trance, which I was buying for myself out of my letter of credit, I walked into the little dining room where the permanent lady guests with old faces and dyed hair and the decay-gentry old men were dining.

There, at a table for one, was the most eminent passenger of the *Vulcania*, reading a book while he plied his food.

Mr. Hugh McDonald had come, or rather returned, to Ravella, which, it developed, was his favorite hideaway, to write a paper to be delivered to a world congress of learned societies to be held in Rome during early summer. This time we drifted easily together.

Coming to know this man of high eminence, high character and erudition was exciting stimulus. His name was known far beyond the esoteric field in which he labored, and was authority. Never before, I may even say or since, had I been in close contact with an intellect that flashed its lightning over such farflung territories.

As a pastime, he was interested in the study of Etruscan ruins, deducing facts which in his judgment would correct certain erroneous interpretations of the historians. He could identify local flora and fauna by their Latin names, trace back to its beginnings the architecture of the huge Gothic cathedral around which the tiny village of Ravella so incongruously huddled, and in his spare time was engaged in writing a book on Etruria, B.C. Still in his early forties, he had lectured at the Sorbonne, delivered the "Lowell" Lectures at Harvard, was the recipient of honorary degrees from American and European universities; his background, foster child of a New Brunswick dirt farmer.

The learning, which he had acquired by way of dishwashing, dormitory heavy work, tutoring, night-shift and odd jobs, somehow belittled me. I found myself suffering a fierce jealousy of his vast self-acquired knowledge which highlighted my lack of it.

He, on the other hand, a master in a rare and not too competitive field, was actually impressed by my kind of success in a highly competitive one, deploring that he had not known who I was, or caught my name, when we met on the ship. It further transpired that we had a mutual friend, Churchill Williams, to whom he had previously expressed a desire to meet me. So here we were.

Stimulated by this man's mind, before the weeks of long walks and talks were over I was something more, flattered by a warming friendship.

I understand more clearly at this distance the attraction and antagonisms that were to characterize my long and stormy relationship with Hugh. My attitude toward him never for a moment collided with mine toward Jack, although over the years Hugh was unwavering in his conviction that, somehow, someway, our destinies would merge.

I was jealous of him, but only of his learning; jealous of his mind. But there were arid places in him. As if bogged down by facts, his imagination scarcely left the ground. He had the scientist's dedication to truth, but he was earthbound, lacking the wing-lift to put what he knew to work.

Admire a sunset and he would solemnly expatiate on the laws of refraction. Rock stratifications that flashed color or formations were geologically interesting but aesthetically nonexistent.

His first visit to Rome had been two years previous for a similar two-week gathering of scholars. I expected to spend a day or two in Rome on my way to meet my party at the ship, and asked him to suggest a sightseeing itinerary. He replied that he had not left his hotel during his entire sojourn, but suggested I read two books while there which he had donated to the hotel lending library upon leaving: *Diophantus, the Man and Algebraist* and *Arctic Icecap*.

On another occasion, Ruth Bryan Rhode, daughter of William Jennings Bryan, and I accidentally encountered Hugh in London. We made up a party to drive to Canterbury. Stonehenge en route was archeologically interesting to him. But when we arrived in Canterbury and set out to see the cathedral, Hugh decided he would rather wait for us in a little teahouse, eat Devonshire cream, and read a scientific weekly.

This is not to detract from his interest, I may say fascination. During those Ravella weeks I picked his brain and most of the time enjoyed his company.

Ravella became an adventure into a strange friendship.

As always up to this dateless now, time continues to be a river, riding me along, life the passing scene, span-of-life a phrase, "life expectancy" something peculiar to insurance companies.

My quick, quick river flows toward eternity, and eternity is the shape of the head of God, wrapped in mists. . . .

Meanwhile, as time and I are passing, I have much. I am greedy for more. More inner satisfaction with my work. I want Jack and marriage and I want to be free. I want the admiration of Hugh. I covet his scholarship and outwardly deprecate it. And, tormentingly, I want to know more of the individuals "out there," built so solidly into the masses. I want to separate them from their tight bee-clusters. They interest me more than I interest myself. And that is a very great deal because I am bulging with my greed to see and be and do, even at the expense of those I love. Even, alas, at Jack's expense. Time has run into years now, and still I procrastinate and still simultaneously I wage the St. Louis battle.

I have never seen Papa so stern. Papa, who had a fine strong nose, looked down it and made repetitive pronouncement: Foreigners beat their wives. Foreigners wear size fifteen collars.

Papa's state of health continues to frighten me. His neck looks so thin. Indeed, his size seventeen collar seems almost the ignominious fifteen. I am killing those I love. I am cheating Jack by telling him too little of Hugh, even though the one conflicts not at all with the other.

These incertitudes are noteworthy, not because they are mine, but because they are one more case history of the off-the-couch labyrinthine mental processes of a human being struggling his way through the maze of himself.

At long last Jack and I agree it is the hour of decision. I hasten to St. Louis with the news. Cates Avenue is blanketed in sooty snow and a north wind howls around our house all of the week I am there.

The Aunts come. They are ashamed for the people. Your father is right. I have seen too many girls marry foreigners, even the nobility, and live to regret it. "Foreigners" think all American girls are loaded with money. Does it occur to you what you owe your parents?

It does, spoke the voice of the tribe deep down inside me.

But, meanwhile, the conviction strengthens that from the day I first saw light in Hamilton, Ohio, a dotted line joined my destiny to that of a ten-year-old lad who was growing up in a city then known as St. Petersburg, Russia.

However, this visit home, to the tune of the same old recriminations, ended on a note of compromise, prompted by increasing sadness for my obviously failing father and graying mother.

Yes, I would wait, I conceded, not admitting even to myself that postponement was also my preference. And, further, I would at least bring "this man" home and have him meet my father.

I cannot understand "this man," said Papa, not wanting to meet your family of his own accord.

I could.

The decade of experimentalists advances. Sex is a discovery. The word, which had lurked so long in the nasty silences, becomes usage. *Lady Chatterley's Lover* is carried in public, without a book cover. *The Well of Loneliness* and *Damaged Goods* are as discussible as *Rebecca of Sunnybrook Farm*. A magazine, in a full-page newspaper advertisement, urges upon its readers its lead story entitled: "Don't Wait to Tell Your Daughter until the Night before Her Marriage."

Judge Lindsey of Denver pulls the rock away from sin and the nation gasps at the facts of the demoralization that crawls out from under.

A Mr. and Mrs. Lynd drag more of the frenetic licentiousness of the period out into the light of day in a study of an average American community, *Middletown*.

The sane hard core of American living, for the most part intact, recedes behind phraseology of the high-kicking twenties. Petting parties. Necking. Trial Marriage. Gin. This is the order and disorder of the day.

Aldous Huxley, Ernest Hemingway, Radcliffe Hall, waving banners for the morality of frankness, perceive something frank and cleansing beneath the postwar decade of decadence.

Some people are accident prone. Why, they reiterate, should that fall downstairs, that automobile mishap, these broken bones always happen to me?

I, on the other hand, seem by some blessed circumstance to have been all my life "nice people" prone. There are no known lawbreakers, social deviators, or delinquents on either side. Nor are there outstanding talents or mentalities. Mine was a conforming world of behavers.

Sometimes I leaned out of the window, peering down into shadowed Waverly Place, wondering what I was missing. Might some of these revelers be the famed and fabulous denizens of the Village?

It did not occur to me how easy would have been my access to becoming one of them.

But I remained one of the millions who lived on, worked on, outside the glittering circus of the "fabled minority" who aimed for the roof of the world but compromised by swinging from the chandelier.

A brilliant young fellow, Princeton's pride and joy, did much to slap a generic label on the twenties which stuck.

This Side of Paradise held up to a dead-eyed, postwar generation a picture of itself, too often dead drunk. Certainly an authentic interpretation from Fitzgerald's point of view, an interpretation which reeled because he reeled.

Here, said Fitzgerald, casting about a myopic eye of despair, was a new generation, grown up to find all gods dead, all wars fought, all faith in man shaken. . . .

And yet that generation, for the most part, developed into the usual quota of law-abiding, God-fearing mature men and women, the one-time flappers and godless young men marrying, building families, becoming the backbone of the nation. The bare-kneed flappers, pushing perambulators, scrimping out of household money for Johnny and Janie's future college education.

No doubt about it, something of Fitzgerald's fabulous twenties did rage in Greenwich Village. I used to lean out of my window as if living in the vicinity of a three-alarm fire, to see if I could feel its heat in my face.

There was the sound of revelry by night, as they reeled down Waverly Place, the bathtub-gin vocalizers, the home-going speakeasy sets, the sobbings of a drunken flapper having it out at two in the morning with her slaphappy escort.

Were such fabulous inhabitants of the Village as Fitzgerald himself, Maxwell Bodenheim, Floyd Dell, Edna Millay, George Bellows "down there" in that Bohemia so near and yet so far?

I would have been tongue-tied in their company, overwhelmed by their status, lacking their powers to extend their exhilarations by way of the cup that cheers. Or, rather, the demitasse that cheers, since part of the technique of the Prohibition era was scotch, gin, or what you will, served in demitasses.

Thus Fitzgerald's era moved on, the millions of us who lived, worked, played outside the circus ring scarcely aware that this era was either "riotous" or "fabulous."

As usual, Shakespeare says it best. "Past and to come seem best; things present, worst."

May Wilson Preston, popular magazine illustrator and personality, had done the drawings for several of my short stories.

At her home I met a smooth-haired, middle-aged woman, Miss Willa Cather, whose vast serenity I was to learn lay over the complicated mechanism of her mind and intellect like a blanket of snow.

The editor in me, she remarked, likes your stories. If I were still with *McClure's Magazine*, I would want to publish them.

This comment hit me on the spot of my almost obsessive sensitivity. Personally she did not like my work, I interpreted, but if the public wanted my stories, her job as editor would have been to give it to them.

She may have meant nothing of the kind, but to me here it was again. Rather be a classical failure than a popular success! A bleeder under criticism, real or implied, I was affected by her words as if a buzz saw were cutting me. Miss Cather had already written *My Antonia*. As the established author of a first-rate novel of literary stature, she could afford her wide popularity, without fear of losing caste with the intellectuals. While I, the author of a few short stories . . .

Fearful and wonderful are the workings of the human mind, but that is the kind of tortuous conclusion mine was putting me through.

I was to meet her in time to come in her quiet and bookish home on Bank Street in Greenwich Village, which was no more a part of Fitzgerald's twenties than Mars.

She was a gracious woman in her aloof way and her culture ran deep and somber. The icy beauty of her writing, its glacial splendor, in contrast to my own ebullience, served to reduce me to self-conscious silence in her presence.

I was to know later, through May Wilson Preston, that Miss Cather was pleased with certain aspects of my work, and remarked that my shyness precluded discussion.

My conviction that she regarded my writing as uncontrolled and effulgent held me rigid. In her presence I felt vulgar. Her mind was a porcelain cup that held its content in perfect balance. I slopped over into the saucer.

Miss Cather was probably in her early forties at this time. I doubt if she had ever been very young, even on the northwestern plains whence she had sprung. Her very adolescence must have been mature. Her era seemed to swirl about her stately intellectual isolation like a noisy storm.

She traveled much, lived her scholarly life, and wrote books as removed from the current sound and fury as she was, books that were to survive long after the bathtub-gin-incited shouting had died down and we had moved into another era of sound and fury in a different key.

Along with Theodore Dreiser, Edgar Lee Masters, Robert Frost, and Sinclair Lewis, Miss Cather's revolt was against the hardened formality of American literature rather than the new postwar cult of freedom or H. L. Mencken's battle-ax assault on the graven images of outworn moralities.

The little red fellow who did the best job of them all was Sinclair Lewis.

The first volume of my collected short stories, *Every Soul Hath Its Song*, dedicated "To Mama and Papa," is published. Hugh, whose scholarly works have established him as an authority in his field, cannot take his eyes off my success. It seems to glitter for him to the exclusion of his own solid accomplishments.

His hankering to write fiction amounts to obsession. This ambition had not lived with him through the years, he confided. It was only after he had heard of me—not met me, mind you—that the desire lifted its head in his latent consciousness.

Time after time he continued to submit his wooden efforts through me to Bob Davis, until Bob finally burst forth: If you don't put this fellow out of his misery with the truth, I will. Tell him his stuff is born dead.

Jack, on the other hand, seemed oblivious of his own talents, concentrating his interest upon my work with an intensity from which he was never to deviate in all the long years.

Certain tortuous doubts live with me. To what heights might Jack not have gone on his own, had he not thrown his interest and energies to me? Again and again I ask myself: Should I have prodded, instead of indulged his resistance to platform appearances? Would a less self-centered woman have thrown herself into his work, as he hurled himself into mine? Had I shielded when I should have strengthened him? Was he, I ponder in those sporadic moments of vain regrets, as happy a man as he appeared to be? Had I, as I so fondly believed, penetrated his reserves until I knew the way into his innermost state of mind and heart? While I had him with me, I was so sure, so secure. But now, in the still world of memory, I reach back over the few years since he left me and ask myself: Did I dwarf instead of enrich him? Did I sacrifice the one I loved? And yet I believe, for reasons that have no place even in this unrestrained analysis of the anatomy of me, that he was happy with me.

Every Soul Hath Its Song sold fairly well. My publishers, Harper & Brothers, had warned in advance that collections of short stories were more or less a drug on the market.

Then, almost overnight it seemed to me—as a matter of fact it was three years of overnights—I had another volume of short stories and a bad first novel to my account, all surprisingly well, if not sensationally, received.

But it was during this period that my multifarious appearances in the magazines were building the "household word" aspect of an author's name. I still had a large backwash of rejected stories to draw on, at least those I considered up to the standard of my continuing output. Therefore, scarcely a month passed that my work did not appear in *Cosmopolitan Magazine,* where I was now under exclusive long-term contract.

Meanwhile, something was happening of which I was scarcely aware. The big, squalid, magnificent, overcrowded, impersonal city was becoming my maestro. I looked about and pondered.

All about me, people were running away from people, shuddering away from people. In the great city blocks of apartment houses, people boasted they did not know or want to know their neighbors. Whites drew aside from darks, dark Negroes from light Negroes. Jews were supposed to deteriorate a neighborhood. German and Russian Jews regarded one another darkly. Spiritual, mental, physical segregation raged. Everybody running away from somebody. I am not Puerto Rican, I am Spanish. Thus obliterating the dignity of racial origin and an entire saga of a people.

The harassed excluder, battling with the science of semantics, cogitates: The name is Klip? What kind of a name is that? He can't fool me. It is Klipstein.

This dawning awareness served well with the passing years to keep life a many-sided, many-splendored affair.

Absorbed by the complexity of a city of unprecedented heterogeneity, life was a concentrated trip around the world, social wrath dividing it into separate countries, even continents.

Avoiding the pitfalls of seeking my own level in the big city and settling there, I was establishing, without conscious effort it is true, friendships and connections from Chinatown to the Bronx, from German Yorkville to an uptown area where Iowans clanned up into coveys of Iowans, from family life in a barge along the waterfront to Negro Harlem and Syrian West Broadway, to Little Italy, to Irish Hell's Kitchen.

There are walled cities within the city, their isolation no less because the walls are invisible. Gypsies, Greeks, Negroes live within their own areas, live what amounts to a community life, with little osmosis into the outside neighborhood, shopping within the invisible walls, seeking their amusements there, often speaking their own languages.

New York is how you want it.

First-rate writers have always seemed fearful and wonderful to me. Sometimes even more fearful than wonderful. Their skills bog me down. My neck aches from looking upward. I yearn to brush the hem of their garments and their minds. And, illogically, I retreat. Certainly not lacking in ego, this anatomy of me is testimony to that, the flashing pen tipped with even the phosphorus of genius reduces me to humility.

As my miscellaneous world expands, my literary contacts, so few at best, remain static or dwindle. With rising evidence of my writing success, my inner evaluations stand between me and the gratifications I should be enjoying.

Zoe Beckley, a popular columnist, comes out with a by-line article in a popular magazine, entitled "Who, among My Contemporaries, Would I Most Like to Be?" I am her choice. "Fannie Hurst has everything. Youth, personality, talent, human interest, and interest in humans. Success."

At least I had some of these and I reveled in them and was grateful. Good, but not good enough.

Nevertheless, the thrill of receiving a letter of acceptance from an editor, even when you regard his intellectual status as not too exciting, continues to this day.

It was wonderful to have Jack thrill with me. I don't know that he ever told me in so many words, but his manner did and his dear blind insistence, no matter what the conflict, that I was always right. What I did was right with him because I did it. What he did was right with me, not only for that same reason, but because he was right so much of the time.

I was in love with Hugh's erudition and scholarly achievements without being in love with him. Jack, I believe, was in love with me and whatever addenda happened to make up the package of me.

Deep in my heart I am sure I never hesitated between the

two widely different men. But I must face up to my guilt in lingering by the wayside between the two whom I had allowed to meet but cursorily, all the while avoiding decision. An avoidance which I have permitted to develop into one of my major weaknesses. Why decide today what can be decided tomorrow, and even then, after decision, still undecided, has been and is my cross to bear.

Too infatuated with the situation to nip in the bud what seemed to be the growing intentions of Hugh, I, who had known what it was to suffer the pangs of wallflower, played for time, sure of Hugh but not quite so sure of the fine sensitivity of Jack and his reactions.

Meanwhile, I was invited to lecture in McMillin Hall, Columbia University. Simultaneously, Dr. Blanche Colton Williams, English Department of the same university, who had included me in her Best Short Stories of the Year anthology, wrote asking me to address her short-story classes.

I was flattered and flabbergasted. Dr. Williams assured me that speaking informally to a group of aspiring young writers could be as relaxing as talking across a luncheon table. I agreed to think it over and ended by accepting both hers and the McMillin Hall invitations.

The short-story classes came first.

Jack said: Don't worry. You'll be the finest speaker they ever had. I saw to it that he never knew how far I fell short.

Hugh, an experienced lecturer, said: What success for a young girl! The magic of the written word. Will you read this little travesty on the insect world I have just finished? It has real popular appeal, I think.

Papa wrote: Those are certainly flattering invitations. Your mother and I are highly gratified and hope you will not fail to avail yourself of this splendid opportunity. Mama wrote: Your father is delighted about the lectures. So am I, but don't let yourself get in with too many teachers. Bear in mind Tillie Strauss, who taught all her life. What will you wear? Do they pay?

In due time I spoke before Blanche Williams' large group of

combined classes. She had asked me to make the talk personal. The students, then as now, wanted to hear my experiences. How I got my start. My aims and ambitions, methods of work. How many hours a day? Where did I get my plots? My opinion of the contemporary short story.

For weeks in advance, I rehearsed various approaches. Each one seemed either trivial or didactic. I wanted to answer their concrete questions, but, more, I wanted to convey to them the unconveyable. The winged moments of conception, the long hours of delivery. I wanted to bare my writing soul to them for what it was worth. Declaiming before my mirror, I was merely long-winded, highfalutin, or ridiculous. I decided to read from a prepared script. I decided to speak impromptu. I decided not to speak at all. I decided to appear, come what might.

Concern over my bulk still lived with me. Now I must stand on my feet before rows of young appraising eyes.

But once before my audience, aided by its warmth, I was able to dispense with all the conflicts of tortuous preparation and talked realistically of the facts they wanted to know.

Hugh was present, but at my urging Jack remained away. I could not bear to risk having him see me in the grip of my insecurity.

Hugh said: Since you are being helpful to all those young aspirants, I am going to ask you to read another opus of mine.

The evening following the lecture, Jack and I dined in a French restaurant. I told him of the occasion in detail. Were any of your friends there? he asked. I was startled by the question. More than that, I was frightened. I used to say laughingly to Jack that he was my benign Svengali and that someday I intended to write a short story entitled "My Dear Svengali." His slightest displeasure was my anguish. To him I could not lie.

Hugh was there, I said finally. But somehow I don't mind talking before him. I care too much what you think. All this was true, yet I could feel confusion reddening my face.

He smiled and gave me a long and curious look that set my

fears racing. I could no longer swallow, much less complete my meal.

Are you angry with me?

No.

He was. He was! How could I ever have placed myself in the position of seeming to favor Hugh? As if my feelings for Hugh had anything to do with Jack. I think he realized that, but it was my evasiveness that made the difference. I belabored the point, protesting too loudly.

He said nothing, and what he did not say was hardest to endure.

As we were parting on the stoop of my apartment house, my fears broke bounds. Was I insane to risk what was paramount in my life by indecisions and the greedy impulse to have my cake and eat it too?

Jack, let's get married!

You don't mean that, Fannie, he said slowly.

I do. I do. I want it more than anything in the world.

You don't know what you want, Fannie.

He was hurt and I felt crazed with having hurt him.

Don't say that! We could go to St. Louis tomorrow and come back married, I insisted.

He was strict and insisted that I be sure it was what I wanted.

I was. I was.

We talked in the shadow of that stoop until two o'clock in the morning, and, in the end, this lovely one, who deserved so much better than these maneuvers of my indecision, capitulated.

I knew he would have given much to sidestep the ordeal of St. Louis, but the clan instinct was strong in me.

Finally it was arranged that I would precede him to St. Louis by two days, give my parents and Hamilton relatives time to forgather, and he would arrive the day, almost the very hour, of a very private home wedding.

I arrived in St. Louis prepared for the glacial reception to my announcement. Mama and Papa received it as if they were listening to funeral instead of marriage plans. Aunt Bettie, Jennie, and Uncle Joe arrived from Hamilton. The inquisition was on.

Ding dong, on deep into the night.

This is no marriage for you. What have you in common with this man who comes from the wilds of Asia? If only you had never laid eyes on Mount Clemens. You admit his earnings are not equal to yours.

What difference does that make?

Such a remark proves you are not in your senses.

Then there were the extra sessions, as one member of the family or another crept into my room through the sleepless nights.

Fannie, give yourself a year to think it over. You have the world before you. Who have Uncle Joe and I got but you? To whom can we leave what we have accumulated but you? But not if you make such a marriage . . .

Both you and Mr.—the young man may feel differently if you wait a while.

Papa simply could not utter Jack's name, never did, and that was bitter tea in my cup.

Incredibly, once more my brief moment of decision began to quaver. Why endure all this? Why hurry into marriage? Things were so wonderful as they were. Why couldn't we just drift on? It was I who had burst out with the suggestion that had led to all this. For all I knew, Jack was content as things were. Besides, time would help Mama and Papa to see the light. Meanwhile, I had work to do. Jack had work to do. It was not as if we did not have one another. Suppose it was a little hard on us, as the old wives' tales insisted. People in love had waited before, and survived it.

Me, trying to establish an alibi for me.

In the end, as if my motives were as unmixed as obedience to my parents, I agreed to postponement and wired Jack to hold everything until my return to New York.

Mama and Papa said I had always been a dutiful daughter, and would live to thank them.

Aunt Jennie took the necklace of oriental pearls off her neck and clasped it around mine.

The bit of dramaturgy which followed that gift I have never

revealed, even to Jack. Perhaps because it was ludicrous, but anything but that to me.

Up in my room, after Aunt Jennie's gift, I jerked it from my neck, the beads flying in all directions.

Perhaps the pseudo-dramatic gesture was more against myself than anyone else. Finally, ignominiously on all fours, I gathered them up and put them in an envelope. That evening Mama came across one of the beads on the floor.

Someone lost a bead, she said casually, and tossed it into the wastebasket.

Anticlimactically, I wrote "Each pearl a tear" across the envelope. It has lain in my safe-deposit box all these years, and, alas, by now each pearl is a tear.

Jack accepted my explanations quietly: Had we not better humor my parents' suggestion that we wait a while, since we will have all the rest of our lives together?

We had dinner that first night of my return at a restaurant on Eleventh Street, and under the crash and bang of the Sixth Avenue elevated trains walked toward my apartment afterward.

He seemed to agree that we should consider my parents' wishes, and my sense of uneasy guilt and fear were in abeyance. Otherwise, I might have been more prepared for what came.

At my corner, Jack suddenly raised his hat, said: This is good-by, and hailed a passing taxicab before I could so much as move from where I stood rooted.

He saw to it that I did not see him for eight weeks. Unable to work, pride down, I wrote, I telephoned, wired, and finally importuned my friend Vera to intervene in my behalf.

You don't deserve it, but I will.

Tell him I must have been insane to appear to be uncertain of the thing in life of which I am most certain. Explain to him that you will go with us at once, tomorrow, to be married. I have no pride left. Tell him I beg him.

Vera finally did reach him over the telephone, while I stood by.

He was gentle but firm. He had his work to do. It had been disrupted by all the confusion and shifting plans. He needed quiet. He was not going to allow his life to be disrupted again. He was very sorry. I was not sure of myself. He had only kind thoughts, but please to tell me to let matters rest as they were. No, it was best that we did not meet.

Despite my despair, Vera was not daunted.

You must go to him.

He won't see me. Besides, he is teaching all day.

Go to him in the evening.

I rang Jack's studio bell that evening. He opened the door himself.

He told me later what it meant to him to see me standing there, but he did not say come in or open wider the door.

You should not have come.

I pushed past him. He was limp-handed and unreceptive and insisted there was no further point in discussion.

Bernard Shaw's Superman theories were rampant at the moment. I felt the part. I was fighting for everything I had been insanely throwing away.

On and on we struggled through the emotional labyrinth where men and women have struggled since the beginning of the time of man.

It is better this way. You do not know your own mind. You want it and you don't want it.

Then let us do it secretly, the way we planned in the beginning. Please Jack? Try it for a year with me. Let us lead both our separate lives and our lives together. It will be a wonderful social experiment. We'll be married in a close and beautiful way. We'll be free that same way. We'll keep the dew on the rose.

Ah me, that fateful phrase. Dew on the rose! Lovely words to eat, but I was to eat them—dew-on-the-rose . . . dew-on-the-rose . . .

Forty-eight hours later, we were secretly married in Lakewood, New Jersey, Vera and a hotel clerk our witnesses, my parents our sole other confidants by long-distance telephone.

Mine was a delayed birth. Actually, I was born on a radiant afternoon in May when Jack and I were married.

All through the writing of this *Anatomy*, its ultimate destiny lies undetermined in my mind. Conceivably, it may remain under lock and key, a shaggy manuscript traveling no further than from the secret places of the heart into the desk drawer.

In that event, thanksgiving because Jack existed will have been privately offered to one who proved the grandeurs of which quiet men are sometimes capable.

From the hour of our marriage, indeed I suppose from the hour of our meeting, my husband, by virtue of his existence, became my remote control, which I promptly realized even if he did not.

In a marriage predicated upon our mutual respect for one another's freedom, which I do not believe either of us ever violated, the fact remains, although Jack would have been the first to laugh it off, that throughout our long years together my busy and many-sided life was to be activated by my desire to keep myself intact in his regard.

For all his humorous nonchalance and easy give, I was well aware of his inner gravity, the melancholy of one who suffers with and for whoever suffers. I knew that at all times, even when least apparent, his eye was upon me, not wanting me to spoil myself in the eyes of others, even in superficial matters.

I wonder if he ever knew to what extent I walked through our marriage in the attitude of looking up.

This was the shape my marriage took from its inception. Little did we realize, on our first secret honeymoon day in the springtime of Lakewood-in-the-pines, that our marriage was to remain secret for five years. My parents, Hamilton relatives, Bob Davis, Vera, not one of Jack's friends, and an editor friend of mine were the exceptions.

The exception of my editor friend occurred on our return to New York from Lakewood. We were crossing on the 7 A.M. ferry from Hoboken to New York, I gala in my honeymoon orchid corsage, when we encountered Churchill Williams, associate editor of *The Saturday Evening Post,* on his weekly trip from Philadelphia to New York. All of my grandmothers must have panicked within me. To clear myself of the deductions that might move through his mind, I confided our secret to him

He never betrayed us

Mama wrote me a chilling kind of letter signed "Mama and Papa," but my father's dictation stood out in almost every word· Now that I had made my choice . . . we pray it is for the best . . . Mama's postscript was all I read to Jack: My dearest children, I am so happy for you The enclosed check is for two thousand dollars, one for each of my children. Please do not let this secret nonsense go on. We are so worried about it. I am ashamed for the people, and so are the folks in Hamilton. When are my children coming home?

Poor Mama, so valiantly wanting what I wanted. Me. Me Me Is my ego as swollen as it begins to appear? Me. Me. Me.

I find myself wondering if these five secret years could have been as pleasant for Jack as they proved to be for me I had everything. On one hand, freedom, to use, not abuse On the other, the silk thread of immense tensile strength that bound me. The paradox of our stolen hours together, when actually they were hours that belonged to us alone! Our secret visits to one another; weekend trips My own happy secure knowledge that I had what I wanted both ways Me Me Me

During this period of our secret marriage, we continued, to outward appearances of course, to live as before, not even my housemate aware of what had taken place

Not wanting to be married, I was superlatively happy because I was. Only the most subtle and giving nature could have fathomed or tolerated what I myself did not, and do not yet, understand.

That nature belonged to my husband, who deserved better, and yet, I repeat with full conviction, Jack had a happy life with me. Time and time again he told me so He acted so He told others so. He looked and was so

He died begging me not to leave him, even to go as far as the telephone to call for help . . .

My insatiable zest may have been responsible for the swiftness with which the city took Miss Hurst of Cates Avenue, connections none, to its fearful and wonderful heart.

The first five years of my marriage might easily be devoted to the kaleidoscopic succession of meetings and repeated contacts with the great and near great, writers, actors, musicians, social, diplomatic, and political figures, so swiftly did my life fan out.

The long plodding hours at my desk, until the fingers and brain stiffened, dominated my time and energies, my workday in no wise altered by the fact of my marriage. By now I am being invited more and more frequently to lecture at universities and before forums.

Only a lusty ego could have managed the extracurricular burdens or faced anew each time the sickening fear of public speaking.

Youth, prosperity, happiness were mine, muddied, it is true, by growing and growing awareness of the inequities, the pain, the defeat, and worse which I encountered in my browsing. Nevertheless, my cup overflowed.

Our marital arrangement was certainly not one from which to deduce a formula. It happened to fit our particular needs. We defied so many of the basic laws for the successful marriage. What a list of "don'ts" we must have supplied for the marriage counselors. Our home life was negligible. We dined out, met when we so willed, or went our separate ways. We talked wishfully of having children, but when it did not happen lived happily and without sense of frustration.

You could liken our marriage to the man who defies every law of health and lives to be a hundred, while his friend who observed all prescribed rules falls dead at sixty.

We were free, maintaining through the years our separate groups of friends, seeing them separately, except when we felt like merging. There were few "musts" between us. We accepted no engagements for one another. We were never "dragged," whether to a dinner party, Europe, or to see that dear old school friend who would be offended unless . . . We had it "nice."

Every Monday morning—Jack died on that day—I write him a short letter, chattily, not in grief and with no feeling that he knows about it in an afterlife. It is a self-indulgence I allow myself. Frequently I dwell on: We had it nice.

While the drudgery of writing never for a moment relaxed its grip, I was already reconciled to what was to become a lifelong awareness. Whatever the heavy penalties of the laborious writer, that kind of punishment was essential to the very meaning of life.

From the long lonely hours of "sweating it out," you learned to be more than repaid by the brief but flashing moment when you began to feel that first faint kick of a story beginning to come alive.

Sometimes I wonder if that was why we two, who had a liking for children, felt little of the frustration usually attributed to the childless. Did the creative aspects of our work compensate? I look about me and draw no conclusions.

We seldom discussed our work with one another. Occasionally I might outline a story taking form, or, after a day spent before a sheet of blank paper, inflict my writing pains upon Jack. That terrible sense of defeat. A story that would not move.

I had very little to bring to Jack in his musical world and actually he dwelt on the periphery of mine. But the alleged desirability of similar interests did not apply to this perverse marriage of ours. It would seem that our sea of matrimony was full of treacherous archipelagoes. But we sailed it for wonderful years of blue waters, blue sky.

Our secret remained almost intact for five years, even though halfway through them Dorothy, my housemate, returned to Baltimore and I moved into a three-room arrangement of my—of our—own. A little paradise, or so it seemed to me, for a pair of adults playing at clandestine existence. We were careful enough about our movements, but I doubt if we realized the social implications that might have evolved from all this. Certainly I did not. And if

Jack, through that somber streak in him, did, it was what I wanted and that was the way it was going to be.

An occasional guest with that kind of mind spoke unwitting and facetious nonsense about the twin beds in my room. Mama and Papa came and were horrified. We had two spaniels, a macaw, and a marmoset, and I acquired a housemaid, or rather housekeeper, who was to remain the rest of her long life. It was an apartment of laughter.

Every time I pass the unusual little Gothic structure on West Sixty-ninth Street in New York that contained those beautiful years, it seems to me there should be a plaque against the building: Happiness Dwelt Here.

To be sure, things like this happened: Gilbert Mallin, the playwright whose friendship with me had developed considerably since the days we first met at the Gobert apartment, and Hugh were still on my horizon, asking me to dinner or calling.

One evening Gilbert burst out: Fannie, for God's sake, is it true? Are you married?

I parried that one with what should have been, but was not, a sense of guilt. How did you get that idea? At the Players' Club last night, someone said they heard you were.

I must have parried successfully, because when Jack and I visited California some weeks later on a belated honeymoon, each going to a separate San Francisco hotel, Gilbert's mother, informed by her son that I was in town, immediately invited me to their fine home.

The entire large family, parents, uncles, aunts, were assembled, obviously to look over the girl in whom the apple of this family's eye was interested. It was horrid. But not three blocks away, my husband was waiting for me in the Mark Hopkins Hotel.

Later, of course, when it was becoming obvious that the time had come when the situation was getting out of hand, I told Gilbert and Hugh of my "engagement." Each is now enjoying a long-time and happy marriage.

Fortunately, Jack was not a "homebody." The vast back-to-the-home movement had not yet swept the American family back into the home with its modern fireside, the television set.

I cannot say that under more normal circumstances and a more run-of-the-mill-minded wife Jack would have chosen our way of life. But once it took shape, it seemed to fit him like a glove. Frequently I offered to conventionalize our living. Perhaps he left the decision to me, but I strongly suspect he preferred it the way it was.

Be that as it may, and at the risk of protesting too loudly, Jack was a happy husband, regardless of how many males may be countering: He can have her!

Considering my slow and laborious writing processes, the output of these five years was good enough. Three volumes of collected short stories and my novel, *Lummox*. One of the natural but banal questions put to authors is: Of the books you have written, which is your favorite? My next novel, of course. But usually one is crowded for a more specific answer.

Interestingly enough, in many instances the author will tell you it is not the book which has enjoyed the best critical acclaim, or by which he is best known.

The reply which seems to be expected of me is *Back Street*. But no, it is *Lummox*, a novel preceding *Back Street* by several years.

As far as it is possible to trace the genesis of a book, *Lummox* was the outgrowth of my groping absorption in the milling masses, all creeds, all colors, which make the narrow island of Manhattan a wide, wide world.

One day, while *Lummox* was only a faint prick against my mind, I wandered into a dark basement on very east Fourteenth Street where two women, obviously Slavic, sat in the open doorway around a large carton filled with buttons of multifarious shapes and colors. Picked up by the handful, they were just a mass. But selected separately, each one claimed its identity. Pink and green buttons, crystal, bone, and pearl. Large, small, medium, oval, square.

In like manner, I had learned—subconsciously, I suppose—to sort faces. Faces in the crowd were no longer just faces melting like wax into one another. They had separateness.

It was out of this milling world of people with no faces in particular, no identity in particular, that my *Lummox* began to take heavy shape. She became the scrubwoman standing in a rain-sheltering doorway, waiting for a bus after a nightlong of swabbing up the million footprints in an office building. She became the woman with widespread knees and sagging breasts on a tenement stoop. She became a composite of many soils, of many climates, of many lineages. Here she is, as she steps into the opening lines of my novel, *Lummox*:

Nobody quite knew just what Baltic bloods flowed in sullen and alien rivers through Bertha's veins—or cared, might be added. Bertha, least of all.

She was five feet nine and a half, of flat-breasted bigness, and her cheek-bones were pitched like Norn's. Little tents. There must have been a good smattering of Scandinavian, and even a wide streak of western Teutonic. Slav, too. Because unaccountably she found herself knowing the Polish national anthem. Recognized it with her heart as it rattled out of a hurdy-gurdy.

In her carpet-bag, an outlandish one with a steamship stamp on it, were a bit of Bulgarian embroidery, a runic brooch, a concertina with a punctured bellows, and an ikon in imitation mosaic. Old world. And yet Bertha had been born in a furiously dark sailors' lodging-house in Front Street, where New York harbour smells of spices and city garbage rides by to the dump on barges. One of those frightening emergency births of rusty instruments, midwifery, and a sinister room made more terrible by the travail of her coming. Of no particular father (although the China seas could probably have yielded up the secret of his rollicking lane), and of a dead mother.

She had died two minutes before Bertha was born, Annie Wennerberg, landlady of the sailors' lodging-house who reared Bertha those first dozen years of her life, that were sopping wet with scrub-water and soft-soap, knew. Horrid scuttling rat-like things that Annie Wennerberg knew.

> Born of a dead mother,
> Secrets of the grave you'll utter.

That couplet could run down Bertha's spinal cord like a mouse.
"I don't know any secrets of the grave, Annie."
"You do. They're written on your face. You got a look in that wide place between your eyes like the sound of a clump of dirt falling on a coffin. You're as full of secrets as a cow's tail is of burrs."

In a way, *Lummox* symbolized my complete breakthrough, by what might be termed the short method, from the circumscribed world in which I had been reared into a new social consciousness.

I felt so completely awake writing *Lummox*. Too awake. I still do. So much to know, to do, to feel, to see, to think about, care about, laugh about. Grieve about.

That enormous waking up was as if the mind had been a house with most of the rooms closed off and, suddenly, new winds were rushing through the corridors, blowing open doors, revivifying dead air.

Write I must and did. But in other directions my selectivity blurred. Extracurricular activities that were too many, too varied, but constantly stimulating, took up where my workday left off.

Just as I had been permitted to have my head as a child, so now my marriage gave me my way. My husband, whose movements I never questioned, nor did I take exception to any sudden plan or need of his which displaced mine, gave me in return the complete freedom I granted him. Between stories or books, I took lecture tours across the country. Special feature newspaper assignments of nationwide interest. National conventions, Hall-Mills murder trial, Lindbergh kidnapping, and, much later, Dr. Sanders' euthanasia case.

New awarenesses burst like skyrockets into my consciousness.

ANATOMY OF ME

I had been walking in my sleep all my life.

Pain, disease, defeat, poverty were imbedded in the current parade through which I moved day after day—most of it hidden deep down in eyes or behind masklike faces.

Irrationally, I came to be considered an authority on subjects unidentified with my experience or knowledge as a novelist. A social study organization wanted a name-author to publicize a fund-raising drive. Why not that girl-author, what'shername? A city slum clearance group decided I was just the person to address a monster mass meeting.

Each of these ventures into fields hitherto unexplored presented new material, new areas, trips across the face of America, invaluable grist to an author's mill, and always that sense of means to an end. Greater good for the greater number. But too often, particularly after addressing a gilt ballroom filled with a gilt audience, the end seemed dishearteningly remote, as through the wrong end of the opera glasses.

But no matter how slight the immediate results, I was beginning to care in a more than disturbing way about what troubled people. What troubled them, troubled me. Discrimination, intolerance, exploitation. Last remnants of the smugness of Cates Avenue were beginning to be blasted out of me the hurting way.

Too many people within the sphere of my daily life were living "down under" on a level of mere existence.

What proportion of the street throngs in the lower reaches of the richest city in the world, even though they put up a good front, had slept on a clean bed the night before, enjoyed a good bath, lived in bright rooms and had good teeth and enough put by to insure decent burial? Why the miles and miles of firetrap tenements, the women old at forty, the dirty stoops, the dirty children?

I did not realize it, but I was merely youth making the old immemorial queries. Youth being young.

The capacity for indignation is as fleeting as youth itself. Too often the immensities of straightening out the human scene bog down the dreamer.

In New York the contrasts were in such incredible juxtaposition! A city block or two separates the marble-lace dwellings of the avenues, the liveried doormen, and the luxury shops from the canyons of slum life, the cats and children among the garbage cans.

I came to know areas in my glimpses into life in New York that seldom crawled out from under the rock, comparable to conditions described by Dostoevski and Gorki. Had these Asians and Europeans imported their misery along with themselves, and brought us a terrible new poverty that we were permitting to thrive in our own country? Were we part and parcel of world inequities?

In St. Louis I had been faintly aware but not particularly disturbed by contrasts of wealth and poverty. Not even the shantied segregation of the Negroes had risen to smite my consciousness, until the spectacle of the tremendous social dilemmas of the human race spread themselves before me on a small island called Manhattan, written there with the high concentration of the Ten Commandments on the head of a pin.

Meanwhile, editors were clamoring for love stories, happy endings, boy-meets-girl. It is interesting that my stories of the forlorn should have met with an undiminishing demand for more. Of course all was not grim in this dirty, poor, gang-infested world. Poverty is as old as mankind. Humor, genius, love, and certainly sanctity also have their roots in its tired soil.

As my public kind of life expanded, I continued behind a false front of pose and poise to be self-conscious and shy of people, especially writers.

There was stimulus in the manifold activities that were extracurricular to the lonely writing hours. But it was to Jack that I looked for strength and serenity. He had both, and withal the playfulness that meant more than any profound intellectual interests we might have had in common.

I wonder if it was because Papa was so unplayful that my gaiety at Jack's gaiety was constantly overflowing.

I would come home, find him at the piano in my—our—apartment and, interrupting Bach or Chopin, clutch a handful of his heavy black hair in a tight grip until he repeated after me: Please, my beautiful wife, let go. If he said "beautiful" without melodramatic intensity, I would tighten my hold. . . .

The dear nonsense . . . life is so stilled now that it is stilled. . . .

Looking back, it seems incredible that the impact of the financial crash of 1929 could have reached me so tardily. Perhaps because at first it hit hardest at the monied interests, before it reached the areas where people had less to lose and where I spent so much of my time.

I was aware, of course, that the country was in a financial crisis. By now, suicides were hitting the headlines, people we knew personally had been "caught" in the United States Bank failure, the country was in trouble, fortunes had been wiped out overnight, taking with them tremendous tonnage in human anguish.

Yet even when it swept up to my own doorstep, the holocaust did not seem to come all the way home to me.

I was not to realize until such tangible evidence of unemployment as apple vendors and breadlines began to appear on the streets that we were in a crisis.

I must have been poor solace to Jack, who was aware that I listened to matters pertaining to finance with half an ear and less than half understanding. There is a type of woman, with whom I must reluctantly admit a one-time kinship, who regards ignorance pertaining to such realistic matters as finance as a charming feminine foible, appealing as a short upper lip or fear of mice. A remnant, no doubt, of obsolete days when she was charming bric-a-brac.

Our lawyer, who, of course, knew of our marriage by now, was telephoning Jack more and more frequently. A guarantee company with whom we held second mortgage investments had suddenly been deprived by the government of the power of guarantee. Tenement houses which Jack had never seen were suddenly our property, their upkeep more than their value.

Our investment was double-edged. The deterioration of our "nest egg," and the fact that these old buildings were in my name at a time when, because of my growing interest in housing problems for those in the lower income brackets, I had been appointed to a housing authority group.

With the bottom out of so many markets, we were advised to bide our time and when, or if, matters readjusted sell the properties at the least possible loss.

But Jack decided to dispose of the houses immediately, regardless of loss. Suppose fire were to break out in tenements so unwittingly owned by a member of the Mayor's Commission for Better City Housing?

One day, Jack placed in front of me a memorandum which he had composed: If I had not sold those tenements, here are headlines which might have appeared in today's newspapers: Three tenement structures, described by Fire Commissioner Jones as traps, were gutted by flames early yesterday morning. Two firemen were severely burned. The structures are owned by Fannie Hurst, novelist and member of the Mayor's Housing Commission. Miss Hurst could not be reached.

Although I did not know about it at the time, indeed until after Jack's death, those were months of financial hazard for us. Our ship had hit, head on, an iceberg that, as far as I was concerned, had been more than nine tenths submerged.

But Mama wrote: Your father has weathered this depression up to now because he is holding onto his securities. But people in this town who could buy and sell him are wiped out. Papa is not well. Naturally, he worries about your affairs, which you never mention. He feels it that you seem to trust your affairs to your husband who is not a businessman, rather than to him. I must say, it does seem unnatural. I worry constantly about the way things are. I cannot understand how it is that your marriage does not leak out. How do we know that people are not saying, God forbid, that you are living in sin with him? I could cry my eyes out. Your aunts blame me, as if I can do anything about it. If you are caught in this depression, you had better write and tell us. I grieve enough to think of you stuck in that little apartment, leading a suspicious-looking life for no reason at all. I just pray you are happy with your husband and that he is making you a good living, regardless of your own earning capacity. What are you writing that takes so long? Isn't there more money in short stories than in such slow novels? Give my love to Jack. I must say, except for Papa, I could feel very happy with such a fine son-in-law.

It was wonderful to have Mama acknowledge my husband!

Now I was prowling more and more about the settlement houses, then at the height of their activity, and coming to know women like Helen Hull, head of Henry Street Settlement, Mary Simkovitch of Greenwich House, Magistrate Anna Kross, founder of Home Term Court, all women who cared and caused their light to shine over dark areas. . . .

The solemn dirge of the depression years had not quite receded when Universal Film Corporation made a package purchase of the motion picture rights to sixty of my short stories.

The day I completed *Lummox*, a snowy one in January, Jack and I had the celebration we usually enjoyed over a finished piece of work. We lunched in my—our—apartment. Afterward, since I employed no secretary, I set about contacting the young woman who usually did my typing. She was in a hospital with pneumonia.

I had a collection of addresses of typists which I had accumulated from time to time. I finally selected one because the address was in my immediate neighborhood, not more than two blocks away. I telephoned the young woman, who seemed experienced in manuscript work, and she agreed to come and see me at once.

A graduate of Hunter College, she typed a sample page with expertness. But she was married, had a young child, and needed to work in her own home.

I hesitated over this last because I had no carbon copy of my manuscript. But since she was so close at hand, and we could also be in communication by telephone if she encountered difficulties, I agreed.

For hours we went over the manuscript and she departed with the bulky tome.

The following day she brought me a few pages which were

competently done. From then on, whenever she had a query, which was seldom, she communicated by telephone.

During this period, a memorable snowstorm struck New York. For days the city stood in a white paralysis, buses and automobiles stalled in their tracks, the usually banging streets noiseless.

It was beautiful, dramatic, and enormously uncomfortable for New Yorkers, who literally had to plow their way on foot or go by subway to places of employment.

For days not a wheel turned. To add to a growingly grave situation, the snowfall continued. In addition to the strange silence, not once during these stormy days had I heard from my typist. But in a way this augured well, indicating that she was encountering no difficulties in reading my heavily penciled manuscript.

But after a week, I telephoned her. There was no reply. I tried intermittently during the day, with no results. Finally, in growing unease, I decided to plow my way around to her address.

It proved to be a stone-front residence that had been converted into small apartments. But there was no name corresponding to my typist's above any one of the six doorbells. I sought out the superintendent of the building. The Kallins no longer lived there. They had moved out the week before. Where was Mr. Kallin employed? Shipping clerk in the garment district, but the superintendent did not know where or for whom. Had they a forwarding address? No, but the local post office might.

The post office had no record of change of address. I stood bewildered in the snow-filled street, great drifts half burying the stalled automobiles. Working my way back to the Kallin residence, I began a round of the neighbors. True to the capacity of the metropolis for anonymity, no one knew anything about them or their whereabouts. Knees almost striking my chin as I plowed, I sought out the nearest express company in the hope that they had moved the Kallins. No. Then the grocer, the butcher, the stationer. A clerk in a drugstore gave me my first clue. Mr. Kallin had been in about a week ago to buy some cigarettes. Said they were moving to Simpson Street, wherever that is. No, the clerk had no idea of the house number. Simpson Street proved to be in the Bronx section of New York, an area least explored by me.

Taxicabs were beginning to cut their way through the streets, but not one of those I hailed would attempt the Bronx.

Finally one of the drivers took time to give me some rather vague directions for reaching Simpson Street by subway. Simpson Street proved to be a long snow-covered procession of fairly modern, flimsy-looking four- and five-story apartment buildings, interspersed here and there with private dwellings not yet crowded out. I had no alternative but to begin a house-to-house canvass.

It did not occur to me to have recourse to the police. In addition, I had decided to spare Jack from knowing. That I had permitted my manuscript out of my sight, without so much as a carbon copy, would have been incomprehensible to him. It was to become that to me, too, but after the event.

All I seemed to realize in those panicked hours was that catastrophe had overtaken me, and to rewrite *Lummox* from memory would have been as futile as to attempt to recapture a dream or a flash of lightning.

For three consecutive days I made a door-to-door canvass of Simpson Street, taking note of the apartments or dwellings where there was no reply to my ring and returning later, usually around the dinner hour. I questioned janitors, superintendents, and also what few neighbors were about. To no avail. The snowstorm might have gulped the Kallins and my manuscript into its white maw.

Toward the close of the third day, as I toiled my way up the flights, I came upon a house painter in one of the long corridors, standing on a high plank stretched between two ladders, sloshing his brush against the ceiling and blocking the door to an apartment. I was returning after having rung the bell in vain the day before.

Nobody in there, miss, he volunteered. And then came the revealing information. New tenants have moved their stuff in, but nobody is living there yet. I'm going in there next, to do a paint job.

After considerable argument and quite considerable crossing of the palm, he agreed to unlock the door for me.

Directly before me in the first of the rooms as I entered, amid debris of furniture, sheeted bundles, kitchenware, hampers, stood a galvanized washtub on a kitchen table. On top of the piled-up tub was my manuscript.

Mrs. Kallin, it developed, who had a history of mental disturbances, had reverted to sudden hallucinations and had been intercepted by her husband in the act of doing violence to their child. She was once more institutionalized and the distraught husband had moved to an apartment in a neighborhood where he could be within reach of his parents, who had the little girl.

It was only as the strain lifted that I came to realize the umbilical cord between author and book.

One late afternoon, came a person-to-person telephone call from Trenton, New Jersey.

Out-of-town invitations to lecture were becoming more than occasional, and long-distance calls were not unusual. But this one went something like this:

Miss Hurst, Paul Degan, Associated Press, speaking. In going over some records here in Trenton, I stumbled across one of your marriage over five years ago in Lakewood, New Jersey, to Jacques S. Danielson of Lexington Avenue, New York City. Is this true?

Wisdom did not come to me until afterward. I panicked. I talked too much, explained too much. I began to enlarge on why we had kept it secret, involving myself deeper with each word. We had not intended to keep it quiet for so long a period. It happened that way . . . wanted a marriage suited to our particular ways of life. We each enjoy our own lives, as well as our common life together.

Does that mean you have separate apartments?

Yes, I blurted, if you want to put it that way.

You mean, you never meet for breakfast?

And then came that fateful phrase, said flippantly: Oh, two or three times a week. Our way of keeping the dew on the rose.

This last hapless phrase flew around the world. Within twenty-four hours the news of our marriage was headlines. Reporters stormed our apartment and Jack's studio. Photographers waited for us to enter or leave a building. Letters, telegrams, cablegrams, appraising, praising, damning, rained upon us. We were news in China, New Zealand, and European capitals. Bernard Shaw, when interviewed for an opinion of our marriage, said: I am for it. Shorter hours and more pay. A term, abrasive to us both, "trial marriage," dogged us every so often. And everywhere for years to come that phrase so punishing to us: "the dew is on the rose" would crop up apropos of matters irrelevant to the subject of marriage. For many a day we shivered away for the connotations that went with the mere sight of a rose. Time has broken down some of the horrendous association. I can even pluck a rose now. But not with dew on it!

Strangely, neither Mama and Papa nor the Aunts were as outraged as I feared. Following my bad example, Mama made gauche and labored explanations to the St. Louis press, which resulted in ridiculous headlines: Mother of Fannie Hurst explains daughter's trial marriage. Fannie is too much of an individualist to do anything like other people. Shoe Executive, Samuel Hurst, Declines Comment.

Today, our way of marriage, which we advocated for no one but ourselves, would doubtless rate no more than cursory notice in the day's news.

We were wind before the dawn. But what a gale!

As one year moves into several, Jack decides, what with our income growing and our quarters seeming too narrow, the time has come for more spacious and gracious living.

Inwardly, I cling to our small apartment, but I go along with his project.

One day he burst in upon me. He had found just the place! Had I not always contended that I had been born in a house, reared in a house, and preferred a house to an apartment? Well, he had discovered a three-story dwelling within an eighteen-story apartment house!

Around the corner, on the famous Sixty-seventh Street of the artists, in a building known as Hotel des Artistes, he had come upon a recently vacated "triplex" studio apartment of immense proportions. Baronial living room, thirty-foot-high ceiling. Wood-burning fireplaces. Balconies. A roof terrace halfway across the building. My workroom, overlooking this terrace, oak paneled, with stained-glass windows, seemed to have a hush built into it.

All this must have stirred within Jack memories of European spaciousness. At his urging we moved into the new dwelling which swallowed our simple furniture at a gulp, leaving us in a vacuum of great reaches of bare walls, bare floors, bare floor-to-ceiling windows.

How we were ultimately to furnish it is another matter.

I could not rise to the move with the ebullience of Jack, who seemed obsessed with the idea that here was the "background" he wanted for me. It is against this same background that this *Anatomy* is being written.

Mama wrote: Thank goodness you are at last going to live like normal human beings. How much rent do you pay? It sounds expensive.

For a while, until we managed to develop an immunity to it, the claptrap dew-on-the-rose, three breakfasts a week, separate apartments, almost forced us into discontinuing our way of life. This we minded not too much, since from the beginning we had been together more than had appeared on the surface. But by now we preferred the procedure to which the first five years had accustomed us, both moving in our separate circles when we so desired, converging when we so desired. Thus we continued what to so many seemed a strange and unnatural relationship, unpossessive yet possessing.

It accomplished little to attempt to explain that we held out no formula for others, indeed advised against it. It was to take many a year to educate our friends to the unnatural spectacle of a wife who did not expect her husband to attend with her functions or occasions that did not interest him; to educate them to feel no hesitancy in inviting her alone. In time, Jack's friends, too, came to accept the fact that his regrettably unmusical wife need not be included in his invitation to join a box party at the Metropolitan for *Parsifal* or attend a bridge game.

Jack's life was quieter than mine, his tempo slower. He lived it with a certain rhythm. Music, good theater, travel, sports, the moderate ones such as ice skating, handball, canoeing, games of chance. This last he practiced with surprising moderation, considering how much horse races, roulette, and the stock market intrigued him. A prodigious walker, he had also a prodigious capacity for contemplation, which I seldom invaded.

People said: Aren't you afraid? After all, he's only human . . . All those pretty girls he teaches . . .

I could not explain, in the world in which I found myself living, that these thoughts never entered my mind, nor could be put there. My domination of him was only exceeded by his domination of me.

No sooner were we established in our immense and underfurnished new home than a common obsession overtook us. Furnishing it.

A phase of myself to which I had never given thought rose now to confront me. A psychiatrist, I suppose, could do things with it.

When I was a student, it was my frequent habit, when walking home from high school, to slip unnoticed into a large cathedral-like church on Lindell Boulevard. Not at the instigation of a spiritual urge, but rather to immerse my senses, to create a mood inducible by the broody silence, the pale faces of plaster and wooden Madonnas, the shape of pain typified by the Christ pilloried to the cross behind the altar.

Mama and Papa would have been no little disturbed by these visits to the vast edifice. A synagogue across the street, and me seated in the shadow of a bleeding Christ . . . moving among the dim votive candles in their red cups, among the imagery forbidden to Jews.

A small exultation resided in these forays into the vaulted splendor of the church. The great dome, the storied stained windows, the imagery, the old smells into which incense had been swung and swung . . . odor of God . . . odor of the terribleness of the unknown.

The synagogue lacked pomp and circumstance. Beyond the trappings, there seemed few differences to justify the deep schisms they had created between men throughout history and still were creating.

Far-fetched as it may seem, it was these nebulous experiences in the Gothic shades of a church that were to direct me in the furnishing of our new home.

I had been reared in the Mission school of interior decoration. Brass beds, oak furniture, cabinets, knickknacks, sideboards, shadowboxes, lace curtains.

At last I was to have the kind of environment for which I had been unconsciously waiting since those hours in the church on Lindell Boulevard. If Jack preferred that we furnish as quietly and elegantly as our purse would afford in Hepplewhite, Phyfe, Chippendale, he made no point of it. After camping for almost three years with what furniture we had, during which time I wrote *Five and Ten*, *A President Is Born*, and a collection of short stories, *Procession*, we decided to embark upon a two-month shopping tour in Italy, the happiest hunting ground for furnishing the kind of home upon which my mind's eye had so long been fixed.

In February of that year, Jascha Heifetz, the violinist, urged Jack to accompany him to Europe on a concert tour. It was then arranged that he proceed ahead with Heifetz, I would remain behind to finish my book as planned, and we would meet in Rome in April.

As a matter of fact, my mission to Europe was twofold that year. I needed to go to France to verify my descriptions of the spa Aix-les-Bains, which I had described in detail in my book without ever having been there.

I arrived in Paris with my completed manuscript. During the

brief stopover there, I encountered Marie Dressler, the American comedienne. She exclaimed how strange that she should meet me in the Place Vendôme, when she frequented my neighborhood in America several times a week without even once seeing me.

I explained that I no longer lived on Sixty-ninth Street but had moved to Sixty-seventh.

Stranger still, she exclaimed!

It developed that Miss Dressler was on her way back to her hotel after having come from the funeral of Mr. X, the friend whose home she so frequently visited in Sixty-seventh Street. A wonderful novel could be written about his story, she said, and you are the one to do it.

Standing on the sidewalk in front of the Ritz Hotel, she outlined her friend's life. He and his wife had lived in a spectacular apartment which he had designed and built for her. The grief-stricken woman who had attended her husband's funeral that day had enjoyed a pampered and happy life with him. But much of his superlative indulgence, Miss Dressler hypothesized, must have been prompted by a sense of guilt, because for the twenty-three years of that apparently sound marriage, another woman, unknown to his wife, had lived in his background.

Wherever Mr. X and his wife traveled, and that was practically over the face of the earth, the other woman followed on another boat or plane, or lived in hotels not far removed from theirs, always out of sight, always within reach.

Even at the funeral, continued Miss Dressler, there she was in the last pew of the church, unnoticed, alone as always, not even entitled to her grief, while the bereaved wife and children followed the bier of husband and father. What a story for you to write, repeated Miss Dressler.

What a story for me! The finished manuscript *Back Street*, which I had brought to Europe to verify at Aix-les-Bains, was precisely that story!

To further twist the long arm of coincidence, it developed that the apartment in which we were living and had come to Europe to furnish had been previously occupied by none other than the late Mr. X and his family.

From Paris I proceeded to Rome, arriving there at midnight Easter Eve, two days before Jack was due, and just as the Hotel Excelsior, where I had wired for a room, was filling up with Americans who had arrived via boat trains from the Italian luxury liner *Rex*.

Most of them, it seemed, had made reservations weeks before and held cablegrams from the hotel verifying them. I had wired the day before from Paris and received no reply.

The overworked room clerk shrugged me off. Hotel full. Hotel no longer able to send arrivals to other hotels. The Easter push was in full swing. But I had wired for reservations the day before. Hotel had been refusing Easter applications for rooms for three weeks.

It looked like an all-night sit-up for me, and I had the galleys of *Back Street* to correct before going to bed, and mail back to my publishers on the steamship *Rex* before it sailed in twenty-four hours.

Suddenly one of the *Rex* arrivals, whom I did not know, stepped forward. Surely, you are not going to turn Fannie Hurst away, he said in a loud voice.

As if by magic, one of those princely managers of European Excelsior Hotels stepped from behind the mail rack, took me in hand and directed the room clerk to split "Suite A," allotting me the sitting room, in which they set up a cot.

And what a sitting room. Oval-shaped, done in pale French Empire, oval-shaped Aubusson rug, arched ceiling done in murals after the school of Tiepole, the adjoining marble bath as large as my bedroom on Sixty-seventh Street.

Tired and grimy, I decided on a hasty bath as a refresher, and then to my galleys and Easter morning in St. Peter's.

But, alas, I reckoned without my Italian plumbing. Tug as I would at the large wheel which corresponds to our faucets, not a drop of water! By then it was three o'clock in the morning, and if I was to see the Pope at St. Peter's on Easter, it meant get to my galley proofs at once.

Slipping into a dressing gown, I planted myself before a table and began work, completing it about six o'clock as a clear dawn began to pinken the roofs of Rome.

As I removed my feet from the rung of the chair, they sank into water which closed about my ankles. The plumbing had worked while I worked, and the place was inundated, the Aubusson rug under several inches of water!

Almost simultaneously, my shocked awareness seemed to race through the hotel. Violent thumpings came from below. Apparently, water was seeping into the apartment beneath; the sound of running feet in the hallways broke the early morning calm.

I looked about the room. Two sofa pillows bobbled toward me on the flood waters. My hatbox and a tan overcoat I had brought at Jack's request lay in a water-soaked hunk beside my chair. One white glove floated like a leaf.

In answer to violent knocking at my locked door, I waded to open it to the burst of housemen in green baize aprons and chattering maids armed with buckets.

Bedlam! Into the bathroom they rushed to turn off the flooding bathtub faucets. Men began ripping up the water-logged rug, maids rescued handbags and helped cart furniture into the hallways, which were also beginning to be flooded. High-pitched voices came from all directions. In the confusion, I managed to slip unnoticed into a closet, get back into my travel-stained clothes, and, clutching my manuscript, slip unnoticed from the scene of havoc.

After all, I was in Rome on Easter! The Pope would ride in sedan chair of state into St. Peter's.

I saw the full splendor of Easter at St. Peter's. But, lock it off as I would, deep down in my consciousness lurked dismay. I had better telephone Jack before he left London to begin raising funds somehow, some way, because we would practically have to buy the hotel to get out of this one.

If only I could run out on the whole experience and not return to the Excelsior. I walked slowly through the Easter crowds of a sun-drenched Sunday, chimes tilting, and all about me the beauty that is Rome.

As I slunk into the hotel lobby, the princely gentleman of the previous evening, in cutaway and striped trousers, hurried toward me, grasping my hand to kiss it again and again.

My dear Signora, he exclaimed, I am full of apology. I beg you will excuse this occurrence. I have had you moved into our manager's suite. You will remain as long as you will with the compliments of the hotel. You will find everything of yours pressed and hung up for you in order. If you will permit, Signora Hurst, I will like very much to give for you a dinner in your honor to meet important people in Rome. With your permission, Madame Safartti, who is Mussolini's confidante and the first lady of the city, will call on you today.

Later that same eventful day, I walked into Ray Long, editor of *Cosmopolitan Magazine*. We lunched together.

When am I going to have a look at the new novel? he asked repeatedly.

But there is no point in showing it to you, Ray. It is not a serial. It is censorable.

Let me be the judge of that.

In the end I sent a carbon copy down to his room in the Hotel Excelsior.

He telephoned me at four o'clock the following morning.

I want to start *Back Street* in our September issue. I'll pay you seventy thousand dollars for the serial rights.

I wanted to dash out into the night and buy Rome.

When Jack arrived, we plunged into the joyous chores of picking up, piece by piece, fifteenth-century refectory tables, hand carved and lacking the sharp precisions of machine production, wall panelings stripped from a villa in the process of being dismantled, inlaid credenzas and berguenos, prie-dieu, chests designed to contain priests' vestments. Savonarola chairs, torchons, lecterns, antique velvets, Italian brocades.

I did most of my shopping "by ear," trusting instinct for the rightness of a triptych or fabric.

In the long run it was to take years more of travel in Spain, France, Germany, England, Italy, days upon days in auction rooms, to put us together into the medieval atmosphere we were finally to achieve. Our mistakes were prodigious and expensive. What we were pleased to call our "chamber of horrors" was crammed with them.

But in the main, intuition combined with Jack's almost impeccable taste produced what we were after.

This summer of crises had not done with me.

Before leaving America, Mama's letters had been theme songs of impatience and disappointments: Can't understand why it takes you so long to finish everything. It is months since you have appeared in the magazines. I read in the *Post-Dispatch* the other day that a man in Belleville, Illinois, wrote a ten-thousand-dollar prize story in six days for some magazine contest. You are surely a better writer than he is.

As if to assuage Mama, *Liberty Magazine* shortly thereafter announced a novelette contest for a fifty-thousand-dollar prize. With Mama in mind, I unearthed a rejected short story I had long ago written for *The Saturday Evening Post*, developed it, sent it in anonymously, with my name in a sealed envelope as stipulated, and forgot it.

One day in Florence, Italy, returning to our hotel footsore and weary from a day in the Ufizzi and Pitti Palace art galleries, a cablegram awaited me. It was from *Liberty Magazine*. I had won.

That night we celebrated at dinner-for-two, served in our room on a little balcony overlooking the river Arno. Let's go to Russia, I exclaimed in the midst of it, taking myself as much by surprise as Jack. We may never be able to afford it again!

It took a pair of babes in the wood like ourselves to scale the unforeseen difficulties which immediately rose like perpendicular-sided mountains of ice between us and Russia.

Russian domestic affairs were in turmoil, foreign travel into this country had reached a new low, and the rigmarole of entry was beyond anything either of us had conceived. It was to require weeks of cablegrams, long transcontinental telephoning, procrastination, interminable waits for visas, credentials, heavy briefing, assistance from American embassies, long waitover in Berlin, and help from Isaac Marcasson and various American correspondents stationed there.

It did not occur to me to seek a commission from a magazine for a series of stories or articles, although after we were in Moscow, *McCall's Magazine,* hearing of my whereabouts, cabled for five articles which I ultimately delivered.

We seemed to have a talent for making matters hilariously difficult for ourselves. Strange caravan we were. Jack, traveling with his clavier, a silent keyboard with legs that folded under it like a camel's. Me, with a full-size typewriter, since my touch is too savage for a portable, and between us an almost life-size fourteenth-century wood carving of Moses, which we had picked up in Berlin, the polychrome flaking and therefore too frail to ship.

There seemed to be no form of Russian frontier holdup and examination to which we were not subjected. By the time we reached Moscow, my typewriter case, so battered from openings and closings that it no longer clamped into place, showed its keys through the aperture in a sardonic kind of grin at the world in general and frontier officials in particular.

In the end, I was obliged to surrender the machine at a border, rather than risk what might have been several days' further delay. I loved that old typewriter. It had no A. The spacer balked. It was like leaving a person behind.

In some respects, the Russian visit proved to be a heartbreaker for Jack. Families he remembered were broken or obliterated, members dead, imprisoned, institutionalized or whereabouts unknown, all traces of distant relatives gone, standards of living reduced to lowest.

He did finally discover two sisters, old friends of his family, still living in their stone house on a residential street that now had grass growing between its cobblestones. There were only two left of a family of eleven, and they now occupied a rear room, the remainder of their one-time dwelling given over to eight families, all using the common kitchen and the one bath that had been kept in condition.

As we entered, we bent our heads under washing which flapped from lines strung across the marble foyer.

In the main we were permitted to move about with a certain amount of freedom, a girl guide assigned us for each day's sightseeing, which was obviously "directed." What freedom we did enjoy was offset by the key of caution in which everyone spoke, as if someone were walking behind them or breathing down their backs. We, too, found ourselves frequently glancing back, sometimes pausing on quiet streets when we thought we heard following footsteps.

One evening we dined in the cramped overcrowded home of a professor at the University of Leningrad, whom we had met through an American correspondent. We were five at a meager dinner, served in the room in which the professor and his wife slept and cooked. Their fiercely pretty young daughter, wearing overalls, was also present. All of the family spoke acceptable English. At the conclusion of the meal, the wife dropped her voice to a whisper: You are leaving Leningrad tomorrow. We will be at the station to see you off. Please, when your train pulls out, look back at me and remember my prayer to you. Get our daughter Tanya out of Russia. There is no God allowed, and where there is no God there is no good. Help us to get her to America!

The young girl shook her head:

I will not go to a capitalistic shambles, she cried. Never! Never!

I wonder where and how she is today.

Although we were unaware of it, our arrival in Moscow followed on the heels of the end of the Trotsky regime. By the simple device of writing a letter requesting an interview from Trotsky, who was already living far from Moscow, I obtained it.

He received me, seated at the far end of what must have been a one-time ceremonial room but was now bare of furniture except for yellow oak chairs, reminiscent of American office décor. What seemed to be a long mile stretched between me and the Grand Rapids desk at the far end of the outside room where Mr. Trotsky awaited.

It was a grilling mile to traverse, reducing the visitor to peanut proportions. With the exception of one object, a book, the top of his desk was swept as clean as an American big business executive's.

He greeted me warmly, in broken English, told me he had lived on New York's East Side for eight years, graciously sidestepped most of the questions I put to him pertaining to state or his personal plans.

Seated beside him, I found it difficult to keep my eyes from returning to that book lying on the clean-swept area of his desk. Finally he reached for it: I am a great admirer of your work. *Lummox* I know so well that I can recite most of it from memory. Would you like to hear some of it?

I would!

He began to recite from "The Cathedral under the Sea" chapter, his voice fine and resonant.

Right? he interrupted himself to ask.

I don't know, I stammered, you will have to let me hold the book.

This sent him into long laughter and we parted in high amiability, Mr. Trotsky inviting me to call on him in case he should ever find himself again in the United States.

That remark must have been unconsciously prophetic, because I was later to visit him, not in the United States, but in Mexico City, where he was living out the last months of his life under machine-gun guard.

During our weeks in Russia, the Greek Church was in process of being practically dispossessed. Tichon, the deposed Pope, was then living in exile in a monastery outside Moscow. After lengthy preamble, an appointment came through and Jack and I drove out one afternoon to see him.

In keeping with practically all of the Russian scene, our car and the roads were rundown and out of repair, the monastery in a state of advanced decay.

We were ushered into a postage stamp of an anteroom, two cells thrown together, bare and once whitewashed. On chairs ranged along the walls sat bearded dignitaries of the church, their habiliment soiled, but most of them still hung with the jeweled accouterments of ecclesiastical royalty.

We settled ourselves for a long wait, but after a few moments a door opened and a white-robed white-bearded patriarch appeared, bending his head to prevent the jeweled cross at the peak of his pointed headdress from striking the door frame.

Everyone rose.

I understand, he said in well-spoken English, that there are Americans here?

We stepped forward, and he advanced, both hands outstretched.

I am happy to see you. Are you from New York? I lived for some years in your wonderful city, on Madison Avenue and Ninety-first Street. Tell me, how are my dear friends, the Norman Hapgoods?

Thus, in a world so strange to me, so lacking in so much of what I loved best in my own country, so heart hurting and nostalgic to Jack, the long, long arm kept reaching . . .

One evening, we passed a motion picture house which carried a large lithograph of little boy Jackie Coogan. I had never seen him in America. We went in. Before the picture began, a boxed paragraph was thrown on the screen which translated: The following picture, made in Hollywood, is not presented for its merits, but as an example of child labor and exploitation in America.

Jackie was probably one of the most carefully reared lads in America, tutors attending him daily, his sports and pastimes carefully provided.

Every morning, in our rather forbidding room at the Hotel Savoy, we awakened to the tramp-tramp of soldiers marching in the street below and singing a Red Army song. It seemed a rather terrible dirge, of slaves singing of freedom in their sleep.

Since the dining room did not open until noon, breakfast in the room was a necessity. We dreaded the coming of the waiter. Kicking open the door, after he had turned the knob, he would deposit the tin tray on a chair and bang out without word or glance.

Those were extraordinary weeks back there, before the changes that have since riveted the Russian people into an even more dictated way of life and threatened the world with the spread of their ideology.

I felt low and depressed during the period of this visit, never at ease.

And yet, as we walked about the streets of towns and cities, visited collective farms, peasant homes, roamed the shops, made purchases of *objets d'art* from homes and churches that were being denuded, I came to dissociate the Russian people from their government, to penetrate to some degree that coating of paraffin which covered their manner and their speech and their fear.

With a sense of guilt, I came to like them. A gargantuan nation had turned upside down, so to speak, a new tyranny replacing an old. And yet, mysteriously, their innate gaiety, their mysticism, their humor, almost absent in their somber literature, persisted.

Following the revolution, a Dr. Hammer, who had lived in the United States for twenty years, had, for difficult and involved reasons, returned to Moscow with his family. As naturalized American citizens, they were rated as foreigners and therefore were permitted to rent one of the city's few remaining private homes, which eventually was to become a sort of clearing house offering hospitality to name-visitors to the Soviet Union.

Foreseeing large business opportunities at this stage of Russia's change of life, Dr. Hammer and his sons, viewing a nation stripped of even the bare amenities, moved in on the industrial scene before restrictions were clamped down.

When the Hammers arrived, Russia needed practically everything from hairpins to tractors. They decided to embark first upon the manufacture of the small commodities, such as electric light bulbs, rope, lead pencils.

In due time, we were invited to the Hammer home, where this latter project, lead pencils, came under discussion. Wood and graphite, said Dr. Hammer, interrogating one of his Russian guests, are easy enough to obtain here, but what about rubber for erasers?

Rubber is out of the question, replied the guest. But never mind about the erasers. No Russian ever admits he is wrong.

Something of this kind of light and shade comes through in Pushkin and even Chekhov, but the song of Russia is somber.

In the villages of the Ukraine, the people followed us about, the women fingering my clothing and asking for lipstick or face powder. They wanted to be friendly, they wanted to ask much. But they were afraid. We, too, were afraid for them, so we refrained from following our impulses to talk to them at length, which was disheartening because Jack spoke the language.

To be sure, on many a village green we answered their eager questions about America, ventured to admire their children, talked of everything but what we most wished to know. Their satisfactions or dissatisfactions. About the broken families, their broken lives. The morale, the morals. The betterment or worsening since come-the-revolution.

But the peasantry dared only to laugh with us, they would not risk being sober with us.

A sense of heaviness took flight when, almost baggage free, having left everything we could spare to the deprived Russians, we stepped off a boat onto Estonian soil, still clutching our fourteenth-century Moses.

Later that same day, we came upon the lone figure of a man standing on a country road, staring in the direction of Russia, from which he stood divided by a hair line.

He proved to be a Russian exiled through the insane displacements of war.

How fortunate for you, said Jack.

No, no, said the man, his eyes filling as he continued to look towards his fatherland . . . over there is my home . . .

Guests find it an experience in contrasts to come from the clatter and miscellany of New York streets into the conventional lobby

ANATOMY OF ME

of our apartment building, enter a conventional elevator operated by an attendant in conventional uniform, and then into the Gothic quiet of architecture, furnishings, and mood, removed by centuries from the scenes eighteen stories below.

Notables of many lands have, from time to time, assembled in our great hall; but since this is not a book of names, I shall reserve them for some future anatomy of notables. Their reactions, however, have been surprise and pleasure and, I suppose, some lifting of eyebrows where my judgment slipped. One lifting of the eyebrow in particular was in the end avenged.

Dr. A. A. Berg, world-famous surgeon and close friend, was dining with me one evening, along with a party of three or four. Jack had a previous engagement. About an hour before dinner, Dr. Berg telephoned and asked if he might also bring Lord and Lady Duveen, then Sir Joseph Duveen, and a Mr. Valentino, curator of the Detroit Museum of Fine Art.

I could only acquiesce, but actually I was thrown into a state of small panic, not because of the last-minute additions to my dinner table, but because Lord Duveen and Mr. Valentino were internationally known art connoisseurs.

I spent most of the intervening period eliminating pieces I knew to be reproductions or doubtful originals, placing this behind a screen, that behind the piano or couch.

My guests arrived, the beautiful Lady Duveen enhancing the scene. During cocktails, we chatted, my dogs were admired, but presently, to my discomfort, Lord Duveen and Mr. Valentino separated themselves from the group and wandered about the room, pausing over various objects, discussing others.

In the dining room, of which I was particularly proud, the refectory dinner table was set and five high-backed chairs in their places.

We had brought virtually this entire room out of a sixteenth-century palazzo, including wall panels and stained-glass windows and monastic bench. There were only seven of the original chairs to be had. To round out the dozen, we had had five duplicates made in America, fairly good ones, we thought.

But, straight as the crow flies, Lord Duveen and Mr. Valentino made for my possessions of doubtful authenticity, peering behind screens, lifting small *objets d'art*, and, finally, wandering into the dining room and pausing behind one of the chairs, a duplicate.

With my third eye and ear I was conscious of all this, and, as my unrest grew, one of my dogs, Satsuma, a white Pekingese, at all times curiously sensitive to my state of mind, began to emit small growls, a curious pallor showing around his black mask.

When the two men returned from their tour of inspection, they were gracious but noncommittal. As if to gloss over their lack of comment, Mr. Valentino leaned to caress Satsuma, who rolled back his upper lip and showed his teeth.

Careful, please, I admonished, Satsuma is a one-man dog.

All dogs like me, insisted the genial curator, and stooped again.

I, too, stooped to interfere, but too late. Satsuma had already sunk a small sharp fang into the forefinger of my guest. Blood spurted.

Dr. Berg took over, asked for iodine and gauze. I sped upstairs to a medicine chest in the bathroom. I was about to rush down again, when I happened to glance into my room. There, across the bed, was Lady Duveen's superb Russian sable coat.

While Mr. Valentino bled, I paused long enough to try it on.

Through the years, that dissatisfaction at the core of so-called success continues to gnaw. The short stories, the novels move slowly off my typewriter, keeping me unsatisfied and apprehensive.

Even though with the march of time I have reason to know that what comes from my pen will be acceptable here or there, the period of waiting for the verdict remains one of suspense. The short envelope of acceptance, no matter how often it may recur, remains the thrill that comes once in a lifetime.

Sometimes the critics lay on the lash, but mostly they praise. Be that as it may, it was and remains my unhappy faculty to remember verbatim the beatings, no matter how slight my regard for my appraiser, and to forget the praise.

After reading a bad review and letting the words eat in and

sear in, I would retire to lick my wounds, praying that Jack had not seen it or that some "friend" would not mail it to my parents.

I am a "bleeder" under criticism and have not done too well in the matter of controlling this mental hemophilia.

It is at least fifteen years since I have read a review of my work, good, bad, or indifferent.

I continued to walk among the apple vendors, the soup lines. The tenements, which at first had seemed so picturesque, began to reveal their inherent and ugly meanings. I no longer thought of them as the breeding place of so many men and women of achievement.

They were in the immense minority. But what of the vast majorities, victims of a monster condition of poverty that seemed so alien to our lush country?

Bernarr Macfadden, the newspaper publisher and food faddist, was establishing restaurants about New York where unshaved men and ashamed women could have a fairly nourishing vegetarian meal for as little as five or six cents. I sat among them and ate among them. The depression was well named. Their mass quiet was not good to hear. New concerns that have never since moved out had come to live with me.

A lady was quoted in a Philadelphia newspaper along lines that interested me. Her husband, one-time Assistant Secretary of the Navy, Governor of the State of New York, was on the verge of a giant step toward the Presidency of the United States. I had never met either of them.

The published quotation exhorted domestic workers in America to organize. Long hours, the author contended, and unfit living-in quarters are largely responsible for the disturbing decrease in domestic labor.

This condition had been borne in upon me even before I left St. Louis. I knew how Mama, along with hordes of women, would retaliate to this lady. Far from misusing, would be their mass cry, we overindulge our maids. Best of food. Every other

Friday afternoon and Sunday afternoons off. Good wages. No living expenses.

I knew this to be true of a percentage of the women. It was of Mama, to a degree. I also knew that our Willie was on her feet twelve to fourteen hours a day, her margin of free time so narrow that she spent most of it in her third-floor room where the ceiling slanted and the day's heat beat through the roof.

I knew that compared to some of the living conditions of maids on our street, Willie's room was de luxe. I knew that maids' quarters in luxurious New York apartments were often Black Holes of Calcutta opening off steamy kitchens. I knew the deadpan tiredness of live-in domestics who had houseworked, cooked three meals for a family, served them, and emerged from their kitchens at ten o'clock at night. I knew the travail of women working for women. I knew my Lummox.

I also knew the almost insurmountable obstacles in the way of attempting to organize the labor of the household. Nevertheless I was struck with admiration for the woman who was concerned with this problem. I wrote my first fan letter:

My dear Mrs. Roosevelt, I am impressed by your recent statement in the Philadelphia *Inquirer* regarding possible organization of women domestic workers. I realize the tremendous difficulties inherent in the problem, but like you I am convinced that unless the labor relations of domestic service and employers is improved domestics will become a vanishing race, thus changing the pattern of the American home.

Time has borne this out.

Characteristically, Mrs. Roosevelt replied at once. Nothing came of her suggested project, but out of the incident grew my long friendship with the great lady of our time.

A new social philosophy was about to evolve in our country. Some attribute it to world trends, others to the election of Franklin D. Roosevelt to the Presidency. Some see in it the advent of a new and better day. Still others regard it as the kiss of death to initiative.

Be that as it may, we were ready and waiting for imperative

change. We were a worried nation, powdered with some of the gilt dust of the roaring decade; dust which now lay scattered in the gutters like morning-after confetti.

Looking back, I try to recapture, in view of the disparity of our interests, what Jack and I found in common to talk about. Not social philosophies. Not music. Not the world of letters. Yet we did not sit through meals with only the monosyllabic remarks that are to a marriage like the blight on the elm. We talked, and were interested! We talked late into the night, when the room was dark. We talked in the morning before dawn became day.

To be sure, in addition to the fact that we shared racial background, the basic and unanalyzable attraction was there.

Yet our major interests did not converge. It is axiomatic that common concerns bulwark a marriage. We were an exception which proved the rule.

I strove for musical literacy, accompanied Jack to symphony concerts and opera, studied the scores. Seated beside me, he would whisperingly alert me to an impending motif or movement. I knew and loved his Chopin, Beethoven, or Tchaikovsky on his own piano, but the symphonies of involvements and immensities poured around me like fog.

Most of the grand grand operas ingulfed me, some of their librettos even striking me as ridiculous. Not so the mass-appeal tuneful stretches of *Aïda, Tosca, Madame Butterfly, Coq d'Or, Carmen, Pagliacci.*

After spending years attempting to bolster me in music appreciation, Jack finally and gently left off. So did I, realizing that outside elementary tune enjoyment, I was beyond my depth. Mama, who had a basic love of music and had one day actually dreamed of a pianist career for me, declared that Papa disliked music, although with heavy fingers he could thump out "Old Black Joe" on the piano. Be that as it may, he had neither feeling nor ear for it.

I felt humiliated, soulless, and lacking in the ingredients which the authentically creative artist must possess.

On the other hand, I do not recall that Jack ever read a manuscript of mine or commented critically. Motion pictures or dramatized versions were another matter. His judgments were quick and wise.

But certainly we were two incompatibles where our respective major interests were concerned, except that Jack did care about people. Not as I did, objectively and collectively. He cared about them in the close and personal way, his sympathy and generosity toward friends—unlimited. Like so many Russians, heavy clouds hung over his memories. He was gay but even in his youth was filled with old sorrows.

That first time I returned to Russia with him he stood on the unkept street on which he lived as a child and tried to reconstruct it for me out of the shambles into which it had deteriorated. If blood and tears can fertilize, he said, this country, which for centuries has been watered with both, should someday be the garden of the world.

He used to tell me out of somber recollections of the peasants who came into the cities on frozen feet that had to be amputated, of pogrom and escapes by night, of Jewish faces that were spat into. He remembered as a very small child, when his father was sculptor to the Czar, that horses were denied water for days, so that they would gulp buckets of champagne before being hitched for the great sleighing parties.

Where I had pity for pain, Jack paid with pain for pain. He knew lower New York better than I, had lived on Second Avenue at a time when that street was still residential although the slum was already beginning to make it dark.

He was hurt through and through with the pain of his family and of old Jews whose faces had been spat into.

The night of Franklin Roosevelt's election to the first term of his Presidency was probably no more than a variation on the theme of many a presidential election. But it was my first closeup. Aside from the Americana and the fearful and wonderful spectacle we make of ourselves on these occasions, it remains a memory that will always have an electric current running through it.

In the dervish dance of New York's Hotel Biltmore that election night, as the early returns began to trickle in, Mrs. Roosevelt whispered to me: Meet me at twelve o'clock in Louis Howe's office on the fourth floor. Be prepared to go home with me to Hyde Park for the final returns and spend the night there. Bring your husband if you wish.

Jack said: No, you go and tell me about it.

I deviate, even in this moment of intense action, to linger over this bring-your-husband-along aspect of a so-called career woman married to a man in private life.

It requires handling.

When Jack declined Mrs. Roosevelt's invitation to what I knew would be to him an exciting occasion, I did not urge. He must have known the invitation was warm and meant. He must have known how much his going would have enhanced my pleasure. But I also knew the workings of his mind.

It was one of those situations when a marriage such as ours required the eternal vigilance of the woman if it was to avoid pitfalls. I learned rather promptly to cultivate the acuteness of that third eye and ear, that extrasensory perception that sharpens Mrs. X to the hazards of permitting her man to become Mrs. X's husband.

Fortunately, Jack's innate dignity and commanding presence minimized such eventualities.

Except there was always the thoughtless aggressor turning to introduce: Mr. Hurst.

On the excoriating occasions when this kind of thing did happen, I did not refer to it afterward or attempt to cover up.

My wishful thinking is that Jack realized how little intent there was in these lapses. Nevertheless I know with my intuition that even though he may have charged it up to tremendous trifles he scorched under them. I hope that he did not know how constantly I was on the protective alert.

At one of the large functions which we, who entertained so

little, felt it incumbent to give once or twice a year, a prominent judge once turned rudely upon Jack, most hospitable of hosts, when he offered him a chair: Let me be judge of when I wish to sit down, he said, and turned back to resume his conversation.

We never mentioned the incident to one another. That judge, eminent and respected, has since died. But after that episode I hated him in life. I hate him now.

I was custodian of something sensitive and not hardened by a life that had not been without its hard side. Every career woman with a private-life mate is faced with this problem in one form or another: the dignity of her male.

I knew that in declining the invitation to Hyde Park that election night Jack was missing an important event. But Mrs. Roosevelt would have understood. She is like that!

Besides Mrs. Roosevelt, Louis Howe, of peculiar and backstage importance to the shape of events about to take place, Steve Early, future secretary to the President, Frances Perkins, not yet Secretary of Labor, Nancy Cook, Miss Dickerman, long-time friends of the family, and I took a late train to the lovely old manor house at Hyde Park, presided over by Mrs. Delano Roosevelt, mother of the about-to-be President. He was already there in a private room, surrounded by various architects of his career.

Our group gathered in the large living room of the rambling house in the Hudson River Valley, the family circle enlarging as car after car of Roosevelts, Delanos, children, grandchildren, cousins, in-laws, friends rolled up the drive.

With the exception of the President's mother, his wife, Louis Howe, and Steve Early, who were with the President-to-be, we sat tense in the living room, listening as the returns came in over the radio.

About two o'clock Mrs. Roosevelt tiptoed in and whispered in my ear: Franklin asks that you come into the room where he is.

Seated around a table, a damask cloth on it, in what looked as if it might be the children's dining room, sat the imminent President of the United States surrounded by about ten men.

Steve Early at his right rose, and the President-about-to-be beckoned me to the vacated chair.

Not a word was spoken. It was growingly apparent that Mr. Roosevelt was "in," but the silence held to the last dramatic moment when bedlam broke, and there I sat at the President's right hand, a chance visitor happening in on history in the making.

It was four o'clock before the elder Mrs. Roosevelt scattered the guests, Frances Perkins, Miss Cook and Miss Dickerman and me to "the cottage," which was about half a mile from the big house. Steve Early directed me to a waiting car in the line of them before the brilliantly lighted house, with messengers still rushing in and out, cars driving up to disgorge excited men laden with portfolios, cameras, documents.

While I waited for I knew not whom, Mrs. Roosevelt suddenly popped her head into the car.

Take us to the cottage, George, she said to the chauffeur, and then bring my Ford around. I must go to the airport.

At four in the morning! I exclaimed. Yes, Elliott is arriving. His plane is grounded at Buffalo but he is due at about five-thirty. I'll just make it.

I'll go with you at this hour!

Oh no. You get your sleep. I have my knitting with me in case there is further delay.

When I came out of my room for breakfast, Mrs. Roosevelt and Elliott were just arriving. She had waited two hours: There was such a nice gentleman from Peekskill waiting for his daughter, she explained, who kept me company, but after a while he fell asleep, and I knitted on. . . .

I am grateful that people, rather than bacteriology, mathematics, banking, or clockmaking, are my job.

At the close of my workday, I put the cover on my typewriter but I leave people on its roll. Then I move out into a world of more people, all grades and varieties.

I read somewhere this query:

Can a man praise his God in the marketplace?
In the midst of his business, can man sing to Him?
The routine of office, the round of each day,
The press of the crowd, the contact with people,
Are these the precluders of contact with Thee?
Can'st Thou not be found in this melee of men?

But "this melee of men" surges with passions deeper than the sea. A tree, lovely thing, is a tree, is a tree, is a tree. Man, responding to the sea, to the tree, to God, is responding to what neither the sea nor the tree possesses—his human soul. Must a man go to the sea, the tree, to find his Creator? Is there no God in the marketplace or in the souls of good men?

Elementary questions plague me. People will not let me be. Why need babies be born blind? What wrongness in our world helped create that alcoholic sodden ruin of a man in the shadow of that doorway? Why need my neighbor's young son, suddenly in khaki, be mown down in a land he has never before seen, by an enemy he has never known or learned to hate?

God's ways are inscrutable, we reply with our faith. He must have an answer that our finite ears are not yet attuned to hear.

And so you ask and you ask and you write and you write . . . and the words dam up in you like leaves clogging a stream. . . .

Your story is published. A reader writes: Thank you for your story in last month's magazine, but why did that wonderful young soldier have to die?

Why?

Book Four

Perplexed in faith, but pure in deeds,
At last he beat his music out.
There is more faith in honest doubt,
Believe me, then in half the creeds.

PAPA DIED while I was on a coast-to-coast lecture tour with Julia Browne, who did so much to fill my place in our Cates Avenue home, and whom I had taken along in a feeble show of gratitude.

We reached home in time. Papa knew what all of us, except Mama, realized. In the brief moments when she could be coaxed from his bedside, he whisperingly put her in my charge, not realizing to what extent they had both been my children over the last few years.

He said lovely things to me that last night of his life. It is good that pain has such a poor memory. As if I had never caused him anguish, Papa thanked me for enriching his years, begged me to humor Mama as he had. Confronted with his hour of immense aloneness as he faced eternity, Papa called up his race heritage and God out of yesterday's two thousand years. Papa urged me to honor my mother and my people. Not mentioning his name, even in the hour of death, Papa prayed that my husband would never fail me. Poor Papa, he died without knowing in what gentle and beautiful hands he was leaving me.

Figuratively speaking, Mama also died that same dawn. Her life line had become too fused with Papa's to bear the severance. Actually she lived five years longer, or rather the shell of her did, but vigor and humor deserted her and, most of all, the will to live. Mama's face became an empty house, all the windows dark because the lights in her eyes were out.

Here was a marriage that had jogged through the years at a clippity-clop. Love that had cooled to companionship of a sort, habit, endurance, and something deeper and unfathomable had held it together. Back in the days when a sober young traveling salesman from Tennessee had encountered a plump pretty Miss Koppel from Ohio, romance may have brushed them with its wing tips; but much inner anguish and, in Mama's case, articulate anguish had also been the lot of both. In the last analysis, the marriage was built on the decencies, and I doubt if either party ever even thought of it as soluble.

Compared with my own marriage, theirs seemed to me a poor thing, but not to them.

With the going of my father, I was face to face with the imminent going of my mother. Only hers was a less merciful going, which I tried to make easier for her over the lusterless years she lived on.

In many respects my doting mother was an object lesson in how not to meet the disaster of the death of a beloved. It had probably never occurred to her, outside of concern for her financial security, to prepare for her later life.

As was the case with wives of her generation, Mama was left in a vacuum that not even I could fill. She had never had a vocation, no avocation, no outside interest, Mama was finished.

We coaxed her to New York to live with us; but, once there, the mothers of my friends did not interest her and, I am afraid, vice versa. Mama was not a reader, and motion pictures troubled her eyes. Our eighteenth-story apartment was like a prison, as she put it, because she could not look out the windows at the street scene.

My anxiety to conserve her failing strength also served to antagonize her. A small incident jerked me to realization of how irritating it must have been to Mama to have someone sit by watching each bite. One day, by the happy chance of being called away from the luncheon table, I learned that once I was gone Mama partook with gusto of foods she had rejected when I urged them on her.

There seemed to be no way to recapture her old spirit.

Loneliness, absence of outside interests reduced Mama's joy of life to minimum. Even I was unable to compensate because, try as I would, and as Jack would, she regarded herself as a fifth wheel.

In a tragic and irrefutable way, that was partly true, and the louder our contradictions, the stronger her intuitions.

I have not the same interests, she would weep. In your hearts you don't want me cooped up here in a New York apartment any more than I want it. And here it came, that tragic theme song of parenthood: Besides, it is never good to live with one's children.

Then take an apartment near us.

And do what? Sit and look at four walls?

It was useless. She would insist that with the going of my father her life had finished, and she wanted to be back in St. Louis where she could live out what was left, her own way.

I yearned for some flash of her one-time naughtiness and spirit, but Mama was gone—gone as if she had flown on wings out of the window of herself, leaving behind her uninhabited cocoon.

My mother, whose quality I feel drearily certain I have failed to convey, chiefly because she was so many-sided and because her high-voltage temperament may have obscured her richness and generosities, met her declining years, at only sixty-four, unequipped to make them worth living.

She had permitted her life to narrow down to my father and me. Empress of her little empire, her home became her mental tomb.

Mama's generation of women took out no insurance against the November and December years. If only I had thought enough about them to forewarn or forearm her.

If only . . .

She endowed me with a warm and cared-for childhood, reared me, it is true, with no technique except a vast mother love.

No doubt psychiatry could detect in me deep fissures in character and scars across my memory that need to be diagnosed in order for me to understand myself. If that be true, they are benign scars, because with all her storminess and even on occasion her terribleness, I loved her and was loved.

I doubt if such phrases as "home environment" or "security" played a role in our contemporary vocabularies. I do not remember that I was even aware of being "teen age" with its attendant problems. In a sense, I and most of my world "jest growed."

People ask: Did your parents live long enough to enjoy your success? What pleasure you must have given them.

I wonder. Gratification, yes. But no sooner could their only child, a girl child at that, spread her wings than she flew out of their nest, out of their interests, and, in a sense, out of their lives. I wonder . . .

Mama lived out her final five years back in St. Louis, my priceless Julia Browne, wonderful Cates Avenue friend, neighbor, and more, who served us all in fair weather and foul, sharing the home with her. No diagnosable illness consumed her. But her will to live ran lower and lower, like the sands in an hourglass, and for years the sound of a telephone late at night was sufficient to send me out of bed, geared to take off for St. Louis.

One morning at three o'clock that summons came. Mama was gone. . . .

The creative writer is usually captive to his next book. This of course is not universally true. I know an author who, midway in a distinguished career, inherited a fortune from a brother and has not written since. But, more usually, we work under our own compulsion, even after economic pressures have ceased.

My own workaday routine, five to six to seven hours at the desk, holds with the years. Like woman's work, the author's work is never done.

The years move on and, with them, my novels and volumes of short stories mount: six novels, seven, eight, nine, ten, eleven!

Each one slow in gestating, then the brief inner excitements of the concept of the book you mean to write. Next that first paragraph onto white paper. The slow grind is on. Weeks, months, years. That painstaking search for the telling phrase, which likely as not the reader may skip, hastening along for the plot. The slow long processes of working your characters out of the clay, and then the mysterious alchemy of breathing life and believability into the clay.

It is a fine thing to finish a day's work "on high," to leave a story on the roll of your typewriter that has come alive. It is heartbreak to return the following morning and find your characters staring at you with unalive eyes. It has been a false birth.

Crushed to earth and rising again is an author's gymnastic. Once he fails to struggle to his feet and grip his pen, he will contemplate a fact he should never permit himself to face: that in all probability books have been written, are being written, will be written, better than anything he has done, is doing, or will do.

The author's Shangri-La must remain that next book!

Thus the shelf of my novels and the years lengthen, years that remain so strangely dateless so far as my time consciousness is concerned, as this timeless and dateless journal doubtless testifies!

While constantly more or less in awe of the skill of other writers both past and contemporary, I do not recall that I ever consciously became the disciple of any one author; instead, following my own pen wherever it might lead me. At one time or another, during my writing life, Sinclair Lewis, Sherwood Anderson, Gertrude Atherton, Joseph Hergesheimer, Willa Cather, James Cabell, Upton Sinclair, Louis Bromfield, Somerset Maugham, H. G. Wells, Rebecca West, Arnold Bennett were in full flower.

It was not strange that I inclined toward authors who labored in the field of the common man: Tolstoy, Dostoevski, Gorki, Dumas, Balzac, de Maupassant, Ibsen, Strindberg, Wedekind, Lagerlöf, Sigrid Undset, Arnold Bennett, O. Henry, Edwin Markham, Edgar Lee Masters. But I felt no need of them except to read, enjoy, or deplore as the case might be.

I wish I could say with Saroyan: "I am proud to be the writer I am." I am not. But I am proud to be the writer who still aspires to be the writer I am not and is ready to struggle on and on. . . .

In a country where the rise from humble or average beginnings is not unusual, I have never learned to take the quirk in my fortune for granted.

That this should happen to me! Cates Avenue to the White House. Cates Avenue to the key of the city of Versailles. Cates Avenue to the authorship of eighteen books. Cates Avenue to honorary degrees, citations, delegate to Geneva Conference of United Nations. Cates Avenue to guest of Canadian and Israeli governments. Cates Avenue to life among so many of the doers and thinkers of my time. Cates Avenue, by now a dream street but still a real street, redolent with the warm fragrance of Mama's cinnamon and raisin spiced *schnecken*.

I returned to St. Louis one blazing summer to receive an honorary degree from Washington University, along with T. S. Eliot and Judge Learned Hand. Three who would have cared most, Mama, Papa, and Jack, were gone and so I stood alone but deeply grateful that aloneness has no terrors for me.

After the campus ceremonies I stole away for a visit to Cates Avenue.

There, after more than a quarter of a century, stood the street, the trees forming a tunnel over the sidewalks, the houses older, many of them metamorphosed into apartments, and of course seeming smaller than I remembered. But all in all, change seemed to have kept remarkably clear of exterior Cates Avenue, although I lacked the courage to ring doorbells to inquire if the Pulliams, or the Saunders, or the Goodyears still lived there.

Our house had shrunk, the white rock façade dirtied, the porch so much narrower than the wide veranda I recalled. And there were two front doors! Our house had been converted into a two-family dwelling.

Now I must reassemble and cram back into my memory the Cates Avenue I had left. I looked up at the second-story front window where Mama used to await my coming from school and on wet days rap against the pane with her thimble for me to go around to the back door when my umbrella dripped. There were fingerprints now against Mama's window and her stiff lace curtains were stringy net. But I saw her, as through the smeared window glass, brightly, her face, so little indicative of the volatile nature behind it, shone round and rosy. And there came Papa's measured footsteps along Cates Avenue: Willie, dish up supper. Here comes Mr. Hurst.

The mists swirl around an alone one in search of her teens. . . .

While Jack was on a brief mission to France, to adjust some affairs in connection with foreign rights to my work, I slept in the White House for the first time. During Mr. Hoover's administration I had attended a luncheon there given for about twenty "key women." Also, I had once testified before a Senate committee, relating my experiences in a Pennsylvania coal-mining town, and afterward there had been luncheon at the White House with President Coolidge. Both occasions had seemed impressive but strictly official.

With the advent of the Franklin Roosevelt family the climate changed. Informality had moved in.

My first weekend there began with a gale of activities. The tradition of "Here comes Mrs. Roosevelt," growing out of her immense vitality and varied interests, had not yet had time to crystallize in the public mind, so I was unprepared for the pace that awaited me.

I arrived early Saturday morning to be met at the airport by a White House car. En route we picked up my hostess at a riding academy, following her early morning horseback ride.

I was assigned to the Abraham Lincoln suite! But there was no time to indulge in the emotional impact of my hallowed lodging. I had been instructed to report for breakfast at once, and when I opened my door to step out into the hall, the President's voice came booming out of his own quarters: Somebody bring me some cigarettes!

Breakfast, served in a screen-partitioned hallway outside Mrs. Roosevelt's sitting room, was a buffet affair, Mrs. Roosevelt deep in a stack of mail and frequently interrupted by secretaries, telephone calls, which included a long talk with one of her sons who had been operated on the day before for appendicitis.

An usher appeared with the seating chart for a state dinner to take place the following week. A miniature church made out of toothpicks arrived from an admirer in South Carolina, and all the while a running conversation with me about myself, my writing, my activities.

Following a conference with the housekeeper, we attended a committee meeting, and she then hurried me to the Library of Congress to give me the thrill of seeing my books there.

At luncheon there were only the President, his mother, his daughter, Miss Marguerite Le Hand, Louis Howe, the First Lady, and myself.

When Mrs. Roosevelt hurried into the dining room, her daughter Anna affectionately adjusted her mother's blouse. There is sometimes a hopeless discrepancy, she said smilingly, between my mother and her clothes.

The years have corrected that. The Eleanor Roosevelt of today is trimly assembled.

I sat between the President and Louis Howe. It was difficult to realize the immensity of problems weighing down upon the seemingly relaxed President. At the time, he was steering the ship of state through perilous straits, following the climax of the depression, cloud banks low on the horizon. He ate with gusto, smoked cigarettes in his long holder between courses, and kept conversation well out of the tension areas of affairs of state.

Louis Howe ventured closest when he related a recent conversation with a member of the State Department who had just returned from Russia. The details of the living conditions he had encountered there were unsavory and Howe apologized for introducing them at lunch. The President listened gravely. At the conclusion, Mrs. Roosevelt senior put down her knife and fork and leaned sternly in the direction of her son: I warned you, Franklin, she admonished, not to recognize Russia!

In the midst of luncheon, an usher entered and handed Eleanor Roosevelt a slip of paper which she read and then turned to me:

You are wanted on the telephone. There is one across the hall.

Wanted on the telephone. How could that be! To be sure, I had mentioned this visit pridefully to friends, but who would presume to telephone? Certainly I was not going to leave the table in the midst of luncheon with the President of the United States and his wife.

Will you ask the usher to take the message? I said.

Nonsense, boomed the President. We will excuse you.

I'd rather not leave. It isn't every day I lunch with the President.

The usher returned with the message.

Queen Mary wishes to speak to you.

The First Family let out a good American gasp, and the President threw back his head for one of his bursts of laughter.

It is a practical joke and of course I am not going.

Go, urged Mrs. Roosevelt. It may be just a quaint custom of the Royal Family to telephone our luncheon guests. The President also insisted. I followed the usher, warily.

Hello.

It was my Jack, homeward bound, and telephoning me from aboard the Cunard liner, *Queen Mary*.

But luncheon was only the beginning of this day. Following it, I accompanied the First Lady to the hospital to see her recuperating son, then on to a board of trustees' meeting at an orphanage, to an opening of a Picasso exhibition of paintings, where she spoke, returning to the White House in time for her to receive a delegation of about forty educators from the Philippines, go into a brief conference with a Negro Baptist minister from Atlanta, before changing and rushing off with me to the home of Henry Morgenthau, Jr., then Secretary of the Treasury, for dinner. The young Roosevelts, home for Easter holidays, were usurping the dining room for a dinner party of their own, while the President dined in his suite.

We returned to the White House at eleven o'clock to see the first showing of a talking picture from a projector which the Metro-Goldwyn-Mayer corporation had newly installed for the President's private use.

It was long past midnight when good nights were said and I found myself alone in the Lincoln suite. Gone was my earlier determination to try to remain awake instead of sleeping away my hours in rooms hallowed by Lincoln.

As I sat on the edge of the Lincoln bed, debating whether to retire without even removing my makeup, there came a knock at the door. It was Mrs. Roosevelt in a bathing suit, towel over her arm, pad and pencil in hand.

What, she asked, pencil poised, do you want for your breakfast?

Then, entering the room, she spread the Turkish towel on the floor: Remember? I was telling you about my yogi exercises this morning.

This morning! It seemed centuries back.

I'll show you the standing-on-my head exercise. Suiting action to words, there she was, straight as a monolith, feet in air.

But I sat stolidly, concerned with keeping my eyes open.

He who would risk the role of autobiographer must first throw himself into a state of conviction that the single universe of himself is worth the telling. And so it is, since each of us is fearfully and wonderfully made, no two identical, our variations wider than our fingerprint differences.

But there come those moments in the process of egotizing when sense of humor rears its head. Of what moment is my particular heartbeat, the secret places of my soul? Of what moment to anyone except myself where I am, why I am, and whither bound in this brief span of my existence?

And yet if only a handful of egos out there look into my ego and find kinship, who shall say my strut will have been in vain?

Regardless of how weary even I may sometimes be of me, there is no escaping the house into which I have been built. The house of me. My spiritual and mental furniture are within it. My ego is taking you on a personally conducted tour through it. It is a perishable structure of flesh and blood, a poor thing but mine own. But, like yours, the spirit which dwells within it has wings.

The wonderer in search of himself, and aren't we all, gropes through the opaque mists that obscure him from himself.

Sometimes it would seem that half-formed memories swim into the consciousness from as far back as the beginnings of life, or leap ahead and become visions.

Each man's concept of God is somewhere in these mists, brighter for some than for others. Buddha equates it: He who causes life also causes death.

My own God concept is tenuous.

The ramifications of theology can have the effect of throwing the seeker into even greater confusion. Metaphysics, Deism, cults, the Oxford Movement, Shintoism, Judaism, Buddhism, Koran, Talmud, Martin Luther, Mary Baker Eddy, Jacques Maritain, John Knox, Billy Sunday, Billy Graham, rabbis, priests.

In fumbling to translate to myself why one concept of God is more valid than another, I stumbled, the kindergarten way, upon an elementary answer.

The late Daniel Frohman, a venerable theatrical producer, a close friend of mine, beloved in and out of theater, was a Jew born in Sandusky, Ohio. His philosophy was as a child's, his capacity for rancor, prejudice, injustice, even less than a child's.

He was a godly man of no particular church or sect, attending churches of any denomination, Catholic, Lutheran, Christian Science, Seventh-Day Adventists, at will, spreading his contributions among them.

All religions have the same objective, he used to say. So what does it matter what train I take to God?

That was his theology and philosophy in a nutshell, and out of that childlike simplification of the basic meanings of life—and death—he had distilled his own humility and compassion.

He once told me of an incident which was a masterpiece of a soft retort that turned away wrath with a velvet wallop.

Driving through the Adirondack Mountains one autumn, Mr.

Frohman decided to spend the night at Lake Placid and drew up in his car before one of the large and fashionable hotels. As he entered the lobby, the manager came forward to meet the arriving guest.

He proved to be a long-time friend of Mr. Frohman, and the two men met with surprise and pleasure.

But when Mr. Frohman asked to be put up for the weekend, his friend's face seemed to fall apart.

I'm sorry, Dan—but I'm afraid we're full up.

In late autumn!

This is about the bitterest tea I have ever had to drink, Dan, but the fact of the matter is—well, damn it, the fact of the matter is—this discrimination business—Jews . . .

Well, if that's the way it is, said Mr. Frohman, I'll move along and the next time you're in New York stop by and we'll have dinner together there.

The unhappy manager insisted upon making reservations at a neighboring hotel for his friend by telephone, loading him with further apologies as he drove away.

Later that day the manager telephoned Mr. Frohman. Dan, he said, I am prepared for a refusal, but it would mean more to me than I can say if you could find it in your heart to come to the hotel this evening and have dinner with me here.

Of course I will. Say no more about what happened. It is I who am deeply sorry. Not for myself, or for my people, so much as for the victims of intolerance. If only they could be brought to understand that no race or religion can claim the right of way to God.

Daniel Frohman's primer philosophy gave me consolation for my inability to pinpoint a specific Godhead. God is a Thought. Each concept, the Bhagavad-Gita, the Koran, the Upanishad, the Bible, a train to the same destination.

The meticulous orderliness of Nature's processes, the rhythm of seasons, of tides, the titanic swing of planets, the tracings on a leaf, the anatomy of the housefly, testify to an over-all God or Thought behind these immutable facts.

Can an intelligent person pray?

Faith in the Image. Faith in the Thought. Faith in God. If God did not exist, says Voltaire, it would be necessary to invent Him.

The creative writer worth his salt does not live by bread alone.

The most pedestrian of us, to whom a spade is a spade and seldom if ever a phenomenon of atoms held together by magnetic attraction, have sufficient wingspread to lift us, even slightly, into the realm of ideas.

There are departments of the creative mind into which the classroom instructor in the novel or drama can never induct his pupils. These are the procreative areas where life begins for the writer's characters.

As these processes work away at him, the author sits at the dinner table, rides buses, shaves before breakfast, gives little Bobbie his vitamin pill, not always aware that his book or play is in the making.

What he has felt, dreamed, thought, hypothesized, experienced, seen, heard, desired, resisted, loved, and hated are stored away in his inner granaries.

Some authors have what amounts to a metaphysical approach. They admit to inspiration. Sudden and unaccountable urgencies to write catapult them out of sleep and bed.

For myself, I have never awakened to jot down an idea that was acceptable the following morning.

Conan Doyle, who was interested in the occult, threw himself, as he put it, into such a relaxed mental state that the stories flowed easily into his consciousness, without assistance from him.

Gertrude Atherton told me that she never began a piece of work until she felt a tug at her arm.

Leonardo da Vinci claimed to have both painted and written by "unaccountable compulsions." And of course we have always with us the Patience Worth of every generation who writes by Ouija board or its equivalent.

People inquire: How do you get your characters and plots? In my instance, the characters usually come first and create their own situations or plots. The reverse is probably true of the writer of the picaresque or mystery story.

But suppose, asks the student of the professor, we follow all your structural rules for writing, what about that "something else" that brings the book alive? What is the formula for that?

The formula for that is not included in the curriculum.

I compose a credo: I would rather regret what I have done than what I have not. Yet my desire to do and be and see and the equally strong instinct to withdraw were in constant head-on collision.

Jack, on the contrary, experienced no such conflicts. He knew so well and so quietly what for him were the values. Whatever in life he may have missed through lack of curiosity as to what might lurk around the corner, he gained in serenity. He walked the pace of a quiet man along a quiet path to his liking.

The marts of men, the race for the slippery peaks were not for him and he knew it.

The eclectic world of the sophisticates was not for me and I would not permit myself to know it. I was no match for this milieu. My intellectual equipment, I think, was there, but I had no repartee, no arts or artifices for men, no turn of tongue for mental battledore and shuttlecock.

I entered a room conscious that there were doubtless man-eaters in it, people who cared little for or even disliked my writing, and who probably also disliked me for the seemingly chilly reserve which coated my unease.

Jack knew how and when to say no. He also knew I knew neither. But he did not attempt to proselytize or pace me to his tempo, for which I was not geared. Neither, it is fair to add, did I where he was concerned. He used to ask: Why did you accept this invitation to do what you are dreading? You don't care for that sort of thing. I cared so little that the coming event could be a load around my neck. But so was the idea that I might be missing something. This teasing conflict has never ceased.

Following the long hours of reading, working, or both, there was eternally that lure of people, places, countries, wide-open spaces, dime-size villages, ships, planes, funicular railways, coal mines, people in mass, people in homes, people in trouble, in festivity, failure, and triumph. A look across a face, somebody's word of wisdom, a personality, a spiritual or intellectual lift that somehow, not so much as a writer but as a human being, a liver of life, I needed in my storehouse. The ivory tower was not for me and yet, in a cruelly paradoxical way, the compulsions that drove me from it were at constant war with my urge to remain in it.

I never attempted to explain to Jack a dual inner battle which I could not satisfactorily explain to myself.

Thus, as we went our separate ways in the world we inhabited, mere dots on the face of the earth, the tongues wagged a bit.

They who wagged could not know that we were together even when going our separate ways, just as we are together now after he has gone the separate way. . . .

The thirties into the forties, the forties toward the fifties, and still my gaze is fastened hypnotically on beyond the horizon—that book I mean to write . . . that great book every author means to write . . .

Decade by decade the evaluators are at work banishing the favorites of yesteryear, but granting survival here and there, tagging the output of an era as if it were so much cargo about to be stored away.

The literary wiseacres prognosticate in many languages, as they have throughout so many centuries, setting the stage for new haut monde in letters and making up the public's mind.

In France, dadaism ink is paling and existentialism's cohorts gather around the same café tables where preceding literary vogues had raged. Meanwhile wars have created temporary stalemate the world over. Then, slowly and surely, the literary impulse of a nation lifts its head. . . .

In American colleges, short-story and novel courses invite editors of periodicals and publishing houses to speculate on what the public wants. Give the beginning writer direction. What is selling best? What's what with editors?

War themes flourish, then become taboo. Historical novels are on the up. Historical novels are on the down. Mysteries become "terrific." Regional writing. Decadence and moral disintegration. Race novels, satire, novels of small indignations, themes plucked off the headlines come, most of them, in order that they may go. The head-and-shoulder survivors, like Hemingway and Wolfe, cast their enormous shadows. . . .

One editor is quoted as having advised a Columbia University class that the writer who dares to feel himself beyond these trends is a goof.

I am a goof. Perhaps because of limitations, I follow my own literary nose, for better or worse.

Give us escape stories, now clamor the editors. No more war stories. Love, adventure, glamour have come back. Through the din I continued to write the way it came, not without success, although more than one editor suggested what George Horace Lorimer came out with: Less red meat in your stories, please, he wrote me. Let us have some delicate white cuts.

All things being equal, I would have gone along, but all things were not equal. Even as a writer who was so far from touching the stars, I wrote as I had to write . . . as a man thinketh . . .

Even authors who protest as loudly as I do are the un- and subconscious disciples of our literary betters, whether they cut their literary teeth on Balzac, Dickens, Tolstoy, Hardy, Hemingway. Art reproduces itself with variations as manifold as nature's. We work in the techniques of our masters. Some more, some less.

I would wish, as an avowed member of the "less" group, I could boast that my literary way of life stemmed out of the conviction that an author who travels alone and on his own travels fastest. Not at all, it just so happened that way.

Meanwhile, our great big phenomenon of a young nation was on the go again, the conveyor belts moving overproduction out of factories and foundries, the majority of American boys back on home soil. Postwar problems, although still with us, had almost lost their implications and seemed chronic, editors were rejecting manuscripts that even remotely had to do with war.

And that way the years between world wars one and two moved through the thirties, packed with events only half indicated here, and on into the forties where once more lurked titanic tragedy. World war two.

One Sunday afternoon, Jack was playing bridge (or was it Bach?) at the apartment of a friend, and I was at my desk, when the telephone rang.

It was Jack. A report had just come over the radio that Pearl Harbor was under attack by the Japanese. Would I verify it by way of a personal friend on the Associated Press and call back?

The idea was too fantastic for credence. But after no little difficulty, I finally contacted the friend. His verification was overwhelming shock. America, the hope, the promise, the fulfillment of millions—violated!

Left foot, right foot, the figurative drums are beating once more. Left foot, right foot, for a fresh generation of boys, theirs not to reason why.

And so with the debris of the first world war still piled up in the hearts of men and in the cities and villages of Europe, with our own amputees and disabled still filling veterans' hospitals, the horrific routine began again.

In no time at all, we were back at the big business of war, practically everybody's way of life altered in one way or another, anxieties for life, limb, and liberty on the march.

Soon we were too, the pacific way. Jack once again doing the morale upkeep job at the encampments, this time on home soil. I on the selling march, writers' groups organized into teams formed to cross the nation, campaigning for war bonds.

My outfit, composed of Ogden Nash, Carlos Romulo, the late Louis Bromfield, and myself, achieved a high sales record on an itinerary that included the major cities, Boston, Buffalo, Detroit, Cleveland, Chicago, St. Louis, Denver.

We moved with the precision of a theatrical troupe, a manager preceding us and arranging for the largest auditoriums available.

Carlos Romulo was the spellbinder of our troupe, climaxing

each occasion with inspirational and powerful appeal. But when we reached St. Louis, I was put forward as the local girl, and was faced with the challenge of attracting large crowds in my home town.

Our advance man had spared no pains to capitalize on the return of the native. A crowd had been assembled to greet us upon our arrival at Union Station, the Sanitation Department's brass band on hand to parade us up Washington Avenue to our hotel.

I was assigned to a front seat in the first of the cavalcade of open cars.

Just before we started, one of the riders in our motorcycle escort turned to me and, lifting his goggles, extended his hand: I did not know you were a St. Louis girl, Fannie, he said. My wife and I and the kids never miss your Baby Snooks on the radio.

It seemed a good idea not to disturb the misconception. The drawing power of Baby-Snooks-Fannie Brice over and above Fannie Hurst would have been considerable. All fair in love and war.

This group of nimble-witted authors gave me my first close-up contact with my species. Ogden Nash, humorist and satirist, with none of that urge to don the tragic mask which so often plagues those with the gift of evoking laughter. Bromfield, famous for novels not as interesting as he was, had comparatively little platform personality but won his audiences.

This expedition did a great deal toward conditioning me to think on my feet rather than about them when speaking. This group of men addressing as many as three and four audiences a day seldom repeated themselves. They gauged each audience, fortified themselves with little localisms, and varied their programs with originality and wit.

I, on the other hand, succeeded only in making about the same plea day after day. After sharing the platform with these men, my lack of versatility was something I determined to conquer and ultimately did, at least to a degree.

This cursory pause over the second world war years does not indicate that they were lived cursorily.

It so happened that neither world war touched me closely so far as family involvements were concerned. But certainly they created disturbances that went deeper than the economic stresses and the upset of a way of life. My mother's brothers were beyond the active service age, and they in turn had no young men to give to war or waste on war.

War, we whistled to ourselves in the bloody darkness, can be purification. We at home tried to keep whistling so that we might sell the bonds to buy the paraphernalia for the devastation. You thought of the two thousand years of Christianity that had been wetted with the war-kill and the tears of women. You tried not to think of it as you exhorted your countrymen to buy bonds for war in terms of ultimate freedom of the human spirit. You downed the impulse for tears and laughter, or the combination of both, which is hysteria.

The writer twirls his pen . . . and twirls . . .

America is still lecture prone, despite competition of modern miracles of communication, motion picture, radio, television. Speakers' bureaus continue to deliver annual contingents of men and women from farflung countries, who mount the platforms with subjects varying from Flying Saucers to The Sagas of Iceland, Graphology, The Abstract in Twentieth Century Writing and Painting.

Despite my attempts to conquer, I am still filled with nervous dread, I am still filled with apprehension when lecturing. The clammy hands, the gulp, the brain immobility continue to precede the occasion.

To be sure, I do it the hard way, permitting myself neither manuscript nor notes. But the ordeal by fire has its compensations. Many lecturers contend that a tour across America has a stultifying sameness. The stereotype of the "chicken patty trail" bogs them down. Cities and towns are monotonously similar, until after a while you are not sure whether you are in Altoona, Albuquerque, or Atlanta.

This may be superficially true. The airport, or train terminal, the waiting committee, the orchid corsage, my unfavorite flower, the meet-the-press in your hotel room are the repetitive pattern.

The view from your hotel window is usually the same. Main Street. Red-front Five and Dime. Supermarket. Department and Specialty stores. Parking lot. The nervous résumé of your planned remarks. The thumbing through the telephone book to see if a schoolmate you know to be living there is listed. The ringing of the telephone: Mr. Brown of the committee will call for you at seven forty-five to escort you to the lecture hall. Telephone: Mrs. Purchase, who once crossed the Atlantic on a ship with you, would like to drive you out to see the new dam. Telephone: Miss Hurst, my maiden name was Hurst. May I come to your hotel and visit with you? I am sure we can trace relationship. Interview and photographs for a woman's page editor. Rushed to local radio or television station for your views on ivory, apes, and peacocks. The Businessmen's League, unable to offer honorarium, wonders, since you are already in town, could you address their breakfast club the following day?

A scant hour to yourself before the lecture. You have dinner sent up, for which you have little appetite. You try lying down on top of the hotel bedspread, which is lumpy with little chenille rosettes. You don't relax, so you pace the floor, assembling your thoughts for the evening. You note that you have neglected to unpack your dinner dress and hang it over the bathtub with the hot water running to steam out the wrinkles. The master of ceremonies of the occasion, a college president, telephones to say that his wife has invited a few friends to their home to meet you following the lecture.

You begin to wonder why you are here in this middle-western hotel, tensed to the hilt because you are to address several hundred reluctant tired businessmen and eager-beaver women. The lecturer's foe, that sense of futility, begins to nibble at you. About here the impulse to telephone Jack overtakes you. But at this hour he is unlikely to be home. You again attempt to assemble your thoughts, dress, and arrange your luggage for departure that midnight.

The backbone-of-the-nation files into the lecture hall. There are few unsophisticated communities left. The kiss of modern transportation, communications, know-how, and prosperity is across the nation. These average Americans are on wheels, in the air, on the seas and overseas.

These are very important people, the vast majority of whom are not in *Who's Who*. These are the people who ultimately make the lecture tour pay off in excitement and fulfillment. They are America in the round. They grow its wheat, build its bridges, roads, and industries. Their children overcrowd the schools and universities and fight its wars. The mental, moral, and material synthesis of the nation rests with them.

The "chicken patty trail" is more succulently the pork and beans, fried chicken, shortbread, lobster, apple pie, ham-and trail.

It requires fortitude and ego and good aim to talk your way into the hearts and understanding of your audience. The rewards are sporadically there. It is no small gratification if even a handful of those present have felt the thrust of your thought.

But it is the questions from the audience that often reveal to what degree you have hit or missed.

After an hour's dissertation on The Novelist as a Historian, if the first question comes something like this: Is it true that William Saroyan has thirty cats, you wonder which has failed, you or your audience. You have labored over that address, sharpened and refined it. The question does not add to your inner gaiety.

Following the reception at the home of the college president, you are taking a midnight train out of town. The train is late and you have finally succeeded in dispatching your kind and wearied hosts home, while you sit in the waiting room.

At something after 2 A.M. you are standing on a lonely windswept platform, no porter to help with your considerable luggage as the far-off loneliest sound in the world, the train whistle, finally hoots into the night.

You think of the townspeople who attended your lecture. By now they are snug and warm in their homes and, after foraging in the icebox for a midnight snack, are doubtless warmly in bed. How many of them could repeat ten words of your lecture? What are you doing here? Why?

You wait on your windswept platform. . . .

The selective processes plague the autobiographer. What to include, what to exclude. What is important, and what is not. Perhaps everything or nothing.

The business of living does not necessarily follow through to neat finalities. On the contrary, how frequently it tapers off like the unfinished song of the nightingale, or the unfinished canvas of an artist who is fatally struck down on his way to his studio.

You meet someone you have never seen since, and yet it is strangely important in your experience. A chance conversation with a stranger in the seat beside you on a plane has no pertinence to your life, yet the incident clamors for inclusion.

Here is a brace of such incidents, beginning with a pair of renowned merchants of laughter, Eddie Cantor and George Jessel, on the day they came to lunch.

The friends I invited to meet them arrived set for merriment. But no sooner were we seated than Eddie Cantor, receding behind his immense eyes, clutched the luncheon roll beside his plate and waved it aloft.

Anticipatory laughter! The fun was prompt in beginning.

You must excuse my friend, apologized George Jessel with solemnity. He eats only when invited out and this has been a slow week for him.

What does this bread mean to you good people? asked Cantor, rolling his glance around the table.

That man cannot live by bread alone, interposed Jessel.

Almost simultaneously it seemed to dawn on us, stopping the laughter and Jessel's persiflage, that Cantor's question was rhetorical and deadly serious.

Want to know what this roll means to me? he said. It means bread that for so many is hard to come by. I've just come from a mountain camp I established for kids for whom it comes the hard way. I've eaten that kind. I know! It came that way for me. I want to tell you about the things these kids haven't got that yours have. I used to be without them myself, and I don't want kids to be that way. . . .

For the full luncheon period, Cantor, flanked by Jessel, with never a banter between them, delivered a sociological tract and a running plea.

Cantor's childhood of poverty was before him life-size and he did not take his eyes off it during luncheon.

In relentless detail he related that childhood, no mere rags-to-riches story, but a personally conducted tour through the mental and spiritual reaches of this banjo-eyed idol of millions who needed to laugh as much as they needed bread. . . .

From the point of view of hilarity, the luncheon went off like a wet firecracker. So far as I am concerned, its detonations, as this inclusion testifies, still ring.

I had been speaking at an Advertising Club luncheon. Following it, I had an engagement to meet Jack at my milliner's. I liked to have him like my hats. We were meticulous about not keeping one another waiting.

The occasion had got off to a slow start and I was the final speaker on the program. Edgy and clock conscious, I finally asked if I might have my talk put forward and leave immediately after.

On leaving the club, I got into a cab. No sooner had we started than the driver turned and asked: Have you heard?

Heard what?

President Roosevelt is dead.

No, no!

He turned up the dial of his radio. There it came in words as big as life: The President is dead.

The five-minute ride to the milliner's and I dashed into the shop. Jack was there, chatting with the manager.

Obviously, they had not heard. The salewomen moved about in routine, a customer or two tried on hats. . . .

Have you heard?

Heard what?

President Roosevelt is dead.

The salesladies froze in position. One of the women trying on a hat jumped to her feet and with it on her head ran crying out into the street—the President is dead!

Another regarded herself in the mirror, a slow smile showing. That means Harry will be President, she said aloud . . . the smile widening.

The King is dead! Long live the King!

Mary Pickford and I were to appear on the same program at a giant rally in Madison Square Garden. Preceding it, we had dinner together at my home.

My apartment house had wind of her coming. The telephone operator remained on duty after hours for a glimpse of her; my laundress and her sister asked if they might peer from behind a portiere.

America's one-time sweetheart looked and acted up to her title, but nervousness was riding her hard. In the midst of dinner she asked if she might withdraw to an adjoining room to study her speech. I held the one-page manuscript as she rehearsed: My dear audience, I am so happy to be meeting you face to face tonight, instead of on the silver screen . . . on behalf of the Children's International Society—I am so happy to be here tonight instead of on the silver screen—— Oh, no, no, that's wrong—let me begin over again.

For an hour she struggled through the one-page script until I too began to feel unease for Miss Pickford's coming performance, wondering how or if she would get through it, which she had not once managed to do during rehearsal.

Over and over again she repeated her opening phrase: My dear audience, over and over again. . . .

Dubiously we left the house for Madison Square Garden where an audience of twenty thousand awaited her. All the way she repeated her text—I prompted—she repeated—her nervousness probably only exceeded by mine.

When the lovely one appeared on the stage, thunders of applause greeted her. Miss Pickford was on her own ground. Miss Pickford was pawing the turf to be off. Without a halt or apparent nervousness, the trouper went through with her memorized and memorized speech, sending it over with dynamic appeal.

And I had stood there in the wings shivering for fear of debacle. Debacle indeed!

Even before she had concluded, the applause rolled over her in rising waves, higher and higher. Stomping, whistling, they would not let her go. The money raising began spontaneously, bringing in one of the largest returns in the history of such campaigns.

One day, to my surprise and pleasure, I received a note from Vilhjalmur Stefansson telling me that his friend Charles Lindbergh had expressed a desire to meet me and would enjoy being invited to dinner.

Characteristically, he wished only himself and Mrs. Lindbergh, Stefansson, my husband, and me to be included.

It was a quiet uneventful evening and with the best intention I cannot describe the occasion as brilliant. A more accomplished hostess might have succeeded in making a better evening of it. Somewhere I fell short. In my eagerness not to appear overeager, which I probably was, I may have added to the natural restraints inherent in both Colonel and Mrs. Lindbergh.

Conversation was inconsequential trivia concerning the trivia of travel. Colonel and Mrs. Lindbergh were like two people each glad to know that the other was there. Their eyes sought one another. Much of his general talk was directed toward his wife. Two on an island.

Try as we might, and did, to lead conversation in the direction of the interests of the Lindberghs, nothing memorable came out of the evening.

The following morning, however, I realized how they must at least have welcomed the undemanding period of relaxation and informality of our dinner, when a maid came in to me with two objects in her hand.

Colonel Lindbergh must have forgotten these, she said. I found them on the hall table.

"These" were a pair of very dark glasses and an artificial mustache.

I will send them to him at once, I said.

You mean you aren't going to keep them as souvenirs! exclaimed the maid.

Slight, unrelated episodes. Unfinished business. I have not seen the Lindberghs since. Mary Pickford never more than in passing. The same for Cantor and Jessel. And yet, they are small bright spots in the vast mosaic of small events that make up the day-by-day of a life.

When all is said and done, they are the life.

This awareness comes squarely before you upon the death of someone close. The day you encountered him so perturbed, because someone else had been selected for the vice-presidency of his firm, rises before you. Those months he had fumed and fretted over a faulty oil burner in his home. His tensions when he missed the five-fifteen commuters' train.

You look upon him in the tremendous immunity of death and marvel at the seeming futility of the small harassments and joyous episodes that held his life together.

We live by them as we live by the love of a man or a woman, despair over a lost wristwatch, and the Joneses to dinner.

Unrelated incidents. Unfinished business, which all together, whether for prime minister or dealer in prime beef, make up the lifetime.

For the postwar writers, the ground-heave of social evolution and revolution bucked and reared under their typewriters. Labor unrest, strikes, displacements, economic crises, race relations, plunging morale and morals. War residuum.

The second world war had ruthlessly exposed American race relations. Negro troops were not only permitted but drafted to spill blood for their country; were allowed to die but not to live with white troops. Outfits were black or white. Not black and white. Gold star mothers were sent abroad by the government in black and white contingents to visit the graves of their sons.

How shocked St. Peter must have been when our colored heroes asked the way to the Negro pearly gates.

My novel, *Imitation of Life*, was born of this consciousness and quickly made into the first of the "race" pictures, and is being at this writing.

People said: Where do you get the vitality for your novels, articles, lectures, motion pictures, radio, television? Housing commissions, Mayor's commissions, committees, United Nations delegate, travel here, there?

The hot and bothered find it easier to be on the move than to relax. I barged through that decade of destruction, despairs, national crises, and literary unrest in order not to sit through it.

Yet who shall say, despite the rather general freeze of the creative impulse, that these years of acting in my capacity of humble handmaiden to the needs of war were in vain?

Louis Bromfield, living through this period of postwar paralysis, said to me: I have two novels contracted for, but I feel like someone lost in a snowstorm. Instead of thrashing about with my arms and legs to keep awake, I want only to sink down into the cold white stuff.

But a fiction writer without people waiting on his desk and their human problems revolving in his mind is a rudderless soul. For a time only, travel, study, play, lazing may half fill the void of the writer who is not writing.

Jack said: Stop for a year. Get your bearings. Let us go to France this summer and dig into a quiet French village. I have work to do. You read and rest.

And then one day the old impulse is back. You dip your pen . . .

The two months in France in a village on the river Loire forty kilometers out of Paris were productive both directly and by indirection. We lived in a lovely old gabled inn whose gardens sloped down to the river. There, except in inclement weather, we had our meals, almost at the water's edge, our view, church spires, châteaux tucked into hills, rustic bridge spanning the river at this narrow point and swans riding under. Jack, with his capacity for spending hours on end at his silent keyboard, worked at his clavier. I planned my next novel, *The Hands of Veronica*, studied French, and spent long hours getting to know the slow-to-accept-foreigners townspeople.

It was an idyllic holiday, except for the rigid diet regime I had decided to impose upon myself, in France of all places. After a long series of adventures in abstemiousness, torturous gymnastics, steam cabinets, a renowned Viennese professor famous for having honed down screen stars to Hollywood's mandatory proportions prescribed a diet which if meticulously followed would, he promised, return me slimmed to New York.

The summer the American writer dined at the base of a garden bordering the river Loire will go down in piscatorial history books. The lineal descendants, grand- and great-grandchildren of the bass, the flounders, the sole, who dined that year on the delicately prepared luncheons and dinners I did not consume, are doubtless reading about it today in submarine libraries.

Many a gourmet, sliding his fork into delicate filet of sole, will never know that its unprecedented succulence dates back to the months when its ancestors lived off the fat of the land, provided by a lady writer from America.

No sooner would I seat myself at the luncheon table than the clear waters of the Loire would come alive. Plop went my appetizer of pâté de foie gras into the water, my escargots, tournedos, truite bleue, my poulet, my mushrooms sauté, thick chunks of the incomparable white bread of France, meringue glacé, petit fours, tiny pâtisseries—Jack, dining well and wisely, regarding all this with a dour eye.

After a summer of grim denial in the midst of the kind of plenty for which gourmets die before their time, we returned to New York. When, luggage-laden, we entered the lobby of our apartment building, the telephone operator looked up brightly. Oh,

Mr. Danielson, she greeted, we are glad to have you back. But you look thinner! Welcome home, Miss Hurst. At me, however, she waggled a forefinger. But you, bad girl, you gained considerable weight, didn't you?

Ten words that shook my world. At that trying moment something petrified in me to a hard core. A resolve. I tossed away diet lists, prescribed bending, jumping, squirming exercises. I cast out a library shelf of do's and don'ts for the reducer, wrote an article for *Cosmopolitan Magazine* entitled "No Food with My Meals," and, defying all rules except my own, proceeded to live by them.

My well-wishers shook their heads, doctors warned, Jack took on a grim look, and the left-to-right movement of the head at dinner became my most important exercise.

Man cannot live by bread alone, but he can live without it. I concluded that three meals a day was an arbitrary man-made mandate which I modified, doctors again warning, to practically one, and that one reduced to bare essentials of protein, green vegetable, and fruit, sumptuous as that may appear, alas, to the millions of undernourished over the face of the earth whose rib cages show.

Life, gastronomically speaking, became an exercise in asceticism and has remained so over the years. Weight reduction is a battle that is never won except by eternal vigilance. People said: But I must have my coffee in the morning. I need a bit of sugar added for energy.

People said: But you require starch in the system. People said: Doctors will tell you candy now and then, and at least one day a week of anything you want, is essential. People said: You will lose your strength and your health. People said . . .

People did not say more of us ruin our health from over- than from undereating. People did not say to rise from the dinner table this side of satiety could be energizing. People did not say we dig our graves with our teeth.

Meanwhile, I have gone my way over the subsequent many years the hard way, up to now the vigorously healthy way, the hungry way, I admit; but I have learned to watch without pangs the overindulgent habits of my land of plenty and to glory in what I have not eaten.

The long walks at dawn, the short fast five hours of good sleep, the disciplined do-it-yourself food regime have not been unrewarding.

The animal of the jungle, the lover, the brain worker are at their desiring best when they are a little hungry for prey, for sex, for pleasure, for success, when they are this side of satiety.

I hold out my formula to no one. This is strictly anatomy of me.

Will power and self-discipline may be stern monastic words, but I have learned to live with and by them.

All these ascetic years I have been described as "slender."

But more important, adventure into restraints has not only given me new shape but has helped shape much of my thinking.

In quest of so little, I stumbled onto so much.

Few enjoy noisy overcrowded functions. But they are a gesture of goodwill on the part of host or hostess, and also on the part of guests who submit to them.

I am repeatedly surprised at the number of people I encounter, both remembered and unremembered, who from time to time have crossed my threshold at such functions, the unremembered usually brought along by friends.

If I were more adept, or had more time to become that way, I could entertain friends frequently, and in smaller groups, but I am obliged to do it the less gracious, mass way. I think I would rather entertain than be entertained. To do without either would be no hardship.

Glancing over some guest lists from the years before Jack left me, there are figures of the arts and sciences, diplomats, industrialists, clergymen, musicians, motion picture, stage, and television personalities, who have crossed and recrossed my threshold, to say nothing of those from miscellaneous walks of life, from a Queen of Romania to Maisie of the Bowery.

Some of them have been close; others, such as the Queen, scarcely brushed by.

Some have shot across the contemporary skies, their names dropping like rocket sticks into oblivion.

One of the compensations of maturity is to be able to observe the lives of your contemporaries in the round, so to speak.

Quite apart from my anonymous public, the handful of intimate relationships that have been carried through the years, even those broken off by death or circumstances, are in my jewel box of prized possessions.

Luster has been added to my life by a rostrum of them. Julia Browne, Frances Windhorst, Lois Toensfeldt, Vilhjalmur Stefansson, Helen Worden, Milton Traubner, Dave and Uranie Davis, Elaine and Margaret Pogany, Benjamin Fine, Harry Herschfeld, Henrietta Additon, Madelaine Borg, Carol Halpern, Anna Kross, Adele Nathan, Jil and David Stern, Robert Davis, Ruth Bryan Rhode, Lucille Tilles, Francine Larrimore, Fiorello La Guardia, Mischa Elman, Barbara Adler, Ethel Shanley, Constance Hope, George Hellman, John Erskine, Stella Karn, Mary Margaret McBride . . . Human Relations.

Now that science has bestowed new longevity, what to do with the additional years is the concern of the social engineers. Are these years friend or foe?

While in the midst of life, warn the therapists, prepare for the impending desolation of old age. In the higher age brackets, interests diminish as contemporaries pass from the scene and the malady of loneliness increases. Build fortitudes against the mounting years. Cultivate a hobby!

Collect Americana. Green glass with warts. Ice tongs. Vinegar cruets. Classify your collection of collar buttons. Learn to build miniature houses out of toothpicks. While away the tedium of the later years in your playpen. Migrate to Florida on your pension, sit in the sun while you wait for the curtain.

Collect green glass! When even from a wheel chair, by the lifting of a book, the turning of a dial, the tired mind can delve into the limitless world of ideas, look in on the phenomenon of the minds of men at work. . . .

Science could not have intended that the gift of years should become the nursery for children with old faces, riding hobby-horses.

For one who has traveled far and to whom the freed mind is the goal and the gold at the end of the rainbow, provincialism, the Cates Avenue in me, still clings.

After all, my roots into American soil are only two generations deep. No farther back than two grandmas and two grandpas, my forebears were tilling European dirt.

Nevertheless, something approaching chauvinism keeps me as close to the home scene as lover to lady. In a thousand moods, I thank America for being America, even when her shortcomings fill me with despair and worse.

Time and time again I have attempted to remain absent from these United States for as long as a year in order to absorb in leisurely fashion other cultures. From Istanbul to Manila, Jack and I have tried to expatriate ourselves for long periods. Seven months in Italy was our peak, and, even despite the idyllic delights, for half of the period I was secretly champing at the bit.

One day at luncheon in beautiful Villa Cristina outside of Florence, where we were staying, I suddenly exploded to Jack: How would you like to cut all this short and fly home tomorrow!

He pushed back from the table: Do you mean that?

Not if you want to stay it out.

Go upstairs and pack. I'll go into town and make reservations. I didn't think you were ready. I have been for weeks.

In vain I ponder the psychology of the T. S. Eliots, Henry Berensons, Henry Jameses, Edith Whartons.

Provincialism has its defenders. The late President Butler of Columbia University opined that Thomas Hardy might not have been the interpreter he was, had he not spent his entire life bound hand and foot, as it were, to his Suffolk soil of England.

Be that as it may . . .

Professor Albert Einstein, who dwelt in abstractions that were timeless, placeless, and vast as eternity, saw to it that his roots were close to the surface of every and any soil.

In a conversation over a luncheon table at Ambassador Morgenthau's home, Einstein retailed to me the long succession of countries in which he had lived. Did he entertain any nostalgia for his homeland? None at all. I transplant easily, so does my wife. Later, I repeated to Mrs. Einstein my talk with her husband: That is true, she said. Albert finds one place as good as another. He sees big because he is big. For his sake I pretend to agree, but my heart is in Germany, my homeland. In spite of all that has happened, I hope to be buried there.

Personally, I subscribe to when in Rome do as the Romans do.

But with good intent and purpose, ye olde knee will not bend in the presence of royalty. To be sure, what with the genus Your Highness a vanishing race, the flexing of the knee is scarcely a major problem in our society, although mine would proudly genuflect to an Einstein or a Gandhi.

The first time I found myself in Florida I was invited to luncheon at the Stotesbury Estate at Palm Beach.

I arrived at the hour designated, only to find myself unfashionably early. I waited amidst the tropical splendors of seascape, palm trees, and peacocks. Presently, several guests, followed by the apologetic hostess, arrived on the scene: I am so sorry, my dear, apologized Mrs. Stotesbury, but the Duke and Duchess of Atholl anchored their yacht last night and all morning we have been practicing the curtsy.

I blurted a rather heavy witticism which somehow raced around Palm Beach and found its way into local and New York columns.

Oh, I exclaimed, I thought what I heard was the creaking of the palm trees.

When Holland's Queen Wilhelmina and entourage visited America, Fiorello La Guardia, then Mayor of New York, gave a luncheon in her honor to about seventy-five guests at the mayoral home, Gracie Mansion.

The Queen, stout, elderly, and able, was conforming strictly to the American way. Up to a point.

I was six or seven removed from her place at the head of the table beside the Mayor. The August day was static and had hung muggily over the preceding ceremonies at City Hall. But in Gracie

Mansion, which stands on a knoll overlooking the river, breeze moved into the dining room.

After coffee, the Mayor made a few informal remarks, introducing the Queen and emphasizing that after the arduous procedures of the morning this was to be a relaxed affair, no speeches, no demands upon Her Majesty.

The Queen responded briefly and gratefully. The midday droned on, the table talk droned on, and the hour moved toward three o'clock. Elaborately casual glances at wristwatches moved around the table.

At four o'clock I whispered to the man on my right that, protocol or no protocol, the hour had come to depart.

We can't do it, he cautioned. No one may leave before Her Majesty makes the move.

Four o'clock into half after. By then the entire table stirring with restlessness, talk dwindled as the Queen sat placidly on, her conversation also lagging.

Amid the growing facetiousness around me I was finally pressured into sending the Mayor a note, explaining that commitments were making the overlong luncheon difficult for us all.

The Mayor, roguish at best, read the note, registered nothing at all. Another quarter hour ticked away while Her Majesty, a bit dozy, sank her head toward her chest.

Finally the Mayor directed his voice down table toward me: Fannie, I am going to exchange places with you and give you the privilege of sitting beside Her Majesty. She tells me she has read your books.

Flatteringly enough, Her Majesty had read *Lummox* and *Back Street* in Dutch, and for a few moments our conversation sustained itself briskly. Then once more her eyes began to droop and she sank, while the party sat captive, into little snatches of naps.

About five o'clock she turned to me: I fear I must leave, she said. It has been so peaceful here. This is the first cool spot I have encountered since I have been in New York. I wish I could remain.

The sun was low as seventy-five victims of the priorities of royalty departed from the Queen's luncheon.

Queen Wilhelmina's visit happened to be closely followed by one from a young King of one of the few monarchies extant. This time Jack and I both attended an occasion in his honor at the Ritz-Carlton Hotel. We planned to combine this private dinner party with a late evening wedding reception to be held at what might be termed one of New York's first-class second-class hotels. The occasion was the marriage of the young daughter of a friend of mine, Mr. Mesnick.

This little gentleman had once befriended me when I was standing in a sudden downpour of rain outside his shop on Delancey Street in New York's lower East Side, where I had been browsing in the city streets.

He came out, held an umbrella over me, and invited me into his stamp-size haberdashery shop to await the end of the heavy shower.

Once inside, he scrutinized my face and, recognizing me, asked if I was Fannie Hurst.

After that, whenever I was in Mr. Mesnick's neighborhood I stopped at his haberdashery store and came to know about him and in time to meet his wife and children. One Sunday he came to visit me, bringing them all along. Hence the invitation to the marriage of his daughter.

The King's dinner was in the tradition. The young ruler sat on a thronelike chair, probably garnered from a theatrical warehouse, at the head of a glittering table, the guests obviously chosen to represent farflung phases of American social, professional, industrial, and diplomatic life.

The wines flowed, but the King's glasses were turned down, so what followed must have been the result of either fatigue or unrepressed boredom.

In any event, His Majesty fell asleep before dessert, his head against the high back of his chair, his mouth slightly open. Following each discreet nudging from his equerry, he would awaken with a start, struggle it through for a period, and then drift off again. Meanwhile, things moved along as if nothing were happening, until the young man was finally assisted to his feet for a few drowsy words of acknowledgment of what must have been an excruciating evening.

The dinner concluded considerably later than we had reckoned, leaving us scant time to put in an appearance at Mr. Mesnick's function.

However, when we attempted to leave the hotel, we found, along with other bottlenecked guests, that we would be unable to depart until the King and his retinue had left the hotel.

For several blocks, in all directions, the surrounding streets had been roped off, mounted police holding back the crowds of curious onlookers. The dinner guests stood patiently awaiting the royal departure. We did the same, but my mind was on Mr. Mesnick, whose daughter, nicely educated out of the long slow earnings from the little haberdashery, was being married.

Mr. Mesnick would be on the lookout for us, on this, one of the most important evenings of his life. Mr. Mesnick had taken pains to let us know how much he wanted us there, had even gone to the extent of offering to postpone the event when it seemed as if the King's dinner might preclude it. And there we stood, traffic frozen in four directions, waiting the pleasure of the sleepy King.

Who was I to deplore a King's keeping Mr. Mesnick waiting?

I was someone standing on the tiny acre of over one hundred and fifty years of democracy.

On a small ship traveling from Bagdad to Naples, I once encountered another brand of Momism for one's country. The passenger in the deckchair beside mine was an elderly, shaggy-haired man of tremendous personality. As casual fellow travelers, we drifted into a discussion of the *White Papers* which were then matters of current controversy between Palestine and England.

A Pole by birth but a man who had lived in various countries, including the United States, my deckchair companion lost no time in hopping aboard the subject of Zionism, declaiming against England with all the vigor of a zealot. He was arresting, informed, and passionately dedicated to the promulgation of the not-yet-born Zionist state. For two hours, while we glided over the Mediterranean waters that lay calm under a summer afternoon, he held me with his glittering eye, riveting my attention with his vehemence, enlightening me with his erudition, convincing me more than ever that it is the fanatics who make the world go around.

Here was a man whose nostalgia for a homeland in which he had not been born dated back two thousand years. Here was a man planning the redemption of a homeland for Jews who yearned for an ancient soil they had never seen. And, more immediately, here was a man not dreaming but about to realize on the rocky Old Testament strip of Mediterranean soil an asylum for Hitler- and war-driven wandering Jews.

Most of the afternoon, too carried away by his exhortation to note that his conversation had turned into monologue, he talked on with the indignation and dedication of a man seeing the vision and the glory.

Finally, in a kind of exhaustion, I attempted to change the subject, but he saw my ruse: Nothing matters but Palestine, he exclaimed! As my curiosity got the better of me, I ventured to ask who he might be.

My name, he replied, is Ben-Gurion.

Meager as my literary trickle seems to me, I contemplate bookshelf-Fannie-Hurst with a kind of incredulity. Thirteen novels translated into more than thirteen languages. A total of hundreds of short stories collected into volumes, translated to the screen, television, and theater. A miniature tonnage of published miscellany, articles, lectures, painfully minted millions of words, still more coming.

Words probably with no great power of survival, and yet the matinal freshness of the impulse is behind each book! That dawn of a new concept. Bright as a new coin. Heads or tails for success or failure. The brain is rearing to go. We're off!

Mama used to say: You'll be old before your time, sitting hunched over that broken-down typewriter all day.

People say: It must be wonderful to be a writer. If only I had the time I would take it up. . . .

Must be wonderful to be a writer. It is!

Ever since I had emerged from the climate of St. Louis, I had been lifting pen and voice against the second-class status of the American Negro, ashamed that my country should bear the ugly tattoo both at home and abroad.

I am not proud of my mental processes or lack of them concerning the long body-and-soul flagellation of another race—my own.

Even discussion of this problem embarrassed me. Generations of the hunted and driven seemed to rise in me; a cold resentment toward the world that had driven them, mingled with a sense of humiliation at belonging to an unwanted people. I am wont to place the easy blame for this phase of me upon my childhood environment of race unconsciousness, except where color made the difference. I wonder . . .

It was to be many a day before I could look upon an orthodox Jew with sideburns and long flapping coat, without a snide sense of embarrassment for him and myself!

Let a Jewish woman appear under an unseemly load of jewels and furs, even though she be only one of a group of women of many races and persuasions, similarly bedecked, and it was she whom I singled out for criticism. Despite the fact that the great financial tycoons of America are not Jews, I deplored the implications that they were. All this while I realized with my race memory, and with my race consciousness, the fortitudes and indestructibility of a people that would not die but chose to live with centuries of pain and transcend them.

I remember when Mama wanted me, at fifteen, to have the expensive baby-lamb coat and Papa had objected: Our people are the first to be criticized for flashy display. We must be more careful than others.

Papa must have known why he despised ostentation and preached the cult of modesty almost to the point of obsession.

In America, where the Jew has not escaped discriminatory practices, he has nevertheless enjoyed his longest period of comparative peace and security and has had opportunity and wherewithal to indulge his aesthetics. He has succeeded industrially and professionally, and the fruits are sweet to a people who have made a torturous journey through the centuries.

The subject of anti-Semitism was painful. But it was something that was happening to them—out there. I regarded it the way we used to deplore famine in China, malaria in Asia, somewhere out there. . . .

To be sure, I was against it as I was against sin.

I hold no brief for the fact that I was one of those for whom it took a Hitler to blast out of regarding the Jew and his problems objectively.

The rituals of lighted candles, dietary laws, fast and feast days mean little more to me intellectually or emotionally than the traditional observances of the Greek or Episcopal Church.

In Israel when I saw the tribal men and women out of Yemen and the long-eyed Sephardic Jews, and Jews who for the first time in their history were not walking the desert sands but the storied streets of the homeland to which they had returned, it came to me as if up from the Biblical soil: These are my people, and Mama and Papa and I from Cates Avenue in St. Louis are their people.

Our people had wailed into the walls of Jerusalem and endlessly trekked the deserts by foot and by camel.

I understand a little better now, perhaps not all the way, why Papa used to ask: Were there any Jewish people there?

I wonder why I feel the urge to reveal these secret places. They do not enhance me. Nor do I do it in the spirit of confessional. I do it because I feel lighter and perhaps a little nicer.

I manage to keep the ungood to myself. As a matter of fact, it requires little management. I am that way. Either it is a natural propensity or it dates back to my childhood and has become that.

Both Papa and I were obliged to remain silent concerning matters that might be disquieting, or be flattened out by Mama's terrible capacity for concern.

She could whirl like a dervish around the simple circumstance of a sore throat, or a bad business break for Papa, or a school disappointment for me, dizzying us with solicitude, apprehensions, and questions.

By unspoken accord, Papa and I learned to be little islands unto ourselves. In some ways I carried this practice over into my relationship with Jack.

The dark times that came to me as a writer, those sterile periods when it seemed that not only the inkwell but the wells within had dried, were suffered alone. There doubtless have been and are creative writers who have not encountered this dark experience. The sense of aridity, the mind a desert, that usually follows the completion of a book. That sudden panic when every theme or plot your brain has cradled no longer so much as stirs.

No matter how recurring these panics, or how false their alarms, you forget they have ever happened before. They strike new terror with each visitation. This is it! There will be no next book.

But to travel about without the impulse to write is akin to carrying about a secret illness. The divertissements of new scenes and peoples anesthetize for a while, but there is always that low-ebb hour when despair will not be detoured. Where am I running? Why?

You question writers, read autobiographies, scan the spacing between the books of the masters. There is the book-a-year, the one-every-two-years, the one-every-five group, the incredibly prolific Elizabethan writers, the one-book authors, the two-a-year serial operators. All put together, they tell you little.

It would be a fallacy to deduce that the slow writer necessarily comes up with superior work. There seems to be scant relationship between prolificness and quality.

Shakespeare, if we accept the slightly controversial fact of the output attributed to him, is one shining refutation. Thackeray, Dickens, Hardy, Maugham have first-class output that compares in bulk with that of so-callèd pulp artisans.

But this form of author malady has its cure. The relief that comes is as specific as easing the nerve of a throbbing tooth. That hour when the pen begins to vibrate, the ink to rise in the well . . .

ANATOMY OF ME

As in every life, there were years, reaching in my case into my thirties, when without my giving it cognizance at the time most of the friends and people I knew were above the ground. Few had died. Death was something remote and impersonal. It came to grandparents or the unknown people in the obituary notices which one seldom read.

Almost imperceptibly at first, this began to change. Like falling leaves, slowly, then in faster drift they came. Papa, Mama, Aunt Jennie, Aunt Bettie, Uncle Joe, Uncle Gus, Uncle Kaufman, Uncle Charlie. Presto, Mama's family gone and also Papa's. Uncle Ben, Uncle Henry, Aunt Emma, Uncle Mich. Then the friends. Pauline Rehbein, Dean Snow, Marion Reedy, the occasional school or college contemporary, on down to this now. Bob Davis, Frank Crowninshield, Rutger Jewett, George Horace Lorimer, Elizabeth Marbury, Anne Morgan, Elsie de Wolfe, A. A. Berg, Fiorello La Guardia, Madelaine Borg, Ruth Bryan Rhode, Willy Pogany, Ray Long, John Erskine.

There had been that period in my early youth when the consuming enigma of my life was death. I wanted to peer into its deep-tunneled eyes, and behind them. . . . My young self, like countless young selves, was in love with the concept of young death.

Then life caught me up into adultness and away from the morbid fascination of adolescence. And then these leaves began to fall faster, faster as the calendars of more and more of my friends moved toward September, October, November. . . .

Even when death struck closely, sometimes with terrible closeness— Papa, Mama, friends—it kept its unreality, still seeming to be happening to someone else, drawing me no closer to the enigma . . . leaving me to faith and faith alone, but without sufficient conviction that we might meet again. . . .

To be sure, we who are left share one irrefutable thought: There someday go I. But the concept is filled with static and midst-of-life interference.

And the clichés ring like bells: You never know from one day to the next. I can't believe it, I saw him only last week looking in the pink of health. Ah me, nothing is certain but death and taxes. So sad, she had everything to live for. Alas, the good die young. The ways of God are inscrutable.

And still it remained something that was happening to somebody else.

Every writer who has proved himself to be more than a one- or two-book author is sooner or later going to find himself pigeonholed in the public mind. There is little the author can do about it no matter how diversified his writing areas.

I find myself classified as a writer largely concerned with women. The impeachment is soft, but it irks. If true, my powers of self-appraisal will bear reappraisal.

It does so happen that I like women.

But women as a whole do not seem to fancy their sex. Their indictments are: Women are feline. Gossipy. Petty. Deadly competitive.

As for men, ah me!

I enjoy liking women. I admire the curve in all of nature's processes. Women have it in body—and mind. The male is given to plane surfaces.

Woman's one-time total dependence upon the male conditioned her for devious ways of winning his support, his largesse, his indulgence, his alimony. Her tenderness for her male, sweet patience, subtlety, and hidden might, have served her well since she was a chattel.

It is possible that because of her circuitous reasoning power and a mysterious sixth sense, intuition, she presents a greater challenge than the more direct male.

It is excitingly possible that, as her participations and experience widen, the creative golden era of woman is about to begin.

Almost up to this now, her horizon has been the walls of the home, from within them her contribution to the creative arts overwhelmingly in arrears.

She is the unflagging reader of the books that are largely written by men, the student and interpreter of their music, the patron of their art.

The unexplored continent of the female creative mind is an exciting frontier that remains to be crashed.

We were again feeling rich. Irving Thalberg, young president of Metro-Goldwyn-Mayer, had read the proof sheets of my just completed novel, *Great Laughter,* and wired a six-figure offer for the picture rights.

I was for acceptance, but Jack and the agent felt otherwise, since no other company had as yet read it.

Our reply to that effect quickened Mr. Thalberg's interest. Jack and I had met in Saratoga Springs for a few days following a two-week lecture tour. Telegrams from Mr. Thalberg awaited me there, raising the original offer. By this time the galley proof had been read by other companies, who had doubtless heard of the Thalberg offer. Long-distance telephone wires between Hollywood and Saratoga Springs began to sing, the competing offers topping each other.

The next thing we knew, every time a bellhop approached me in dining room or lobby, the guests at the Gideon Hotel sprang to attention, necks craned, ears cocked.

As if the spectacular figures that came over the wire were not sufficient, rumors, as false as they were fantastic, were flying about to the effect that I was being offered one million dollars for the picture rights.

After a week of high tension, I suggested that we escape the atmosphere of the price war into which we had stumbled and drive across country to a secluded inn in a village we knew and loved in the mountains.

But news in the form of forwarded telegrams had preceded us there and the grapevine system of a tiny community had thrown it into a state of excitement before our arrival. We drove up to the inn through a group that had gathered to stare.

At the close of the following day, the deal was closed, Mr. Thalberg topping competitors and acquiring the rights, and by the conclusion of the week the contracts signed and delivered.

The day following this consummation, the young Mr. Thalberg, the wonder boy of the motion picture industry, died very suddenly.

Meanwhile, my *Great Laughter,* holding both its sides no doubt at the going agley of the best-laid plans of mice and men, has lain unproduced these many years since, gathering Metro-Goldwyn-Mayer dust on Metro-Goldwyn-Mayer shelves.

It was following this negotiation that Jack and I decided upon a trip around the world.

Because of the eight-month absence we planned, our preparations were more extensive than usual. There was the apartment to close, Jack's and my business affairs to be ordered and allocated, the case of books and my own full-size typewriter to be crated, and the processes that went with taking along a small dog.

Weeks of the usual routine and, after considerable pressure, a visit to the doctor with Jack, who was looking and acting a little fatigued although he did not admit it. He received a good bill of health, but as we walked away from the doctor's office he seemed strangely subdued. You don't seem happy over your good report, I commented. I had reason to recall his reply, although at the time it bounced off: I know how I feel, he said.

A shining September morning found us walking up the gangplank of the steamship *Ile de France,* the usual gala paraphernalia of a great liner departing from New York Harbor in full swing.

We went aboard a full two hours before sailing time in order to be settled before the arrival of friends.

As our luggage came into our stateroom we went at the unpacking, then sat about in our ordered quarters, reading the sailing list.

Suddenly, out of a netherland of my consciousness, I blurted to Jack, who was seated with his hands hanging loosely: You don't want to take this trip!

He smiled in his indulgent what-you-want-I-want manner and asked: Why do you say that?

Because it has come over me that for some reason you haven't wanted to from the beginning, and it has only caught up with me now.

What an idea, he said, but his voice had no resonance and I knew its every inflection.

I walked over, locked the door, and sat down beside him.

You haven't wanted to go from the start but didn't want to spoil things for me, and I've been too crazily full of myself to see it until now. Me of all people, the one who has always railed at the women who drag reluctant husbands. Why don't you want to go?

He looked away, and to my heartbreak I saw that his eyes were glazed with tears.

I have a ridiculous feeling that doesn't make sense. It will pass as soon as we get started. Come, let's go up on deck.

I was not satisfied.

We don't have to sail, even now.

He was so gentle. Nonsense, he said, of course we are going.

It isn't too late. No one is waiting for us in Europe. We owe no one explanations here at home. We have changed our minds, that's all. You just don't feel up to going. Please let me unravel the trip. There is time to get our luggage off. . . .

He continued to protest, but with that lack of something in his voice.

When he finally conceded that he did not feel physically up to long and arduous traveling, I realized his mental block against this journey and took matters into my own hands. As he actually permitted me to proceed, I understood to what extent he had been dreading it.

Later that morning, from our own windows at home, we watched the *Ile de France* sail off into the blue. . . .

He was crestfallen and I was strangely happy. In time to come I was to know why.

It did seem, however, that my decision had been hasty. After what must have appeared to our friends a rather far-fetched explanation of Episode-Ile-de-France, life resumed as usual. Jack seldom referred to the debacle, except on occasion to remark: Today we would have been in Bombay or Seville. His vigor had come back, but I kept on being glad we had canceled. Subconscious misgivings, however, must have had hold of me. Often at night I would awaken, sit up in the darkness and peer through it to him. Sometimes it seemed to me he was not breathing. I would touch him lightly and, reassured, slip back to sleep.

Like most writers, I suppose I was finding it difficult in a zone of cold war, which in some respects seemed more cruelly insidious than the shooting wars that had preceded it, to recapture serenity.

In the bone-chilling dawn before what might possibly become a storm more terrible than wars had ever been before, it was a matter of half hoping that, if it had to come, it would come quickly and end the fears and uncertainties of the young men and women and of the human race in general.

People were in trouble. I could not seem to have enough of moving among them. People still asked: Do you do this to get material? And I still tried to explain. . . .

People were disturbed as perhaps they had never been in their long history. A new and terrible atomic force had been released and men were deadly afraid of one another.

Once more I haunted New York's docks and airports as more and more displaced people disembarked, accompanying many of them into their first American homes. Walking in a kind of high-walled inner gloom, I carried on in the heterogeneity of the five boroughs of Manhattan what I had planned to do in the heterogeneity of around the world.

People. The fearful and wonderful human race that had produced a Socrates and the village idiot, saint and sinner, Einstein and Hitler, Gandhi and Stalin, the Jones boys and the Zilches. Millions and millions of the Joneses and Zilches, powdered with mediocrity and, crazily enough, with a kind of sublimity.

The Zilches and the Joneses snapped their fingers at security. The unsure world had destroyed it. The atom had destroyed it . . . sufficient unto the hour . . .

Papa used to say to me: Remember, we are saving only for you, in order that you may be secure after we are gone. He was never to know the amount of elegantly engraved paper, whimsically called "securities," that still occupy space in my safe-deposit box. They were to dwindle in value to the vanishing point. I am glad he did not live to see the Dead Sea fruits of his thrift.

One day in the pouring rain I stood under an umbrella on a corner of Fifth Avenue, enjoying the downpour and waiting for a bus. Well-intentioned friends, acquaintances, or even strangers are forever rescuing me from public conveyances, not knowing that I am a public conveyance addict, riding them on every possible occasion, managing to seat myself in front of two in conversation, and eavesdropping.

Rescuing the orphan of the storm this time, and inviting me into his car, was the nation's number one private citizen, Mr. Bernard Baruch, whose wisdoms have made him adviser to presidents and prime ministers and empire builders.

At the time, Mr. Baruch, who is warm and human and therefore bleeds when pricked, was smarting under a sharp encounter with President Truman on subjects pertaining to national security.

Security, said Mr. Baruch, quoting his words to the President, is not alone a matter of the times but of the manner in which we meet them. Security, he continued, no longer quoting himself, is not so much a man's mount, regardless of how ticklish or nervous, as it is of the level head of the rider and how he controls his horse. At the moment, Mr. Truman is the man on horseback. Let me explain:

We were interrupted by our arrival at my door, a rainy-day traffic jam of taxicabs honking behind us.

We will continue this later, he said.

I have been waiting ever since, but up to a point he had already made his point.

What kind of people have two world wars and a current cold one made of us Americans who, unlike the people of so many countries, have not been conditioned by centuries of battle and blood-spill?

I think of Papa at twenty-one, whose hair allegedly turned gray overnight, when he was bound and gagged by safeblowers in the office of the Memphis firm which employed him. One of the marauders, shot in the act, had fallen dead across my father's bound body.

I ask myself into what kind of people have these tempestuous gales of our era fashioned our generations, which have probably been called upon to weather more changes than any in the history of the world. Horse and buggy into jet age. Pre-atomic into this nuclear era of the triumph of man's impulse for self-destruction. As for the younger ones, it is the kind of world into which they were born.

At this stage of the so-called span of my life, do I like myself? I did not set out to be any particular type, but had I the power of self-determination, am I the person I would will to be? Certainly not.

What has my kind of harassed era contributed to, or subtracted from, the potential of me? Probably no more, no less, than would any other. The mental anguishes that strife has induced have left their mark on all of us. We are apprehensive, disillusioned, even embittered by the incredible capacity of man for cruelty to man. For years world tension has been in the air we breathe. Hating warfare, we live with it and, alas, die of it. Our souls are bony from malnutrition.

Even though this America is still removed from the bloody theater of war, its travail and the stench of its blood have bogged down the world morale of our time.

Nevertheless, this period, irrigated with human blood and terribly enough perhaps fertilized by it, has produced its aspects of the rich full life.

Ours has not been a golden age of Pericles. No small part of our culture has been designed by engineers. Archeologists digging us out a thousand years hence may catalog us as the "plug-it-in age." The major memorabilia which we bequeath to the future may be the deep freeze, stocked with Cornish hens, corn on the cob, needing only to be thawed for twenty-first century consumption. We have hitched our wagon to the gadget, more concerned with what money can buy than with what it cannot buy.

Even with the lively march of the arts during the first half of this century, I could wish that the lyre of poetry had been struck more resoundingly, and that a closer procession of literary, art, and music Olympians had passed this way in our time.

But when I ask myself the barnacled old question, would I have chosen to be born in another century, I would not! Come periods when of course I feel born out of time. To conjure up the horse-and-buggy age, the pre-radio, gaslit evenings, reading beside an open fire, is a kind of sedation. The good old days, but may they rest in peace with yesterday's seven thousand years.

It is idle to hypothesize on the kind of me I might have become in another era. Here in my own, certainly, I have not found enough of the answers. Why are we put here in this interlude between life and death, not knowing—except by sense of faith and many concepts struggling through the darkness of the human heart— whence we came and whither we go?

The light of that faith seems to burn for some with a pure and steady gleam. It flickers for me. Why, I ask myself in the flickering darkness . . . why?

Once, when I was a guest in a country house in Sweden, I found an ailing seagull in a meadow, a good twenty miles from the coast. I nursed it back to health and then one day my host and I went out behind the house and released it. Off it went. How will it find its way? I asked. We are set down in life that way, he replied, and most of us somehow find our way. . . .

We guess in the misty dark, we think with the faith we muster. We want so passionately to know whence, and thus we create our separate concepts of the Father image.

I pull my faith as you would a blanket up over all these restless queries, covering them. Yet their contours show through my thinking. I want the serenity of God-sure people. Even the doubters must falter as they doubt. The cornea of the human eye, the functional journeying of pollen, the behavior of planets, the seasonal thickening of the coat of a squirrel . . . the pattern has a Master. The people, said Isaiah, who walk in darkness have seen the light.

Men and women under the duress of sickness and poverty, apprehension and panic, turn prayerfully to catch the eye of God. These are not always the serenity people who live by and in their Father-faith.

I wonder what God's thoughts must be concerning those who turn their faces to Him chiefly in times of calamity. The askers. Give me, God. Help me, God. Do for me, God. Protect me, God. Does God separate them from the givers? Has God too much grandeur to look askance at those who come seeking and never bearing gifts? Or is Faith in itself the great meaning, the white cane of groping mankind?

Once in a library reference room, I found myself seated beside Theodore Dreiser. We fell into a loudly whispered discussion of a book by Aquinas he had taken down from the shelf. Our hisses became disturbing to those around us. I explained that I had to interrupt the animated discussion, which had largely to do with philosophies of his own, in order to catch a four o'clock plane for St. Louis.

I'll go to St. Louis with you, and we can continue our talk on the way.

I took it for persiflage, but when I reached the terminal where Jack was waiting to see me off, Dreiser turned up.

I introduced him to my husband, and Dreiser said: I thought I would ride to St. Louis with your wife in order to finish up a conversation we started in the library. I'll take the next plane back. Do you mind?

Not if it is all right with Miss Hurst, said Jack.

I threw Jack a dagger of a look. Seven hours was a strong dose of a man of Dreiser's intellectual ferocity. In the end, he and Jack walked over to the ticket office.

Incidentally, this throws a revealing light on my wonderful kind of marriage.

The trip proved amusing and exciting. We, or rather he, talked straight through it.

I was met at the St. Louis Airport by Mama and Papa. I introduced Dreiser, who immediately went his way.

Mama said: You do manage to get acquainted with the strangest looking people. Who was that man?

The name Theodore Dreiser meant nothing to her. When I explained the circumstances, Papa said: I am surprised you would permit such imprudence. Mama said: Eminent? He didn't look eminent to me. I never in my life heard of such a thing. A man following a married woman to another city. Is that considered artistic? I don't put it past his being married too. If I were your husband I would have put my foot down. Don't tell anyone here at home. I'm ashamed for the people.

But a remark from Mr. Dreiser on that trip lingers on in my memory.

Damn it, he growled, up to a year ago I lived all of my life without God, and I might have had Him always. . .

There I sat, twenty thousand feet up, with no words to console the massive Dreiser, who had almost missed God.

He died a few months later.

Where were intuition or premonition?

Where were intimations of things to come?

I awoke that Monday morning, without deviation from the normal.

There had been a small dinner the night before at the home of a dear friend, Ethel Shanley.

In this rapid personally conducted tour into the interior places of a wonderer in search of herself, there has been too little time even to pause before such close and long-time friendships as mine with my Ethel.

Jack and I enjoyed the relaxed and undemanding atmosphere of her attractive little apartment which overlooked an expanse of Hudson River and George Washington Bridge. Her other guests were also old friends, Uranie and Dave Davis, teachers in the public schools of New York.

It was not unusual that the little occasion revolved around Jack. He was like that, a special person wherever he went, and here he was among friends who knew him well and loved him well.

I was always proud of him. This night, as I sat opposite him at dinner, he was so straight and handsome and . . . quiet, so arresting in gray suit and lavender necktie. He told light inconsequential jokes and all through dinner the conversation was light inconsequential happy-talk. Even the waitress, when she served Jack, indicated the choicer cuts.

We seem so tiny in retrospect. Five specks surrounded by cloud formations as tremendous as eternity.

We were home before midnight, a bit of television, of feeding our Yorkshire terrier the slice of Cornish hen Ethel had wrapped in wax paper and sent to him, and so to bed. Life was right, without our being particularly aware of it.

I awoke as usual on the stroke of five-thirty, then up for my usual hour-and-a-half morning walk. More of the routine . . .

Our terrier, who like Jack refused to bestir himself at that hour, to be lifted from the foot of my bed over onto Jack's; the windows to be closed, while Jack turned on the radio for the weather report so that I might dress accordingly.

Then down the long hallway to my dressing room.

Once, through the sound of running water into my bath, I thought I heard a call, paused, heard nothing more, paused, and then went on. After a moment I heard it again, shut off the water, and went into the hall.

Did you call, Jack?

No answer, and now in sudden terror I flew.

There were six words left in his precious life when I reached him and found him in a convulsive twist of pain, his clutch around my arm so tight, so terrible. I tried to ease him, and began unlocking his digging fingers one by one.

Everything will be all right, I said quietly. I'll get a doctor.

Don't leave me, he gasped, beads popping on his brow, don't leave me.

I had to! I had to! And to regret which lives with me and always will, I rushed for help. When I returned, he had left me. . . .

My wreath to his memory is entwined out of thanksgiving for all the things he was, for his beauty of body and soul.

I have learned, in the dark hours since, not to grieve because he is gone but to thank God and rejoice because I have had him—and still have him. . . .

My love is dead. Long live my love.

I walk alone, all dear ones gone, but the warmth of the herd still emanates to me, their vast impersonality chills me not.

No block of marble marks Jack's grave. He has no dug one. His ashes belong to everywhere.

He has two monuments. My heart and a living, working laboratory, in the Albert Einstein College of Medicine, dedicated to heart research, which I have established in Jack's name in eternal gratitude because he passed this way.

The sole hobby I have, people, has kept life many-splendored. Those tightly packed anonymous masses, composed of "the people," are dynamite and sweat, poetry and senility, genius, beauty, and sainthood. They break down, each one of them, into individual biographies on two feet, wearing hats, sweaters, jodhpurs, khaki, robes, bikinis, campaign buttons.

Almost any published author who will read, or listen, is beset by those who claim to have an unusual life story to tell. More often than not, they are badly written: This story of my life is so unusual that I am sure it will be of great interest to the world, if only I can get it published. I have read your books. I am certain I can write as well as much of what I read. Will you help me get it published?

From the editorial angle, the chief value of most of such submitted work is nuisance value.

But from another vantage, even when the dignity of a man has almost reached its vanishing point, every human of us is a living chapter in the Book of Us, worth recording because it is a life being lived, if only on the low plane of existence. Not even the meanest is a throwaway sheet.

"Little people" is a man-coined phrase. I doubt if we were meant to be graded as eggs. White. Brown. Large. Medium.

Small. Made in the Image, we trudge the allotted span on clay feet of different admixture. . . .

People. I love them because I am so separate from them and yet so a part of them. I love the loneliness they are inflicting upon me as well as their nearness and often their dearness. I love them for their weakness and their strength and the strength they bring to my weakness.

After Jack's going, my personal house was left empty. But I had also dwelt long in the polyglot family of people, a second home with a doorway the span of the wide wide world. . . .

How dare I sink into the broody depths of personal bereavement!

No world, people being people, will ever be in order. To be sure, it can be less and less disordered. Brick and mortar slums, and at least some of the slums people carry within themselves, may go down. You may shift the power of the dictator, but beware lest the one-time oppressed then turn dictator.

Yet imagine this planet without them, the people. A sterile magnificence without power of soul or imagination to create cities, ships, hi-fi violins, fire, the wheel, books, newsprint, Venetian blinds, zippers, symphonies. Without people, waterfalls unseen, unheard, unsmelled flowers never to perfume the tips of a non-existent woman's ears.

What if there were no one to sing, no one to hear "Ode to a Skylark," no one to capture a sunset on canvas, no brain of man to harness water, evoke out of the immensity of his brain power the transformation of forest into newsprint, into cities, gas stations, into churches where men seek for meaning . . .

Life, whether I have one hour or one decade of you left, I salute you. To have lived you up to now, to have attempted to interpret you in books made out of forest-primeval, to have known and to know people good and bad, great and puny, eminent and anonymous, is already to have lived you close to the jeweled hilt.

My bright author's dream is still unfulfilled. But there is always the next book—and the next—and the next . . .

ANATOMY OF ME

The going is stony. The going has wings, and the heart sings.
I salute you, Life, for the riches and wonder of you.
The dark and private hours in the secret watches of the night are not too much to pay. . . .

922.96
Hu 94

89-129

The Temple Library
UNIVERSITY CIRCLE AT SILVER PARK
CLEVELAND, OHIO 44106